RESEARCH METHODS

in TOURISM, HOSPITALITY & EVENTS MANAGEMENT

Sara Miller McCune founded SAGE Publishing in 1965 to support the dissemination of usable knowledge and educate a global community. SAGE publishes more than 1000 journals and over 800 new books each year, spanning a wide range of subject areas. Our growing selection of library products includes archives, data, case studies and video. SAGE remains majority owned by our founder and after her lifetime will become owned by a charitable trust that secures the company's continued independence.

Los Angeles | London | New Delhi | Singapore | Washington DC | Melbourne

RESEARCH METHODS
in TOURISM, HOSPITALITY
& EVENTS MANAGEMENT

Paul Brunt, Susan Horner & Natalie Semley

Los Angeles | London | New Delhi
Singapore | Washington DC | Melbourne

Los Angeles | London | New Delhi
Singapore | Washington DC | Melbourne

SAGE Publications Ltd
1 Oliver's Yard
55 City Road
London EC1Y 1SP

SAGE Publications Inc.
2455 Teller Road
Thousand Oaks, California 91320

SAGE Publications India Pvt Ltd
B 1/I 1 Mohan Cooperative Industrial Area
Mathura Road
New Delhi 110 044

SAGE Publications Asia-Pacific Pte Ltd
3 Church Street
#10-04 Samsung Hub
Singapore 049483

Editor: Matthew Waters
Assistant editor: Lyndsay Aitken
Production editor: Sarah Cooke
Copyeditor: Sharon Cawood
Proofreader: Lynda Watson
Indexer: Silvia Benvenuto
Marketing manager: Alison Borg
Cover design: Francis Kenney
Typeset by: C&M Digitals (P) Ltd, Chennai, India
Printed in the UK

Library of Congress Control Number: 2017931613

British Library Cataloguing in Publication data

A catalogue record for this book is available from
the British Library

ISBN 978-1-47391-914-3
ISBN 978-1-47391-915-0 (pbk)

At SAGE we take sustainability seriously. Most of our products are printed in the UK using FSC papers and boards.
When we print overseas we ensure sustainable papers are used as measured by the PREPS grading system.
We undertake an annual audit to monitor our sustainability.

This book is dedicated to all the students past and present
who have engaged in the research process.

CONTENTS

LIST OF FIGURES, TABLES AND IMAGES

Images

ABOUT THE AUTHORS

 **Professor Paul Brunt** is head of the School of Tourism and Hospitality at the University of Plymouth, UK. Paul wrote *Market Research in Travel and Tourism* (Butterworth-Heinemann) in 1997, which was based on his teaching at the time. This book helped many a student project and was used extensively in teaching across colleges and universities in the UK. Paul was a co-author of *Tourism: A Modern Synthesis* (Thomson) in 2001 and has also written book chapters, journal articles and research papers on his research area of the linkages between tourism and crime.

Paul helped develop the first tourism and hospitality degrees at the University of Plymouth in the early 1990s. Events management and cruise management were later additions to the portfolio, and the programmes are now delivered by the school to around 1,000 students in Plymouth, Hong Kong and Sri Lanka.

 **Dr Susan Horner** is associate professor in Hospitality, Tourism and Events Management at Plymouth University, UK. Susan wrote her first book, *Marketing for Hospitality* (International Thomson Business Press), in 1996. Her key texts include *Consumer Behaviour in Tourism* (3rd edition, Routledge, 2016), *International Cases in Tourism Management* (Routledge, 2003), *Business Travel and Tourism* (Routledge, 2001) and *Leisure Marketing: A Global Perspective* (Routledge, 2004), all written with John Swarbrooke. These books are used internationally and have been translated into a variety of languages including Chinese.

Amongst her other skills, Susan has an interest in the learning styles of hospitality students and relationship marketing and management issues for hospitality. She has also developed an international reputation as a marketing specialist and been responsible for the academic content of hospitality courses at undergraduate and postgraduate level that have been delivered both locally and internationally. During her academic career, she has encouraged both undergraduate and postgraduate students to publish their research at various academic conferences.

 **Dr Natalie Semley** became a lecturer at Plymouth University in 2008, after successfully completing her BSc (Hons) and MSc with a first and distinction, respectively. Since joining the teaching team, she has completed her PhD and become a Senior Fellow of the HEA. Natalie is currently the programme leader for the under-graduate Tourism pathways and is the module leader for the Tourism, Hospitality and Events management research methods module at Plymouth University. Her research interests are broad and include visitor motivation, the impacts of tourism-related crime and community responses to tourism impacts, alongside specific areas of special interest tourism.

PREFACE

This book has grown out of our collective experience of teaching research methods on undergraduate, postgraduate and doctoral programmes. Twenty years ago, Paul published *Market Research in Travel and Tourism*, a text that was widely used in research methods teaching across the UK for many years. Twenty years on, the use of technology in research methods has considerably expanded, especially in terms of data analysis, and this book is very different in many respects. However, the text is similarly intended for undergraduate and foundation degree students who are faced with a substantial piece of independent research, often for the first time, as part of their course. Such courses, if appropriately aligned to the subject benchmarks, will require students to undertake some sort of research investigation, which in turn will require an understanding of methodology and analysis. This book will provide some useful guidance throughout the whole process from initial ideas to writing it up and presenting the findings. We use real illustrations taken from our own and our students' work to help the reader understand how to manage and present their research, and, in doing so, perhaps give an indication of the standard that could be achieved.

There are nine chapters which begin by outlining the nature of research and the methods typically used by students of tourism, hospitality and events management. Chapter 3 provides some guidance on how to plan a project, and Chapters 4–6 give practical suggestions in terms of sampling, questionnaire design and data collection. Chapters 7 and 8 provide details of approaches to data analysis in both quantitative and qualitative contexts. We provide some information for those using computer software packages such as SPSS, NVivo or Qualtrics. However, how to handle analysis 'by hand' is also covered. The final chapter shows how to write up and present findings in a variety of settings.

At the end of each chapter, we give suggestions for selected further readings. Our intention here is to provide some key references you can turn to, which we use and recommend to our students, rather than to provide an extensive list of all possibilities. Here and there, where appropriate, we provide some exercises, which, having read the chapter, you should be able to tackle. As mentioned above, the book is littered with examples from our own work and those of our students.

For many students, the final project can be feared and seem overwhelming. However, if it is done well, it can be your proudest achievement of your course. We hope this book will help you secure that sense of achievement.

Professor Paul Brunt, Dr Susan Horner and Dr Natalie Semley,
School of Tourism and Hospitality, University of Plymouth

ACKNOWLEDGEMENTS

As authors, we would like to extend our thanks to numerous individuals. We are particularly indebted to our colleague Jennifer Phillips, who assisted us greatly – especially with Chapters 3, 7 and 9. Jennifer developed the text and authored several of the illustrations. Rob Giles, our IT specialist, has provided much guidance and assisted with the illustrations associated with Qualtrics.

We appreciate the assistance provided by our colleagues within our school: Dr Graham Busby, Dr Steven Jakes, Dr Christina Kelly, Dr Charles Mansfield, Richard Parkman, Derek Shepherd, Tanya Bellingham, Dr Andreas Walmsley and Dr Craig Wight; similarly, colleagues from other institutions: Matthew Yap, Goran Yordanov, Aliaksei Kichuk, Adele Ladkin; and, of course, our students, who kindly allowed us to use some of their work: Julius Anders, Danielle Chapman, Antonio Galogero Nobile, Rohit Reji George, Callum Haines, Kimberley Anne Kirk-Macaulay, Chloe Locke, Emma Macphie, Rebecca Makepiece, Lauren Polhill, Avantikka Raghunandan, Lauren Read, Luke Slater, Rachel Stevens and Rebecca Young. Finally, we also extend our thanks to those organisations which have given us permission to reproduce text: SPSS, NVivo and Qualtrics.

WHAT IS RESEARCH?

1.1 What is research?

Research is boring. Research is something that somebody else undertakes – other students and other managers. Research is that subject area that you have to study at university, but you have never really understood why you are made to study it. Research has no place in your day-to-day life; after all, you are not a technician; you are studying towards a tourism, hospitality or events management degree. So, why do you need to know what research is? These are just some of the comments and questions which are raised when asking students about research. Well, listen up – research is of great value to your area of expertise.

Research is what we do when we have a question or a problem that needs to be answered or solved. Research helps you to answer questions, specific questions you may have about your subject area. Research enables you to complete their honours project or dissertation. Research helps managers to make decisions about their business. Research helps individuals harness their curiosity. Research helps *you* to understand your marketplace, your target audience and your future goals and aspirations. Research helps *you* to discover something new about your consumers, your product and your marketplace. Research can help *you* to make well-informed decisions and to successfully develop your career. Research is, after all, knowledge – knowledge of people and knowledge of place. Is that not what you came to university for? To learn about, research and manage a business within your chosen subject area?

For example, in studying tourism, you may be curious about why people move to destinations away from home and why people undertake the activities that they do whilst on vacation. Hospitality students may also be interested in the movement of people, but they may be focused on consumer behaviour and researching the expectations and satisfaction levels of each consumer. Then, events students may consider motivation – the motivation to attend a concert or a community festival – or even develop their ability to think to the future, to create new events and opportunities for people. Either way, what you are is a researcher who has principles founded within the social sciences. These are situated within the social sciences because we are talking about people – the study of human society and the manner in which people behave. Those people can be booking a holiday, choosing a hotel or determining which event they wish to attend, but they, the people, are the common connecting factor. Therefore, we should all be interested in finding out information about people and their behaviour, their decision-making process and their level of expectation/satisfaction with experiences and products.

The point being, whatever knowledge you may need to acquire, you can do so by undertaking research. You can acquire knowledge and/or advance knowledge (Brunt, 1997; Veal, 2011). Therefore, regardless of your preconceptions about research, your subject stream, or the necessity to actually undertake research, you need it. You need to undertake research and you need to understand it; research is of importance to you.

Undertaking research is not simple; it can be challenging and confusing at times. However, it can also be fun and exciting. To actually find out the truth, to apply general principles to practice and to know why something happens the way it does, is very rewarding. However, it can only be rewarding if you undertake research in an appropriate manner and if you can understand the reason for carrying out specific forms of research to answer explicit questions. Therefore, it is important that you understand the logic and rationale behind adopting the different research strategies and ensure you pick the right, most effective method for your research question. For example, as a manager, you may wish to gain knowledge solely about the consumer or you may choose to gain a broad understanding of the organisation (e.g. its various products and the consumer). If that is the case, then you need to be specific about the type of research you are undertaking. After all, 'research methods' is a standalone academic discipline that warrants careful consideration.

To provide you with an insight at this stage, research should be:

Reliable – research should be accurate and credible.

Ethical – research should be fitting and principled.

Stimulating – research should be thought-provoking.

Evidential – research should be based on evidence; be undertaken and then substantiated.

Arduous – undertaking research is not simple; it can be challenging at times.

Rewarding – to actually find out the truth, to apply general principles to practice and to know why something happens the way it does, is very gratifying.

Conscientious – it is a researcher's duty to be diligent and thorough when undertaking research.

Handled – research should be controlled and managed effectively and ethically.

Consequently, an understanding about the various guises of research is needed, and clarification of the chosen focus and process of research is required to ensure valuable research is undertaken. It is not sufficient to just 'do' research. What you need to develop is a clear understanding of the different approaches that are available to you as a researcher, and to make well-informed and logical decisions, based on your current circumstances and constraints. Then you should be able to effectively discover answers, solve problems and make decisions about research and ensure it is reliable, ethical, stimulating, evidential, arduous, rewarding, conscientious and handled.

1.1.1 Research as an academic discipline

Research is viewed as a subject area in its own right. Research is an academic discipline that requires a systematic approach and is about undertaking an investigation: thinking carefully about a topic area, discovering the principles of it and exploring the topic area. Undertaking research should therefore help you to understand, explain and predict things that are of interest to you and/or your organisation.

Research can be descriptive, helping us to describe/list/report a phenomenon by finding things out. Research can be explanatory, helping us to explain phenomena. Research can also be evaluative, combining both descriptive and explanatory research to suggest a course of action and make a judgement. Within the literature or company reports and the like, it is very rare that the terms 'descriptive', 'explanatory' or 'evaluative' will be used to title a piece of research or a report. Nevertheless, all research is concerned with one or more of these categories.

There is unfortunately not just one type of research that can be undertaken. Instead, there are many different types of research to consider. It is therefore important to stop and think about exactly what form of research you are planning to undertake, why you are undertaking it and who you are conducting the research for. By reviewing the various types of research outlined below, the logic for doing this should become clear.

Scientific research

Scientific research is research that is conducted according to strict rules of logic and observation. A scientific approach is one where research is conducted in a systematic fashion. Normally, this is associated with conducting experiments where, if researchers follow the same methods and techniques, they will gain the same results in their experiments. This aspect, often termed replication, is particularly important in scientific research. Although the conditions of experiments may not always be replicated, scientists strive to achieve them to give weight to their conclusions.

Social science research

Social science relates to the scientific study of society and social relationships. Social science research is therefore much more about people and how they live. As people are often subjective and irrational, it is more difficult to carry out experiments in social science that are capable of being replicated. Social science research therefore focuses on people and their behaviour.

Applied research

Applied research uses the same methods and techniques of science or social science research but the research itself is undertaken for a specific purpose that goes beyond solely advancing the body of human knowledge in the area. Therefore, applied research is designed to be put to a particular use and to solving practical problems. For example, an organisation may need to solve a specific problem and to solve that problem they need to undertake some research, the outcomes of which they will apply to the original problem. Applied research therefore focuses on the application of the research findings.

Pure research

Pure research is mainly for academic interest alone. This is because, typically, the researcher chooses the topic of research with the aim of publication in academic journals and books. Alternatively, pure research is sometimes undertaken for higher degrees, such as doctorates. Whatever the circumstances, the aim of pure research is the advancement of knowledge in the area rather than an attempt to find an industry application. For instance, a PhD candidate needs to offer an original contribution to the subject area for the title to be awarded; this is a clear example of pure research.

Illustration 1.1　Pure research in the events sector

Donald Getz is an acclaimed international academic and leading scholar within the fields of tourism and events management. On numerous occasions, Getz has developed theoretical knowledge about the events industry, which at the time of undertaking had no practical purpose in mind. This can be viewed and categorised as pure research. For example, Getz (2008) reviewed 'event tourism' as a field of academic study. Within this article, there is a clear focus placed on the theory of events, and the paper produces a conceptual model (a framework) for future research – advancing and encouraging the development of theory in the subject area of events management. In later publications, this theory is tested and applied, but the original article had no practical purpose in mind. Following on from this publication, as the knowledge of events management has progressed significantly, Getz and Andersson (2016: 1) have more recently published a conceptual paper that 'draw[s] upon organizational ecology theory' to develop knowledge about festivals and events. The article offers an alternative perspective on how groups of festivals and events within a single location can be viewed (the event portfolio as such). The paper does discuss policy implications, nevertheless the theoretical (not practical) focus of it means it is still a good example of pure research.

Action research

Action research is about combining academic understanding with industry application. Often, the researcher undertakes work with a client or sponsoring establishment and both have agreed goals as to the outcomes of the research. Both parties have control of the research and agree necessary actions. The results may still be published by the researcher, perhaps with the support of the sponsoring establishment.

Illustration 1.2   Action research in the tourism sector

Working alongside Visit Somerset and the Dartmoor National Park Authority, two academics from Plymouth University, Semley and Busby (in 2014 and 2015, respectively), undertook some action research. Having established a research connection between the organisations, work was undertaken to examine the impact of tourism on two diverse rural areas. The objectives were set by all parties involved, the research was designed and executed by the academics and then the findings were disseminated back to industry. Broader dissemination was also undertaken through academic publication.

Consultancy research

This is research undertaken specifically for industrial or commercial purposes. The company or establishment sponsoring the research defines the problem and the researcher enters a contract as a consultant. The results are normally not published as they are very often commercially sensitive. Consultancy companies exist within all areas of expertise and it is these organisations who reply to a call for tender and compete with other consultants to win the tender and actually undertake the research.

Illustration 1.3   Consultancy research in the hospitality sector

When considering the development of the global hospitality industry, a balanced approach to operational issues and real estate decisions is required. Consultancy research can help in this domain, from reviewing the alignment of existing facilities to determining competitiveness and considering the feasibility of new developments. Commissioning tailor-made research can ensure competitiveness, provide business solutions and/or appraise the property market; depending on the need of the organisation at the time of the investigation.

Consultancy companies, such as Knights Frank (international focus) and Humberts Leisure (UK-based expertise), have specialist knowledge about the hospitality industry and, therefore, have the prospective to analyse trends, conduct feasibility studies and offer impact assessments. However, the information disseminated within these reports is confidential and commercially sensitive at times, therefore the best way to gain an insight into the specifics of consultancy research within the hospitality sector is to view the various case studies found on the consultant's website.

1.2 Marketing research or market research?

Research has purpose; the type of research that is undertaken is guided by the requirements of the individual or organisation who identifies the initial need for the enquiry. Despite there being many different types of research on offer, there is also a debate over the variety of activities that can be undertaken that you will need to consider. As a manager, you need to be clear – for example, are you undertaking marketing research or market research?

Within the literature, there is a debate about what constitutes 'marketing research' as opposed to 'market research'. Holloway and Plant (1988) indicate that marketing research (the broader perspective of the two) involves a wider variety of aspects, including research into new products, price, distribution channels, publicity and consumers, whereas market research (the narrower perspective of the two) focuses on the consumer and their patterns of behaviour. Consequently, if you were undertaking market research, you may talk quite informally to a few colleagues or clients, or you may devise a highly formalised and complex series of multiple surveys to understand your consumers. This market knowledge may even go on to support marketing decisions, but it is different to marketing research.

Marketing research is concerned with the whole marketing process (Horner and Swarbrooke, 2016), not just the market. Research in marketing relates to the study of a market condition by methods which go beyond simply using factual information which arrives at the organisation as a matter of course. In this context, the research is planned with thought given to the collection, analysis and presentation of data. The results of the research are then often used as an aid to management decisions. This said, an executive who is about to conduct a research project either himself, with company staff or through an agency is likely to be less concerned as to whether the market research project is truly a subset of marketing research. Similarly, the student on a professional tourism/hospitality/events management programme facing an assignment is likely to be (rightly) more concerned to demonstrate rigour in the methods of data collection, application in the analysis and synthesis in the presentation. Nevertheless, it is important to realise that these debates exist, and that you understand the need for clear articulation of your research goals, purposes and, eventually, outcomes.

1.3 The importance of market research

As a student learning, or as a manager making decisions, it is important to acknowledge the role of market research further than the debate above. Market research enables an individual or an organisation to understand their market and their consumer.

We need to stop and think about people then: how people identify a need, review possible options, finalise choices, make actual purchases and then go on to evaluate those products. The purchase decision-making process, as highlighted by Horner and Swarbrooke (2016), is not simple or straightforward. There are complex issues to understand and subjective feelings and tastes to consider. Nevertheless, if we can unlock some of the rationale behind consumers' decisions, then we are a step closer to understanding the market and determining our consumer's future behaviour. The main question is, how can we unlock such knowledge? What would be the best research method to adopt, and what exactly could it tell us about the people? Throughout the discourse of this book, these topics are questioned and examples are provided to get you thinking about research methods in a more detailed manner. As all the specific industries being discussed within this book are people based, it is imperative that we acknowledge some important facts: people are heterogeneous and their actions are subjective. Once these characteristics are acknowledged, we can consider just how market research can feed through to other areas of interest (like marketing research) and allow evidence drawn from research to be influential in our understanding of the subject area.

Reflection 1.1   Purchasing a convenience good

You are at home preparing lunch and you realise that you have run out of bread – an essential component to your midday snack. You decide you need to go to a shop to purchase a fresh loaf.

Now, take a few moments to consider your behaviour as you envisage this simple scenario:

- Do you go to a specific shop? Which shop do you go to and why?
- Do you walk straight in and pick up one specific loaf that you buy each and every single time, or do you check the labels and price tags to determine which

is the cheapest and/or the freshest and buy that loaf? Perhaps you are health conscious and so you review the nutritional value before you make a choice.
- Whilst in the shop, were you distracted by another food item, and did you decide to eat that for lunch over the sandwich?

These questions are just some of those that are designed to get you thinking about the subjective nature of buying a convenience product. If you ask a friend to undertake the same reflection, they may play out a totally different scenario to you, even if they are the same gender and age as you. Now just imagine the complexity of buying a luxury item; this could get very tricky!

1.4 Market research in tourism, hospitality and events management

When we consider the tourism, hospitality and events management (THE) industry as a whole, it is easy to identify with the statement that we are dealing with people. Tourism is about people (Brunt, 1997), hospitality is about people, and events management is about people. Between the three industries, there is a focus on people's movement to a venue or a destination, the activities which they undertake whilst away from home, the level of satisfaction they gain with various services and facilities they encounter, their general motivation for travel, and, in general, consumer behaviour. People are the customers and each and every person has a different expectation to the next, and their satisfaction level and aspiration differ. Furthermore, tourism is also about travel to and staying in places outside people's usual environment for business as well as leisure purposes, and event management is also about seeking to shape the future (Getz, 2007) through developing new experiences.

Given this explanation, it is clear to see how research in THE has its roots within the principles and practices of social science. Still, it is necessary to ask how market research within THE differs from market research carried out in other industries. There are common grounds, in terms of theoretical knowledge, but differences are evident through the application of theory (Middleton, 1994). This concept can also be applied to the more narrowly defined area of market research. The general theories, methods of data collection and analysis of market research are similar in all industries; however, when applied in this context, they must be sensitive to the specific characteristics of the THE industry.

Smith (1989) provides a valuable insight into some of these particular characteristics in his book *Tourism Analysis*, which is developed further by Brunt (1997) in his book *Market Research Methods in Travel and Tourism*. Taken together, it could be said that:

1.   Tourism, hospitality and events are a special type of human experience.

Tourism, hospitality and events are particular types of human activity, and the purchase of a holiday/hotel room/ticket is unlike the purchase of most other products. It involves the individual giving up their time as well as their money. How individuals reach their purchasing decisions in tourism is more complex than, for example, the purchase of a television because so many more aspects are involved. Moreover, many of these aspects are very difficult to measure as they are related to the individual's personal opinions, experiences and values.

2.   Tourism, hospitality and events are more strongly linked to advertising.
3.   Linking the first point, it is often the case that an individual's awareness of a THE product can be much lower than for other types of purchases. You cannot test-drive a holiday nor send it back. You cannot attend an event before purchasing a ticket either. Unless the experience is known through previous engagement, the individual is likely to be making a significant purchase of something completely untested. The role of advertising based on sound market research is, therefore, crucial for THE success.
4.   The tourism, hospitality and events-based industries are particularly vulnerable to outside forces.

One aspect which distinguishes the THE industries from many others is its vulnerability to outside forces, which range from political instability to changes in fashion. The favourability of a particular destination or event can change quickly. The outbreak of a disease, a rise in tourism-related crime, an act of terrorism, a swing in exchange rates or even a widely reported bad experience can subsequently drastically affect the level of business to that organisation. Whilst research can assist with some of these aspects, for example in estimating the political stability of an area, it is often the case that the THE industries are highly susceptible to change as a result of outside forces.

5.   The tourism, hospitality and events industries create a variety of impacts.

The economic, environmental, social and political impacts of THE are well documented. As such, they may have a more widespread impact than many other industries. Market research information (alongside other forms of information) can help to understand these impacts to enable planners and governments to reach appropriate decisions.

It can be seen, therefore, that a variety of factors begin to distinguish the nature of tourism, hospitality and events and the THE industries from others. When conducting market research in the field of travel and tourism, these differences become apparent when traditional methods are applied.

Reflection 1.2   Purchasing a luxury good

You have been working hard, saving money and you need to get away. You decide that you want to use some of your annual leave and go on holiday.

Now, take a few moments to consider your behaviour as you envisage this complex scenario:

- What is the first thought that jumps to mind? The where and when of the holiday, or a determinant that means you may not be able to travel (you may have a pet after all!)?
- What would be the first thing you did when you made this realisation? Book leave? Pick up your phone and message a friend to see if they wanted to travel as well?
- Where would you go? For how long? At what cost?
- Where would you initially search for information? On the internet, at the travel agents, in a magazine?

These are just a few possible questions that may be asked about this scenario. The questions are designed to get you thinking about the complex and subjective nature of buying a luxury product like a holiday. It is luxury because you do not purchase a holiday on a regular basis, like you might do a loaf of bread! You may find that it takes you a long time to come to a final conclusion about which trip to book, and with whom. If you ask a friend or a family member to undertake the same reflection, they may play out a totally different scenario to yours.

1.5 Ethical considerations

Research is undertaken because of the need to know facts or opinions. However, the participants in any research have rights to their individual privacy or even to be completely anonymous. People may wish to keep their feelings confidential and researchers need to be sensitive to these types of issue. The following is a list of aspects which should be considered to ensure that the rights of participants in research are reasonably dealt with. Research should therefore be fitting, and principled, and ethical values should be central to any researcher's plan as a matter of good practice.

Informed consent – the researcher should always inform potential participants in advance of any features of the research that might reasonably be expected to influence their willingness to take part in the study. Where the research topic is sensitive, the ethical protocol should include verbatim instructions for the informed consent procedure and consent should be obtained in writing. Where children are concerned, informed consent may be obtained from teachers acting in *loco parentis*. However, where the topic of the research is sensitive, written informed consent should be obtained from individual parents.

Openness and honesty – so far as possible, researchers should be open and honest about the research, its purpose and application. Some types of research, for example in the area of social psychology, require deception in order to achieve their scientific purpose. Deception should only be approved in experimental procedures if the following conditions are met:

a) deception is completely unavoidable if the purpose of the research is to be achieved
b) the research objective has strong scientific merit
c) any potential harm arising from the proposed deception can be effectively neutralised or reversed by the proposed debriefing procedures.

Failing to inform participants of the specific purpose of the study at the outset is not normally considered to be deception, provided that adequate informed consent and debriefing procedures are proposed.

Right to withdraw – all participants must have the right to withdraw from participation in the study at any time and must be clearly informed of this right at the outset. No attempt should be made by a researcher to persuade or coerce participants to remain in the study. In the case of children, those acting *in loco parentis* should be informed of the right to withdraw the child from participation in the study.

Protecting from harm – researchers must endeavour to protect participants from physical and psychological harm at all times during an investigation. Where stressful or hazardous procedures are concerned, obtaining informed consent, whilst essential, does not absolve the researcher from responsibility for protecting the participant. In such cases, the ethical protocol must specify the means by which the participant will be protected, for example by the availability of qualified medical assistance. It is also important for the researcher to protect themselves from harm, informing others of their schedule and whereabouts to ensure their own safety, especially if conducting interviews in the homes of respondents.

Debriefing – researchers must provide an account of the purpose of the study as well as its procedures. If this is not possible at the outset, then it should be provided on completion of the study.

Confidentiality – except with the express written consent of the participant, researchers should be required to ensure confidentiality of the participant's identity throughout the conduct and reporting of the research. It may be necessary to specify procedures for how this will be achieved. For example, transcriptions of interviews may be encoded so that no written record of the participants' name and data exist side by side. Where records are held on computer, data protection legislation may apply.

Gender, race and culture – procedures must always be sensitive to issues of race, gender, sexual orientation and disability. Researchers should respect the rights and sensitivities of religious groups and cultures of all kinds. If researching within a different cultural setting, it is important that intercultural communication skills are developed and that consideration is given to cultural differences and distances. Communication apprehension should be explored and, when researching a sensitive topic like race, additional consideration should be given to developing a suitable procedure.

1.6 Summary

This chapter has introduced the main approaches to research in terms of the distinctions between pure research, action research and consultancy. The role of market research has been demonstrated to assist in the better marketing, planning and management of tourism, hospitality and event facilities and enterprises. The focus of market research in these industries has shown that distinct qualities exist. In addition, it is important that researchers in any field, including THE, must learn and follow certain ethical principles.

Exercises

1. Explain the differences between scientific, social science and applied research.
2. Outline the principal distinctions between pure research and consultancy research.
3. Review several textbooks on marketing and contrast the definitions of marketing research with market research.
4. Write some briefing notes for new interviewers which outline the ethical considerations necessary for a street survey on consumer behaviour.

Further reading

Fox, D., Gouthro, M.B., Morakabati, Y. and Brackstone, J. (2014). *Doing Events Research: From theory to practice*. London: Routledge.
This book (pp. 39–42) offers an events perspective on the principles of ethical research, including a reflection on ethics in e-research.

Getz, D. (2008). Event Tourism: Definition, evolution, and research. *Tourism Management*. 29 (4): 403–28.
This article advances knowledge in the field of event management and acts as an example of pure research.

Getz, D. and Andersson, T. (2016). Analyzing Whole Populations of Festivals and Events: An application of organizational ecology. *Journal of Policy Research in Tourism, Leisure and Events*. 8 (3): 249–73.

This online article draws on organisational ecology theory to advance knowledge of festivals and event portfolios; acting as an example of more recent pure research.

Semley, N. and Busby, G. (2014). Film Tourism: The pre-production perspective – A case study of Visit Somerset and the Hollywood story of Glastonbury. *Journal of Tourism Consumption and Practice*. 6 (2): 23–53.

This article showcases action research between academics at Plymouth University and practitioners at Visit Somerset.

Semley, N. and Busby, G. (2015). War Horse or Not? A study of the Dartmoor visitor. *European Journal of Tourism, Hospitality and Recreation*. 6 (2): 49–65.

This article showcases action research undertaken between academics at Plymouth University and practitioners at Dartmoor National Park Authority.

Horner, S. and Swarbrooke, J. (2016). *Consumer Behaviour in Tourism*, 3rd edition. London: Taylor & Francis.

This book considers the purchase decision-making process in detail and offers understanding of both theory and practice in consumer behaviour.

References

Brunt, P. (1997). *Market Research in Travel and Tourism*. Oxon: Butterworth-Heinemann.

Getz, D. (2007). *Event Studies: Theory, research and policy for planned events*. Oxon: Routledge.

Getz, D. (2008). Event Tourism: Definition, evolution, and research. *Tourism Management*. 29 (4): 403–28.

Getz, D. and Andersson, T. (2016). Analyzing Whole Populations of Festivals and Events: An application of organizational ecology. *Journal of Policy Research in Tourism, Leisure and Events*. 8 (3): 249–73.

Holloway, C. and Plant, R.V. (1988). *Marketing for Tourism*. London: Pittman Publishing.

Middleton, V.T.C. (1994). *Marketing in Travel and Tourism*. Oxon: Butterworth-Heinemann.

Semley, N. and Busby, G. (2014). Film Tourism: The pre-production perspective – A case study of Visit Somerset and the Hollywood story of Glastonbury. *Journal of Tourism Consumption and Practice*. 6 (2): 23–53.

Semley, N. and Busby, G. (2015). War Horse or Not? A study of the Dartmoor visitor. *European Journal of Tourism, Hospitality and Recreation*. 6 (2): 49–65.

Smith, S.L.J. (1989). *Tourism Analysis: A handbook*. Harlow: Longman Scientific and Technical.

Horner, S. and Swarbrooke, J. (2016). *Consumer Behaviour in Tourism*, 3rd edition. London: Taylor & Francis.

Veal, A.J. (2011). *Research Methods for Leisure and Tourism: A practical guide*. 4th edition. Harlow: Prentice Hall.

(MARKET) RESEARCH METHODS

2.1 Approaches to research

There are many different approaches to research and each approach is determined by the researcher's intention in and perspective on collecting data. Each researcher is expected to make a number of decisions which will determine the nature, focus and process of their research project. These choices can stem from personal habits to current beliefs and they represent the causal puzzle of the researcher. Now, this may get confusing, because as philosophers develop their understanding of practice, over time we have seen the rise and descent of particular approaches, and a refocus on specific beliefs and principles around conducting effective research.

This chapter is, therefore, devised in a way to lead you through the thought process of philosophers and to give you a basic understanding of the various paradigms that may (or may not) determine the design of your causal puzzle. From positivism to post-positivism and beyond, this chapter will familiarise you with the key terminology that is deemed of significance to the tourism, hospitality and events management industries. Taking you through the perspectives of your ontology and the positioning of your epistemology, this chapter will help you to determine what methods you need to utilise to help answer your research question. Therefore, it is important to try and digest this information before you design your project, to ensure you are making well-informed decisions and that you are able to express your beliefs about research design.

In essence, when you discuss your causal puzzle, *your approach to research*, you are devising a POEM – expressing your feelings and your intentions about data collection. The research POEM (Guba, 1990; Pernecky, 2007) entails the following attributes:

> *Paradigm* – your beliefs and principles around conducting research
>
> *Ontology* – your perspective on existence; representing what you believe to be 'real'
>
> *Epistemology* – the relationship between the knower and the known; representing what you count as knowledge
>
> *Methodology* – the actual methods you use; the most suitable methods to address the positions and perspectives outlined by the previous factors.

The consideration of a research POEM is the same as if you were composing a narrative poem; in so much as you are deliberating a series of chronologically related events that all contribute to the whole, to the project itself. Furthermore, the POEM acronym implies an order in which consideration should be given, starting with the paradigm.

Each aspect of the POEM will be discussed in this chapter. However, to distinguish the differences posed about the POEM, it is also important to acknowledge the dichotomies which exist. Dichotomies are a division of two opposing parts, and, as you will see, as each paradigm, approach and method are discussed there are contrasting perspectives to discuss. This raises your awareness of the debates which underpin the philosophy behind each component of your causal puzzle.

2.1.1 Paradigm, ontology and epistemology

The initial three elements of a POEM will lead you to an appropriate methodology. But what do the terms mean and how can you decipher your position as a researcher? It is important here that we do not get weighed down by the jargon; there are numerous terms to define and it can be a rather complex thought process. However, it is something you may need to consider if you are planning to undertake your honours project, your dissertation, or to commission a piece of research. The important thing here is not to be able to recall the specifics of each aspect, but to be able to determine your own set of beliefs and then utilise the appropriate terminology to express your beliefs. So how can we draw knowledge from this gobbledygook?

There are three terms to become familiar with here – **P**aradigm, **O**ntology and **E**pistemology (the **M**ethodology will follow):

1. The term *paradigm* is used to classify your basic set of beliefs which will influence the way you 'do' research. The intention here is to have your own principles, but to acknowledge how they conform to a broader way of thinking. In essence, you are applying your beliefs to a typical example, a model of beliefs that then, in turn, defines the nature of the world through your own eyes. It is important to consider the paradigm because it does help you to make well-informed decisions about the design of your research. For example, you might want to think about how you view the world because it will influence your selection of a paradigm: are you a realist, a relativist or a critical realist? Meaning: are you a person who accepts a situation as it is and you deal with it accordingly; or a person who believes that knowledge is not absolute (complete) but shaped by culture and society; or are you somewhere in between? A realist, a relativist or a critical realist, respectively.

2. *Ontology* is a term which is used to describe your position as a researcher on the research you are undertaking. It helps you to describe what you perceive as being the 'social reality' (Mason, 2002: 14) at the time of your investigation. In essence, it asks you to consider what your research is really about. It may seem fundamental and obvious, as noted by Mason (2002), but it is important to give it sufficient consideration. For example, are you focusing on people, feelings and attitudes, or are you concentrating on texts, discourses and codes of communication, or societies and groups? The list of examples here is infinite, to some extent, so don't stop at just these few examples; read Mason (2002) and develop a deeper understanding.

3. *Epistemology* is a term used to convey your perspective on the research you are undertaking. It helps you to express what you view as representing knowledge and/or evidence of the 'social reality' (Mason, 2002: 16) you are investigating. What, from your perspective, acts as evidence? What evidence can you collect or consult to generate data? Literally, it is about your theory of knowledge (Mason, 2002).

Once you have developed your knowledge about these three terms, you should be able to connect your thoughts (Mason, 2002) because the ontological position should be supported by your epistemological perspective and these, together, should lead to your paradigm (Mason, 2002; Wahyuni, 2012). After all, paradigms are based on ontological, epistemological (and methodological) assumptions (Guba and Lincoln, 1994). However, this does not make for a simple and straightforward acronym!

Moving forward then, the three main questions we need to ask of our research, as noted by Guba and Lincoln (1994), are:

1. The ontological question
2. The epistemological question
3. The methodological question

These questions will be discussed in light of three specific paradigms (positivism, post-positivism and interpretivism) before methodologies in general are discussed in section 2.2.

Positivism

Here you are thinking like a realist. You are thinking that the situation is what it is and that you need to work with it in that way. This means that you are a factual person and you believe these facts are objective and that if you were to generate data from these facts, another person could come along and replicate the 'experiment' and gain similar results. If this is the case, then you are a positivist. You believe you can observe and describe reality from an objective, impartial viewpoint. You like rules and you believe phenomena are measureable and predictable. You form a priori hypotheses about social reality and you verify these statements through appropriate testing. You believe that statistics are a necessity and that applying a similar research process in investigating a large sample is appropriate (Creswell, 2009). You search for patterns and you are concerned with causality (connections).

As a positivist, you are likely to have a realist ontology and an objective epistemology, meaning that you view the social world as a matter of fact and you remain impartial regarding the way you generate knowledge – after all, it is what it is!

The fallout from these beliefs is that you are likely to conduct research that is deductive in nature; deduction is something that will be discussed in the final component of the POEM (the **M**ethodology), alongside induction (the other half of the dichotomy).

Interpretivism

Interpretivism is seen as an alternative to positivism. It can be called many things (constructivism, naturalism, humanism, and so on) but, in essence, as an interpretivist you believe that the meaning of the social world is hidden. You believe reality needs to be brought to the surface through deep reflection (Creswell, 2009). Therefore, you think like a relativist (not a realist). You do not have the same beliefs as a positivist. Instead, you believe that reality, as you know it, is constructed by social actors and people's perception of reality. Consequently, you believe that individuals are different: they have different backgrounds which shape their interpretation of reality; they have different experiences, which contribute to their interpretation of reality; and, due to the attributes of society constantly changing, the construction of reality is ongoing, developing, as people engage with society. This means you do not believe that measures of reality are observable (from the outside) because it (reality) is imperceptible (needs to be viewed from the inside), and therefore you are unable to make predictions or state a priori hypotheses because you do not know what exploration (e.g. data collection) may reveal. You therefore believe that reality is a product of subjective experience and that knowledge about this reality should be 'created' as you go. Then, perhaps once you know, you can devise tentative hypotheses about the phenomena.

As an interpretivist, you are likely to have a relativist ontology and a subjective epistemology. This means you view the world as a connected place, whereby phenomena within that world influence other phenomena and all are connected through intersubjectivity. You view the interconnected elements as one, having influence over one another – after all, the reality of what is seen is not clear cut.

The outcome of these beliefs is that you are likely to conduct research that is inductive in nature; induction is something that will be discussed in the final component of the POEM, the **M**ethodology. This is in contrast to deduction. The differences between interpretivism and positivism are summarised in Table 2.1.

Table 2.1   **A snapshot of POEM**

Paradigm	Positivism	Interpretivism
Ontology	Realism	Relativism
Epistemology	Objective	Subjective
Methodology	Deductive	Inductive

Post-positivism

Post-positivism is the third paradigm to consider, which falls somewhere in between the two paradigms that have already been discussed. This does not mean that it is just a mixture of positivism and interpretivism; it is a standalone paradigm that helps a researcher to articulate their beliefs when these beliefs do not fall into the extremes noted above.

Post-positivism is a belief system that is neither naive (positivism) nor subjective (interpretivism). Nevertheless, it is about gaining explanation and making predictions and maintaining control (very similar to positivism). Post-positivism, in essence, acknowledges the belief system of positivism, but then modifies the objective assumptions. So here you still develop hypotheses, but these may be fabricated from the outset, without the actual reality being known. This means you have an idea about reality (it is still observable like positivism) and you still want to test it statistically, but you know that some things may not be exactly as they appear, so falsification is necessary at the start.

As a post-positivist, you are likely to have a critical realist ontology and a dualist/objective epistemology, meaning you view the social world as a matter of fact and you remain impartial about the way you generate knowledge, to some extent, because you interrogate reality until knowledge has been gained. You think you know but want to be certain, before you state something as being a matter of fact. You challenge reality.

The upshot of these beliefs is that you are likely to conduct research that is both deductive and/or inductive in nature; again, something that will be discussed in the final component of the POEM.

Therefore, by considering the three paradigms noted here, we can summarise the differences. The POEM for each is noted in Table 2.2.

Table 2.2   **A summary of the POEM**

Paradigm	Positivism	Post-positivism	Interpretivism
Ontology	Realism	Critical realism	Relativism
Epistemology	Objective	Objective	Subjective
Methodology	Deductive	Deductive/Inductive	Inductive

Illustration 2.1   A personal account – constructivism (AKA interpretivism) in tourism research

Whilst undertaking my PhD in tourism-related crime, it became very clear to me that I had a certain set of beliefs regarding the subjects of my investigation. I was aiming to evaluate the extent to which a community can influence residents' perception of tourism-related crime, and as a result I knew I had to talk to people from 'the community'. Now, before thinking about the methodology, I had already done an extensive review of the literature and determined the multiple meanings of the term community – it isn't just the people who live in the same street or town as you, it is also about groups of people who you actively engage with and share an interest with (like members of an online forum).

I then started to think about how people retain information (or fail to!) and how people recall matters through conversations. But, if we take any person out of their natural setting, they feel uncomfortable, and once we feel uncomfortable we fail to recall all the details, influences and complexities of our experiences and lives. Therefore, I did a little reading (in particular, Mason, 2002) and I made a series of assertions: people (community members) hold actions, reactions and behaviour, which are considered as meaningful components of the social world I was investigating; data could be collected from the knowledge these people hold (as long as they had the ability to reconstruct and remember!); and, in a familiar environment, people would be more willing to share their views, experiences and beliefs if I were approachable, as such. These assertions reflected my ontological position and epistemological perspective, as well as my choice of paradigm.

Consequently, I conformed to the constructs of constructivism. Constructivism allowed me to be actively involved in the social world as a researcher, and for conversations with a purpose (Burgess, 1984) to be undertaken with community members and within familiar surroundings. Constructivism also allowed my relativist belief to be acceptable; that people do not just tell you about their world, but they were (and still are) also actively living in their world and influencing that world. The paradigm also reflected my lack of constraint in terms of defining the boundaries of 'the community' (meaning it reflected my belief that a community is not just a geographical location, but also an ever-changing and complex entity). So, the thought process was much more complex than described here, but, in essence, I believed each person was an individual and would have a story to tell (think about subjectivity, changeability and the possibility of having multiple recollections – this was the start of my POEM!).

2.1.2 Methodological choices

Once you have established your paradigm, your ontological position and your epistemological perspective, it is time to consider your methodology; to complete your POEM. At this point, there are a number of choices you will have to make as a researcher – some are guided by the paradigm, whilst others are guided by the information that is available to you as a researcher and/or the requirements of your project brief. To simplify some of the decisions you may need to make, this section outlines three dichotomies (remember that word – opposing parts – contrasting perspectives) that you may need to discuss with your supervisor, manager or executive team prior to data collection. The three dichotomies to be discussed are:

1. Inductive and deductive approaches
2. Primary and secondary data
3. Quantitative and qualitative methods

There are numerous other dichotomies that can be discussed within the realms of research. However, for the purposes of this book, the discussion is limited to these three, more practical, discussions about undertaking research. To gain additional insight into the various other dichotomies which exist, you may wish to read Veal (2011).

Inductive and deductive dichotomy

The inductive and deductive dichotomy represents two different approaches to collecting data. One approach means you wish to generate theory (induction) about a subject area, and the other implies you wish to test the knowledge you have already gained (deductive). For a moment, just consider that last sentence: theory; knowledge. Where do you gain an understanding of theory and develop knowledge from? Research. Therefore, when determining which approach you are going to follow, it is assumed that you have already done a little research. You may have conducted a quick literature search online to see what theory is already in existence in your subject area. You may have read a piece of research that you wish to follow up on, or you may have developed an awareness of something which is considered to be a new phenomenon. It is this understanding of theory and knowledge that will help you to decipher which approach you may take: inductive or deductive? Furthermore, having worked out your POE(M) to this point, you should have a specific perspective on which approach you wish to take.

However, by presenting research in this way, as a dichotomy, it is important that you do not think you can only do one or the other; because in reality some things are not so clear cut. In fact, some research frequently involves both approaches in a circular way where theory leads to observations, which lead to new patterns of understanding, which in turn lead to new theory. So, instead of seeing this dichotomy in a linear manner (Figure 2.1), it is worth considering it as a circular process (Figure 2.2).

Figure 2.1   **A linear perspective of the dichotomy**

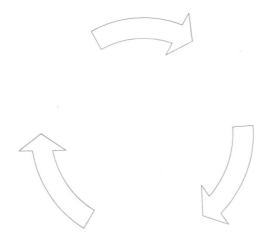

Figure 2.2 The circular process of the dichotomy

So what are induction and deduction? Both are orientations. Both are an approach to undertaking research. Each has a different feel when you are conducting research, mainly because each results in different methods being adopted, as the suitability of each method is determined by your orientations; hence why your methodological decision here may be influenced by your POE(M).

Induction is a process which derives general principles from specific observations; a process which generates theory; a process which starts with observation and moves towards making a broader generalisation. Also known as a bottom-up approach to research, induction is associated with qualitative research and the paradigm of interpretivism. An inductive approach is undertaken when little is already known, you are researching a new phenomenon, you start to detect patterns and then you wish to induce knowledge from the subject(s) itself/themselves (see Figure 2.3). Therefore, the process starts when you observe a matter, decipher patterns and explore that matter in more detail, resulting in theory that may or may not be tested in the future. The process of inductive research is open-ended and exploratory.

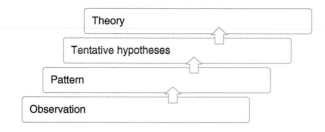

Theory

Tentative hypotheses

Pattern

Observation

Figure 2.3 Inductive reasoning

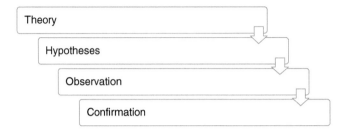

Figure 2.4 Deductive reasoning

Deduction is a process which is based on reason and logical analysis of the available facts; a process which aims to test theory; a process which starts with general understandings and works towards gaining specific insight. Also known as a top-down approach, deduction is associated with quantitative research and the paradigm of positivism. A deductive approach is undertaken when knowledge exists about the subject area and you wish to test that knowledge within your specific subject area, to see if that theory can be applied to your subject matter (see Figure 2.4). Therefore, the process involves you stating hypotheses (drawn from the known theory) and proving/disproving them through statistical analysis. The process of deduction is narrow in nature and is concerned with testing and confirming hypotheses. After all, by collecting data you are narrowing down even further in a very specific subject area, one which may only have a single application.

More specifically, when considering the circular process of the inductive and deductive dichotomy we can really start to think about the two alternative approaches to undertaking research and how they can be viewed more as a process. For example, if you take Figure 2.5, you can see each process involves three stages (A–C). From the content perspective, it could be argued that there are seminaries between the two processes. However, the difference sits exactly where the research process begins (at point A, B or C). The inductive process begins at point A, proceeds to point B and arrives at point C; whereas the deductive process begins at point C, proceeds to point A (gathering data to test the hypothesis) and arrives at point B.

Each approach is frequently used within research. There is no right or wrong or preferred process to undertake. Instead, it comes down to suitability. It is important that when you make this methodological choice, you carefully consider the POE(M) and you ensure you select the most appropriate paradigm to follow. As long as you have a clear rationale for the choices you make, and your choices are substantiated with an understanding of the approach, you will make the right decision for your research. Remember, you may be a realist or a relativist, and that may influence your choice – so you may make a different choice to others.

In terms of detecting each approach within completed research agendas, it is useful to consider what the study focuses on. This can be determined through the

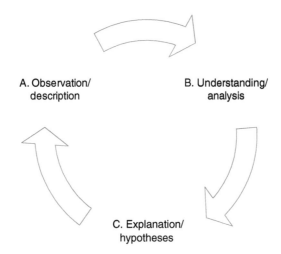

Figure 2.5 **The inductive/deductive dichotomy**

methodology (because qualitative research is more favourably associated with inductive research, and quantitative with deduction) or through the level of knowledge that can be ascertained prior to data collection (remember it is where the research process begins that dictates its actual process). An example of how this can be determined is outlined in Image 2.1 which displays two extracts from tourism-related crime journal articles; one is inductive, the other deductive. But can you decipher which is which?

Extract A within Image 2.1 clearly states it is an exploratory approach to the subject area of gay victimisation. The authors uncovered a theory (they were not testing it). Therefore, it could easily be claimed that Extract A is inductive, because it did not start with a hypothesis; instead it generated theory (an A, B, C process). Extract B, on the other hand, started with the theory of tourism-related crime and

This study examines the phenomenon of gay tourist victimisation

A review of literature suggests that
has only recently become a focus of research

The paper questions whether

The findings suggest that

The exploratory nature of the research

A specific link was uncovered

Extract A (Brunt & Brophy 2006)

Tourist victimisation and the fear of crime on holiday

This paper reviews research undertaken in the field of tourism and crime

which suggests that there is empirical evidence that

tourism does contribute to an increase in crime

The paper also focuses on research aimed at assessing the nature of tourist
victimisation and the fear of crime exhibited by British holidaymakers.

not a new phenomenon.

It would appear that, on balance, tourism does contribute to an increase in crime, and tourists may be
particularly susceptible to crime especially where they
involve themselves in risky behaviour.

The questionnaire itself covered 90 questions

Extract B (Brunt, Mawby & Hambly 2000)

Image 2.1 **Induction and deduction in action**

worked with empirical evidence to test theory in a specific setting. Therefore, it is easy to suggest that it was deductive because not only did it test hypotheses, it also used a questionnaire for data collection (and that is associated with a deductive approach). So, sometimes, you can determine the approach of other researchers, and this may also lead to the methodological decision you make here – to follow a deductive or an inductive approach. The main question to remember and to ask of research is: where does/did the research start?

Primary and secondary data

The primary and secondary data dichotomy represents two different approaches to collecting data. One approach means you are inclined to see what is already known about the subject matter (secondary data), to determine if knowledge already exists; and if the data you require has indeed already been collected by someone else, you use it. Because why would you just wish to replicate a study to find out nothing new? Primary data collection means you are looking to collect your own data about the subject matter because the information does not exist elsewhere and you wish to explore the subject matter further. So, the real question here is, does data already exist or are you collecting new information? To summarise:

> *Primary data collection* relates to the collection of new information. This is the case where the researcher requires specific information which does not exist elsewhere or in another form. For instance, at recreation sites if information is required about how people regard the attractions, then it is only practical to ask them directly. It is, however, often sensible to consider whether it is worth going to the expense of collecting new information.

> *Secondary data collection* relates to the collection of data from sources which already exist. Thus, the researcher is the secondary user. The use of census data, minutes of meetings or financial records are some sources of secondary information. In the THE industries specifically, there is the World Tourism Organisation (WTO), the Organisation for Economic Co-operation and Development (OECD), the Economist Intelligence Unit (EIU) and the Office for National Statistics (ONS), who all publish invaluable sources of THE data on a global and national level. Moreover, government departments and public sector agencies, like Visit England and Visit Britain, undertake surveys for a wide range of purposes which may provide valuable secondary information for the THE researcher. Furthermore, many organisations keep a variety of information or records which could be analysed. All of these examples are valuable sources of information.

When considering which of the two approaches to adopt, it is important to reflect on a number of constraints, including both time and money. It may be that data exists and obtaining the secondary data is easy and timely. Many companies find that the cost of collecting data first hand is such that managers need to consider whether data collected by others can be used for the purpose outlined. However, secondary data can involve financial costs as well, because not all data sets are free and open access. Furthermore, you may have to trade off other attributes as well, like your level of control over the research process and the quality of the data set, because you were not involved in the original data collection process. As you begin to weigh up the advantages and costs of utilising secondary data, you may foresee the other option (primary data collection) as a more viable possibility. Primary data collection is not without its own set of constraints though. For example, setting up a research schedule is time-consuming (and reflected on in the next chapter) and costly. Therefore, it is important that you review all of your options and that you make well-informed and timely decisions, to suit the nature of the project you are planning to undertake. No research methodology is without its imitation, however it is up to you, as the researcher, to ensure careful thought and consideration go into all the methodological decisions you make.

Illustration 2.2   The use of secondary data in research

Andreas Walmsley is a reader in entrepreneurship at Plymouth University and he specialises in youth employment within the tourism sector. From a review of his more recent publications (Font et al., 2012; Walmsley, 2011, 2012), it is evident that secondary data contributes to a large proportion of his research. In a number of publications, he has utilised data to establish international comparisons of tourism wages (Laborsta – an International Labour Office database on labour statistics), youth unemployment from a European perspective (the European Commission's Eurostat resource) and CSR policies of specific hotel chains (individual company websites). The sources of secondary data illustrate the range of possibilities that are open to the researcher – from online databases to individual websites.

Quantitative and qualitative methods

The quantitative and qualitative dichotomy represents two different approaches to collecting primary data. A quantitative approach means that you, to some extent, are focusing on statistics, numbers and making generalisations about a broad population, whilst a qualitative approach means you are focusing more on depth of knowledge, interpretation of evidence (like words) and transference. Therefore, each approach has distinctive attributes and consequently leads to a variety of advantages and limitations that need to be considered prior to data collection. However, by this point in developing your POEM, you may have already considered these issues and made your methodological choice: quantitative or qualitative? After all, the paradigm can dictate and influence your choice at this stage (e.g. positivism, deduction and a quantitative approach). Nevertheless, you may still be pondering the decision and wishing to ensure you have made the right choice. Therefore, this section is designed purely to give an overview of the dichotomy. It is in the next section (2.2) that the details and depths of each approach are explored, with further decisions to be made and justifications contextualised to the THE industry.

Quantitative methods involve numbers: statistics and statistical analysis. This means that the results of studies using quantitative methods (from perhaps a survey) could be used to generalise about the broader population with a certain degree of confidence. Quantitative methods rely on numerical evidence to test hypotheses (Brunt, 1997) and are commonly used to be sure of reliability in statistical tests. Data are gathered, the information is coded into numeric form and computers are used to analyse the data. Therefore, the main attributes of a quantitative approach include: the use of identical questions and methods of recording the answers; a large sample that is representative of the population under consideration; the statistical analysis of data to draw conclusions; and specific consideration given to questionnaire design (whereby most questions are closed and attitudes and opinions are measured by the use of rating scales). On the back of these attributes, there are numerous advantages and limitations which also need to be considered, as noted in Table 2.3. There are further possibilities to consider, because sometimes quantitative methods are actually used on small

Table 2.3   Advantages and limitations of quantitative methods

Advantages	Limitations
• Large sample sizes commonly used are more representative of the population. Thus, statements about the population can be made with a degree of confidence.	• Samples may not always be representative because of the problems associated with those who decline to take part in research.
• Much information in the tourism, hospitality and events management industry is required in a quantitative form to enable managers to make decisions or to conduct meetings in an informed context.	• Quantitative methods are often impersonal. Often, a relatively small amount of information is known about people's life history or experiences.
• Data are easily summarised and analysed using computers.	• Bias may be caused by poor questions or interviewers, which affects people's answers.

numbers of people where the aim is not to generalise widely. This discussion will be left until section 2.2 though.

Qualitative methods give rise to non-quantitative information, meaning they focus on collecting a great deal of 'rich' information about relatively few people rather than more limited information about a large number of people. The techniques adopted include in-depth interviews, group interviews and participant observation alongside ethnography. The term 'ethnography' (or ethnographic research/ethnographic fieldwork) in this context is a type of research which uses a range of techniques rather than being a single technique itself. The word *ethnos* derives from the Greek word meaning people, and therefore ethnography is about the study of people. The term has been 'pinched' from anthropology – essentially about the study of groups of people and, by a variety of qualitative methods, leading to an understanding of how a community works and what makes it 'tick'. Consequently, the main attributes of a qualitative approach are: to gain in-depth, open-ended answers rather than yes/no responses; and for the interviewer to get people to share their thoughts on a topic with the minimum of guidelines about how they should answer. Due to the level of researcher involvement, there are specific advantages and limitations which need to be considered here, as noted in Table 2.4.

Table 2.4   Advantages and limitations of qualitative methods

Advantages	Limitations
• Provide 'rich' information about people: their experiences, motivations, behaviour, needs and aspirations.	• Small numbers of people are normally involved, thus generalisations about the population at large cannot be made.
• Are able to encompass changes over time.	• The measurement of qualitative material often requires judgements to be made by the researcher, hence questions of objectivity arise.
• Are more personal.	
• The information is understandable by the majority – statistical tests are less important.	

Taken as a methodological choice, it is at this stage that you need to review your POEM and identify the most suitable means for collecting data. Every research project has its limitations, but for your project you need to ensure you have clearly justified your decision and choices. As noted before, you may get to this final decision and your POEM has already dictated which approach you need to follow. However, if you are unsure and you are reflecting on your stance – your set of beliefs which influence the way you plan to 'do' research – then the content of Table 2.5 may be of value to you. Table 2.5 highlights some of the common dichotomies within the quantitative and qualitative debate and refers back to the initial

Table 2.5   Common dichotomies within the qualitative/quantitative debate

Quantitative	Qualitative
Objective	Subjective
Deductive	Inductive
Sociology	Anthropology
Science	Art
Explanation	Understanding
Predictive	Descriptive

construction stages of your POEM. Furthermore, it may be that you are not picking just one approach to data collection; you may be opting for a mixed-method approach to triangulate the findings (see section 2.3).

2.1.3 Overview of the research POEM

Section 2.1 reviewed a range of different approaches to research, which are determined by the researcher's intention and perspective on collecting data. Whilst considering your belief set, and the methodological choices that are open to you, the POEM was identified. Now your feelings and your intentions around data collection have been expressed, it is useful to review your decisions and ensure you are clear on their implications. Table 2.6 is designed to provide an overview of the content of this section, and offer clarification as to how each POEM may differ depending on the paradigm that is followed.

Table 2.6   An overview of a research POEM

Paradigm	Positivism	Post-positivism	Interpretivism
Ontology	(Naive) realism:	Critical realism:	Relativism:
	External	Social conditioning	Socially constructed
	Objective	Objective	Subjective
	Independent	Independent	Changeable
			Multiple
Epistemology	Objectivist assumption	Modified objectivist assumptions	Subjectivist assumptions
	Observable phenomena only	Observable phenomena only	Observable phenomena (and/or)
			Subjective meanings
Methodology	Quantitative	Qualitative (and Quantitative)	Qualitative
	Deductive	Falsification of hypotheses	Inductive
	Verification of hypotheses		Tentative hypotheses
Examples	Survey	Ethnography	In-depth interviews

2.2 Methodologies for tourism, hospitality and events-based research

The main methodologies used in the tourism, hospitality and events management (THE) industry has evolved and expanded in recent years as new knowledge has been gained and additional insight has been sought. Even though there has been a broad range of unique studies that have explored various key issues within THE, there are some common and more frequently used methodologies. The most commonly utilised methods in THE fall within the qualitative and quantitative dichotomy, and will therefore be identified and defined within the next two sections. The focus will be placed on quantitative, questionnaire-based methodologies and qualitative, in-depth interviews. Nevertheless, consideration will also be given to qualitative focus groups, case study approaches and observational tools. For a more complete guide to this dichotomy, and help with collecting data via these techniques, please see Chapter 6.

2.2.1 Quantitative methods for THE

The most commonly used methodology in the THE industry is the questionnaire survey. Questionnaire surveys are used to gain information from respondents (i.e. people) who answer questions about themselves, their knowledge of a particular subject and their opinions. The questions in the questionnaire are structured so that each respondent answers in exactly the same way. This enables the researcher to compare the answers of each respondent in a quantitative way. For example, pie charts and histograms can be constructed from the results to show the spread of answers to the questions. Therefore, each technique has unique attributes to consider and creates its own broad implications for questionnaire design and delivery (see Chapter 5).

In general, there are two principal types of questionnaire surveys found within THE, relating to the methods of the data collection process itself:

1. Personal interviews (sometimes referred to as a face-to-face questionnaire)
2. Self-completion questionnaires

The difference between these two types of questionnaire surveys relates to whether interviewers conduct the interview and complete the questionnaire on the respondents' behalf, or whether the respondents themselves complete the questionnaire. These two methods have different advantages and limitations to consider, which are listed in Table 2.7.

In fact, the choice of approach may be dictated by how the questionnaire is distributed. For example, if you devise an online survey, you will need to undertake a self-completed questionnaire because you will not be present to tick the boxes for the respondents. However, if you are on-site at a festival, for example, you will have the

Table 2.7 Advantages and limitations of self-completed and personal interviews

	Personal interview	Self-completion
Advantages	• Personal contact with the respondent. • Verbal explanations can be given by the interviewer, as necessary. • Misunderstanding can be reduced because the interviewer can gauge if the respondent has understood the question(s). • Problems of limited literacy can be avoided because the questions are verbally articulated to respondents. • Unhelpful or inadequate replies can be probed. • Unanswered question(s) can be avoided.	• Large number of questionnaires can be distributed quickly and cheaply. • Training of staff need not be as intensive as for personal interviewing because the respondent is completing the questionnaire. • Respondents can complete the questionnaire at leisure (in their own time). • The possibility of interviewer bias can be removed.
Limitations	• The approach is subject to interviewer bias because the way a question is worded, or answer responded to, may influence the respondent's answer. • It can be costly to implement personal interviews because training interviewers is costly and they can only interview one person at a time.	• The questions have to be simple and not open to misunderstanding. • No probing (further clarification) is possible. • There are costs associated with distribution and/or postage (depending on how it is distributed). • There is little control over when the questionnaire is completed and by whom. • Failure to answer questions is more frequent and the quality of answers can be variable.

option to record the information on behalf of the respondent, or allow the respondent to complete it in their own time. In general, there are different types of situations where a specific type of questionnaire is deemed as being most suitable. For example, the personal interview survey can be sub-divided into three suitable categories:

1. On-site/street
2. Home/office-based
3. Telephone-based

Whereas the self-completion survey can be sub-divided into two suitable categories:

1. Postal
2. Online

Of course, as noted above with the festival example, there may be situations that defy these categorisations. However, for the purposes of identifying and defining the various techniques, the sub-categories are applied to outline the basic process alongside the advantages and limitations of each technique.

On-site/street questionnaires

Within the THE industry, we can identify a range of attractions, places and destinations which people may travel to. We can also recognise a number of places where people pass by. For example, there are numerous tourist attractions, hotel complexes and festival sites (to name only a few). There are numerous transportation hubs, shopping centres and recreational facilities whereby you may find THE participants and non-participants. This means that, depending on the nature of your enquiry, you may be undertaking either an on-site survey (at a specific destination where users can be found) or a street survey (whereby you may be interviewing non-users of a specific product, site, facility). Simply put, if you foresee yourself in situ at the location of your enquiry, then you are conducting an on-site survey. If you are not, then you are on-street. Whether you decide to complete an on-site survey or a street survey, there are numerous considerations to take on board. The foremost consideration is the question of suitability, which can be determined by reviewing the advantages and limitations of this technique in Table 2.8.

Table 2.8   Advantages and limitations of on-site questionnaires

	Advantages	Limitations
On-site	• The interviewer will gain direct access to the site users. • There is a minimum time lag between questions about behaviour and opinions about the site, and the respondent's actual behaviour taking place because you are asking on-site itself – leaving little time for recall to become distorted or fail. • Rapport can be built with the respondent.	• The questionnaire needs to be kept relatively short – normally under 10 minutes and, as a consequence, the range of questioning techniques is limited. • It can be difficult to carry out rigid sampling on complex sites because you may need to be situated at an entrance and an exit and elsewhere to capture data.
Street	• The interviewer has the potential to gain access to users and non-users of a THE product. • Consequently, a range of perspectives can be gained because non-users (for example, those who would not be selected by a site survey because they have not visited the site) can be included.	• Depending on the focus of the study, there may be a time lag between a respondent's actual behaviour and their surveyed behaviour and opinions of a THE product/experience. • The non-response rate may increase due to the access to non-users.

Home-based or office-based questionnaires

Depending on the focus of your investigation, you may need to interview people within their home and work environments. For example, you may have determined that people are more capable of recalling their thought process and actions if they are comfortable and are surrounded by familiar objects. You may in fact be researching professional standards and/or business matters and therefore feel that to uphold a level

Table 2.9   Advantages and limitations of home-based and office-based questionnaires

Advantages	Limitations
• The interview can be arranged at the respondent's own convenience.	• Time is involved in contacting each respondent individually to arrange a suitable time and date for the personal interview.
• The interview can be longer – up to an hour.	• Information about behaviour and opinions is retrospective.
• A wider range of questioning techniques can be used.	
• Non-users (for example, those who would not be selected by a site survey because they have not visited the site) can be included.	• May only include a small number of users (as opposed to a site survey).
• Sampling can be strictly controlled.	• The approach is costly in terms of the interviewer's time and resources.
• Response rates are higher than other questionnaire surveys, especially if prior contact/appointment is made.	

of professionalism and to ensure the respondent gives an appropriate reply, you wish for them to be at work, to keep them focused. Alternatively, you may want the respondent to comment on a lengthy questionnaire and to give answers that are reflective of their personal life; you may therefore choose a home-based questionnaire. In essence, these types of questionnaires do not differ from the above; they just place emphasis on the interviewer accessing respondents within a different environment. The main thing is that you choose the most suitable type of environment that helps you, the researcher, gain the most apt answers. This may be pre-selected due to the aim of the project and who is supporting the project financially. However, for some it will be a choice, and an open choice that needs to be considered in detail; a choice that is well informed and considers the advantages and limitations noted in Table 2.9.

Telephone-based questionnaires

Telephone interviews are frequently conducted when there is a desire to target a broad range of users, from different geographical areas, but travel to them is not feasibly possible. Although the interviewer and the respondent are not face to face, the process is the same as the other personal interview types described above. The interviewer is using the questionnaire as a script and is recording the respondents' answers on their behalf; the main difference is the level of interaction over the phone rather than being in person. Another difference is the fact that the researcher can directly input the answers into the appropriate software programme; but, on reflection, with the aid of Wi-Fi and tablets, this is also now possible with on-site and in-street surveys. Perhaps then, the differences are minimal, other than the nature of rapport that can be gained over the phone and the way in which trust can be built between the two parties to ensure effective communication takes place and appropriate answers are gained. A variety of advantages and limitations are listed in Table 2.10 for consideration. One of

Table 2.10 **Advantages and limitations of telephone surveys**

Advantages	Limitations
• Reduces the costs involved in travel. • Answers can be easily computer coded as the interview progresses. • Sampling can be strictly controlled.	• Rather anonymous; respondents may be less willing to recount experiences on the telephone. • Only involves respondents who have a telephone.

the key points, however, is access. How can you gain access to a database of relevant phone numbers and, if you can, how much will it cost? There may be minimal costs associated with the technique if, say, a hotel has a list of customer details (customers who have agreed to have their numbers stored and shared – just consider data protection for a moment!) and all that needs to be paid for is the call itself. However, should you be purchasing a data set, this may add undue costs to the project; and, hence, as the researcher, you need to know if this is worth the additional cost.

Postal questionnaires

Postal questionnaires are the first of two self-completed questionnaires that are being discussed here. In this case, the respondent has time on their side and they are in control of how and when the questionnaire is completed, and even by whom. Just stop and think about this for a few moments. You are at home, and through the door with your postal delivery you receive a questionnaire. Do you sit straight down and respond to the questionnaire? Or do you judge the necessity of completing the questionnaire and make one of two decisions: to complete it or put it in the bin! This is a natural response, because as you sift through the mail you judge the questionnaire and determine if it is of value to you, personally, to actually respond. If it is, then you may decide to put it on the side and fill it out later when you have time. Then, when later arrives, you may get around to filling it in. You may not fill it in, after all, if it is not of value to you, personally, in which case you may decide to recycle it with the other junk mail. If you do complete the questionnaire, the next key issue is how you return it. In general, postal questionnaires can be returned to the interviewer in a number of ways, either via post or by having a deposit box in a communal location, thus helping to remove interviewer bias (Brunt, 1997).

According to Bryman and Bell (2007), postal questionnaires are one of the main instruments for gathering data in the social sciences. However, I am now starting to question the frequency with which postal questionnaires are used, especially within THE. With the rise of online surveys, surely it is not still the case that they are the main instrument. Postal questionnaires are still of value to a researcher and can yield appropriate and reliable data, as displayed in Table 2.11. However, there is no longer evidence to support the claim that they are the main instrument.

Table 2.11   Advantages and limitations of postal questionnaires

Advantages	Limitations
• Can be completed at leisure.	• Lack of control over the question order.
• Allow large number of respondents to be surveyed in a relatively short period of time.	• The possibility that many questions go unanswered because the interviewer is not present to direct.
• Allow time to be taken by the respondents to answer the questionnaire.	• No control over date or time of response, or in fact who actually answer the questionnaire.
• Give the respondent greater assurance of anonymity.	
• Insulate the respondent from the expectations of the interviewer.	

Online questionnaires

The second, and final, self-completed questionnaires that are being discussed here are online. Here we are hosting and posting our set of questions on the internet and utilising online software, like Qualtrics, to design our questionnaire which is then distributed to our chosen audience via many different means. By no means is Qualtrics the only online software package that may be used; there are many to choose from (like Google Docs and Survey Monkey, to name just two more) and your decision may depend on your available resources. Your institution or organisation may have a subscription to an online software package; you may have money constraints and choose not to pay for a lengthier questionnaire, or choose to export your data to your chosen analysis software (i.e. SPSS); or you may have previous experience of using just one platform and you decide to stick with the known entity. Whatever your choice in software is, you are creating a self-completed questionnaire that allows your respondent to take their time over filling in the questionnaire. Based on this fact then, there are many things you need to consider in relation to adopting an online survey.

First and foremost, who is online? According to the Office of National Statistics (2016), over 10% of the UK population have still never used the internet which equates to a population of 5.3 million people! Of those using the internet more recently, they fall within the age category of 16 to 24 years (99.2% are users) and not aged 75 and over (only 38.7% are users) (ONS, 2016). You should find an even usage between the genders online, but not between age groups (older women have seen the largest rise in recent internet use). Consequently, you need to determine who your target audience is for your questionnaire and deem if it is suitable to distribute it online to them.

Second, should you be targeting specific consumers, or are you just asking the general public? In terms of collating information online, you need to consider the unique qualities of the THE industry and determine who, how and when you are planning to distribute your hyperlink to them for maximum effect. Let's just stop and think about each strand of THE. From an events perspective, ideally, if you are focusing on one specific event, then you should be conducting research at the time of the event. However, if a list of attendees is available to you, then they can be contacted online after the event (Fox et al., 2014). From a hospitality perspective, an organisation may wish to assess the guests' level

Table 2.12   Advantages and limitations of online questionnaires

Advantages	Limitations
• Allow respondents to complete the questionnaire at leisure.	• Only involves respondents who have a computer/smartphone/access to the internet.
• Allow a large number of respondents to be surveyed in a relatively short period of time.	• No control over date or time of response, or in fact who actually answers the questionnaire.
• Allow time to be taken by the respondents to answer the questionnaire.	• The data may not be honest because some people answer questionnaires for incentives, and not because they have genuine insight into the experience/product.
• Give the respondent greater assurance of anonymity.	
• Insulate the respondent from the expectations of the interviewer.	
• The process can be faster, cheaper and quicker than other methods.	

of overall satisfaction with their experience. The hotel is likely to have a contact email address (because we share our information with the hotel upon check-in!) and then they (with perfect timing before people forget) will be able to gather feedback after the experience. From a tourism perspective, the provider may, again, be interested in gathering information following the tourism experience, and therefore after the visit they will be able to gather feedback on experience, satisfaction and expenditure. However, a key concern here is timing. When is the right time to send an email and who is likely to actually respond to the request? Customers who are happy or have a complaint to make? If you are working for a tour operator who targets the ageing market, then the majority of your audience will not be online, so why would you create an online questionnaire? These are all key questions to consider and are reflected in the advantages and limitations noted in Table 2.12, although a much more detailed discussion about online surveys is held in later chapters. This note here is just about providing food for thought, because online surveys are extensively used within THE, but they are not always suitable.

2.2.2 Qualitative methods for THE

The group of techniques listed in this section have been put under the banner of qualitative methods, because the purpose is more likely to develop tentative hypotheses concerning behaviour or attitudes (so is more inductive) and to understand how people feel or react (so offers a depth of understanding). These techniques are commonly used within the THE industry and offer an alternative, rigorous, method of data collection to quantitative techniques noted in the previous section. Some of the main techniques used within the THE industry include:

1. In-depth interview
2. Focus group
3. Observation
4. Case study approach

An overview of each technique will be outlined here, with both the advantages and limitations of each approach being highlighted from a THE perspective. For a fuller discussion, subsequent chapters can be reviewed.

In-depth interview

As a qualitative technique, the in-depth interview with a respondent is designed to gather 'rich' information (Mason, 2002) from a relatively small number of respondents, rather than to statistically generalise from a large sample (Brunt, 1997). The interaction happens on a one-to-one basis between the researcher and the respondent, and engages in a conversation with a purpose (Burgess, 1984).

The in-depth interview has specific characteristics because the respondents are given the opportunity to discuss their experiences, in detail, of something which is common to them. To give respondents this freedom to recount their experiences, prior analysis of the subject area needs to be undertaken, and the nature of the questionnaire needs to reflect not only the objectives of the research, but also the level of formality being applied to the situation. For example, formal interviews tend to be guided by a structured questionnaire, whereas informal interviews tend to be guided by a semi-structured or unstructured questionnaire (literally a few bullet points!). The level of formality suggests the nature of the encounter between the researcher and the respondent, and other situational factors that need to be considered. For example, formal in-depth interviews may be conducted in an official setting, to put the respondent in the right frame of mind to offer insight into the subject area. Just imagine you are interviewing a tourism official – you are likely to develop a structured questionnaire, send the questions over to the respondent before you meet, and, upon arriving at the tourism office, you sit at a desk to 'talk business'. This is a very different scenario than if you were to interview a local resident about the impacts of festival tourism that they have personally been experiencing in their home environment. Here, you may develop a less structured questionnaire (because you do not know what the resident might wish to reflect on), arrange to meet in their home environment and make yourself comfortable on

Table 2.13   Advantages and limitations of in-depth interviews

Advantages	Limitations
• The technique corresponds with the nature of the phenomena being studied.	• The respondent, if not made to feel comfortable, may be unwilling to reveal information.
• The researcher can access a large amount of data quickly, through each and every interview.	• The interviewers may not ask questions that evoke long narratives.
• In-depth understanding is sought and the researcher is able to probe deeper into information.	• The technique is time-consuming because, on average, an interview lasts for more than 30 minutes.
• Allow respondents to say what they think.	• The recordings are also time-consuming to transcribe.

their sofa to conduct the interview. This second example is rather informal in comparison to the first, but has the same purpose in mind. Both examples are putting the right person in the right frame of mind to talk about the subject matter being discussed, in their natural environment (Marshall and Rossman, 1999). Respondents are comfortable and in a location that helps them, as an individual, to recall the most appropriate information that will assist your investigation.

Another element to consider is that interviews tend to be recorded (audio only) and then transcribed by the researcher. This process is common (given consent by the respondent) because it is difficult to have a meaningful conversation whilst writing detailed notes to ensure you, the researcher, can recall all the appropriate information. There are, like other techniques, a range of advantages and limitations to consider, as noted in Table 2.13.

Focus group

Focus groups are similar in many respects to the in-depth interview (Savin-Baden and Howell Major, 2013) but are conducted with a small group of people, not just an individual. The group formation enables interaction on many levels – both between the respondents and between the researcher and the respondent. These supplementary levels of interaction form an additional part of the data collection process. Normally, the researcher will act as the group leader (the facilitator) and initiate the discussion with the group. The facilitator then allows conversation to continue between group members, rather than maintain the discussion throughout the session themselves. This aspect differs from in-depth interviews. However, in a similar manner, the discussions of the group tend to be recorded – both audio and visual elements can be recorded (with consent from the respondents).

The group itself is made up of between 5 and 12 respondents (Brunt, 1997; Bryman and Bell, 2007) who have something in common with each other. For instance, they may all have stayed at a particular hotel, attended the same event or decided to engage

Table 2.14 Advantages and limitations of focus groups

Advantages	Limitations
• The technique can be used as a process of fact finding as it allows thematic interests to naturally arise.	• The researcher has less control over proceedings because interaction happens on many levels.
• Quick and detailed information can be gained from the group.	• Due to the richness of information gained, data may be difficult to analyse; furthermore, the researcher needs to assess what is by whom!
• In general, focus groups can be less expensive and time-consuming than individual interviews because the researcher may only need to conduct two or three group meetings.	• A focus group can be difficult to organise because of the number of people who need to come together in one place at one time.
	• The recordings are time-consuming to transcribe.
	• There can be problems of group effects (e.g. the bandwagon effect).

with a specific tourism product. Saying that, the common factor may be that they are all non-users of the specific product! The atmosphere of the focus group is also of importance. The meeting should be designed to be as relaxed as possible, so that members feel at ease and are happy to recount their experiences. Consideration should also be given to the range of advantages and limitations noted in Table 2.14.

Observation

Observation is often a neglected technique within the THE industry (Brunt, 1997) but the results can be of great value to all involved. For example, much can be learned about human behaviour by observing it, even at a distance. In essence, there are three main types of behaviour that can be observed:

1. *Non-verbal behaviour:* this includes observing information about movement, which can serve to repeat, emphasise or even contradict a verbal message being shared. For example, the face is used a great deal during communication and hand signals, shrugs and head movements can be employed. This non-verbal movement is often subconscious and can be used for things such as expressing emotions and conveying attitudes.
2. *Spatial behaviour:* this refers to attempts by an individual to structure space around themselves. For example, people move toward or away from, maintain closeness to or distance from, others and objects. All of these are significant acts of spatial behaviour which may reveal a great deal about the phenomenon under study.
3. *Extra-linguistic behaviour:* words only contribute a small proportion of verbal behaviour, and it is other factors, such as the rate of speaking, loudness, tendency to interrupt and pronunciation, which constitute a rich source of data.

Illustration 2.3   Examples of what can be observed

To observe *non-verbal behaviour*, you can pay attention to the emotion that is expressed by a respondent (e.g. smiling to show happiness), determine if the respondents are conveying attitudes (e.g. are they staring to show aggression?) and highlight any personality traits being conveyed (e.g. open palms show accepting qualities). In essence, you are paying attention to the body language of the respondents. Body language is a sign of the subconscious thinking of the individual. Such behaviour is of significance when behaviour, as noted above, is displayed at the same time (in clusters) and when it is unlikely that the person being observed is trying to control their non-verbal behaviour (e.g. being asked an embarrassing question).

To observe *spatial behaviour*, you can pay attention to where people are positioned in situ (e.g. on a beach, why do people all group together down one end of the beach when the rest is free space?) and to how people position themselves in relation to others whilst communicating (e.g. are they conveying a personal space between themselves and another?).

To observe *extra-linguistic behaviour*, you can pay attention to vocal pitch (this is an accurate measure of an individual's emotional state). Try and replicate some of these suggestions, so that you can acknowledge the differences: talk fast and then slowly, talk quietly and then loudly – can you associate each one with a different emotional state (e.g. loud is aggravated)?

However, for observation to be a reliable technique it must be systematically planned and relate to the precise aims and objectives of the research proposal, the planning of which requires careful consideration of the actual type of observation which will take place and the ethical implications of each approach.

There are two different types of observation (Bailey, 1987) to consider:

1. *Unobtrusive observation*: in the field, researchers can place themselves in suitable positions to watch the behaviour of others. For example, researchers can use cameras or one-way mirrors to observe the activities being undertaken. In airports, the queuing behaviour of people, as they check in, can be observed to make assessments of staff and tourists. In recent years, the use of television cameras in tourist resorts has become common to help reduce crime.

2. *Participant observation*: in this type, the researcher becomes part of the group he is researching and participates in the activities of the group. For example, the researcher can become a tourist, attend events or join a hospitality organisation and become the 'other'. In this way the researcher can feel the frustrations or enjoyments of the other and gain experience of and background material on how things function.

Furthermore, there are two types of observation which implicate the ethics behind the observation:

1. *Covert observation*: this involves the researcher participating fully without informing members of the social group of the reasons for their presence. The research is carried out secretly or covertly.

2. *Overt observation*: this involves the researcher being open about the reason for their presence in the field of study. The researcher is given permission by the group to conduct their research.

Table 2.15   Advantages and limitations of observation

Advantages	Limitations
• Behaviour is studied as it occurs. Instead of asking people what they do, the researcher can observe it as it happens.	• The researcher has little control over the interactions, environments and therefore the data gained.
• Data is collected in the setting in which the behaviour or actions to be studied are taking place.	• Due to the richness of data that can be collected, there are analysis difficulties.
• The relationship between an individual and their environment is reflected upon and non-verbal behaviour can be gleaned.	• Gaining entry to an environment can be an issue, especially if overt and unobtrusive. After all, who enjoys being knowingly watched!
	• This technique is inappropriate when studying opinions and attitudes.
	• Striking a balance between subjectivity and objectivity during data collection is an issue.

Once these decisions have been made, the advantages and limitations can be acknowledged, as shown in Table 2.15. The advantages include those noted by Nachmias and Nachmias (1996) of directness, the natural setting and contextual background, whereas one of the main difficulties associated with observation as a means of data collection is the amount of judgement that the researcher must apply. This is because human behaviour is extremely complex and an amount of inference from the researcher is required. Despite these worries, observation can be a useful method of data collection. Sidney and Beatrice Webb (1932: 158) were early researchers in this area and stated that 'an indispensable part of the study of any social institution, wherever this can be obtained, is deliberate and sustained personal observation ... from which the investigator may learn a lot. He clarifies his ideas ... revises his provisional classifications ... tests his hypotheses ... or even more importantly by watching committees etc., picks up hints that help him manifest new hypotheses.'

One of the main difficulties with the methods of observation is the balance between subjectivity and objectivity. On the one hand, data are collected which are rich, in that the observed may be unaware of the study and will therefore act naturally. On the other hand, the level of judgement that the observer has to introduce into the recording of the observation may bring into question the accuracy of the results. In order to overcome or minimise these difficulties, a systematic method of recording the observation is required. The level of control necessary to introduce into an observation study depends on the topic and the difficulty of judgement in the observations. One method would be to use an 'observation schedule' where the observer records the actions of others according to definite pre-arranged plans (Brunt, 1997). The development of an observation schedule can be complex and requires trial and error, if the data produced are to be reliable. An example of an early study was reported by Bales (1950). Bales' (1950) method of 'interaction process analysis' involved the systematic recording of the interaction of small groups of people.

Case study approach

A case study is the intensive examination of an individual or a small number of examples. The approach may involve techniques such as the scrutiny of secondary sources, in-depth interviews or focus groups. It can be considered as being opposite to large-scale quantitative surveys. For example, if a researcher was investigating holiday decision-making, they may choose to confine their attention to an intensive study of a small number of families rather than a large sample survey. In the latter case, the results would inevitably be more superficial. Thus, case studies allow the researcher to 'get inside' the subject under study, but in doing so they lose the opportunity for statistical generalisations.

Case studies enable the intense study of one particular case (Fox et al., 2014) – for example, an event, a festival, an organisation, a business, an attraction. There are six different types of case study (Yin, 1993) approaches which can be taken, split over two axes: single case (focus on one individual, business or organisation) and multiple case (focus on two or more individuals, businesses or organisations). The categorisations are then separated by the level of depth and detail being designed into the purpose of the research, as illustrated in Figure 2.6.

From reviewing these options, it is clear to see how different types of case studies could be developed to suit the research agenda of the researcher. After all, you would only select one of the six categories noted above if it was suitable – suitable in the sense that you believed that data could be effectively generated from that specific type of case study to answer the research question.

	Single case	Multiple case
	1	2
Exploratory	Focus on one individual, business or organisation to develop research questions and objectives.	Focus on two or more individuals, businesses or organisations to develop research questions and objectives.
	3	4
Descriptive	Focus on one individual, business or organisation to describe the case as a complete project.	Focus on two or more individuals, businesses or organisations to describe the cases as one complete project.
	5	6
Explanatory	Focus on one individual, business or organisation to explain the cause of the phenomenon within the case under study.	Focus on two or more individuals, businesses or organisations to explain the cause of the phenomenon within the cases under study.

Figure 2.6   Overview of the different types of case study investigations

Source: Adapted from Yin, 1993

Table 2.16   **An overview of THE case study methods in academia**

Author	Topic	Case study area
Tarlow and Muehsam (1992)	Impacts of gambling on tourism	Mississippi
Lawson, Williams, Young and Cossens (1998)	Tourism impacts	10 towns from different parts of New Zealand
McGehee and Meares (1998)	Tourism development	3 co-operatives in central Appalachia
Brunt and Courtney (1999)	Socio-cultural impacts	Dawlish, South Devon
Barton and James (2003)	Contested perceptions of risk	Newquay, Cornwall
Gjerald (2005)	Socio-cultural impacts	North Cape Community, Norway
Agarwal and Brunt (2006)	Social exclusion	Ilfracombe and Torquay, Devon
Wickens (2002)	Tourist typologies	Chalkidiki, Greece
Ohmann, Jones and Wilkes (2006)	Social impacts of a major event	Munich, Germany

The case study approach has been widely used within the THE industry, especially from an academic (pure research) perspective. This usage is acknowledged in Table 2.16 which provides an overview of THE orientated case studies which have been undertaken over the past 20 years.

Table 2.16 is not an exhaustive list of case studies, as there are many more to note and they can be found in more recent publications as well. However, the table acts as evidence that case studies are in existence within academia. Each of the examples offers new knowledge about the phenomenon under investigation and proves to incorporate many limitations. However, there are also distinct limitations to choosing a case study approach and these are summarised in Table 2.17.

Table 2.17   **Advantages and limitations of case study approaches**

Advantages	Limitations
• Case studies take an in-depth look at a particular phenomenon(-mena). • Attributes that are unique to the setting can be described. • The technique allows for the transference of knowledge from one case study to another.	• Generalisations cannot be made about the data from the case study location to the broader population.

2.3 Triangulation

In the previous section, attention was paid to individual methods and to either side of the quantitative/qualitative dichotomy. Here, the focus is placed on viewing a phenomenon from more than one perspective, known as triangulation. This could still mean the study is a qualitative or quantitative one, as you choose to select multiple methods to triangulate your findings. However, it also implies that the study could be

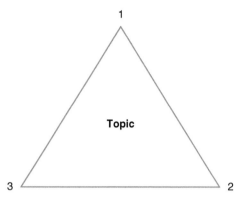

Figure 2.7   Visualising the process of triangulation

a mixed-method approach to data collection. Some of the thinking behind triangulation can be related back to the paradigm discussions in section 2.1.1. Post-positivism, which falls somewhere in between the two paradigms of positivism and interpretivism, may, for example, require (depending on the extent of your belief system) both quantitative and qualitative data to feed the curiosity of the researcher. This means you may opt for a mixed-method approach, to triangulate your findings.

To triangulate means to trace and measure a phenomenon, in order to determine the relative position of each perspective against the others. This means you are viewing a topic from more than one perspective, and you are able to check the findings against additional points of reference, to arrive at a reasoned conclusion about the research area in question. By using multiple data sources, you are validating your findings and strengthening the answers given.

Personally, I like to view triangulation in its literal sense – as a triangle, noted in Figure 2.7. When viewing the process as having three perspectives, we are in a position to acknowledge the research that is initially undertaken prior to the collection of data itself (e.g. the literature review) as being one perspective on the topic under investigation. Then, depending on the chosen paradigm, the initial data collection exercise can be undertaken (e.g. interpretivism may lead to observation being undertaken) to offer a second perspective on the topic concerned. Once the knowledge has been gained about the subject matter from the primary data collected, the researcher can then undertake a second stage of data collection to validate the findings of the first (e.g. in-depth interviews with those who were observed to clarify the meaning of the non-verbal behaviour which was observed). This final stage offers a third perspective on the topic. By viewing the topic from all three perspectives, you can effectively measure the phenomenon under investigation and merge your findings based on a range of perspectives. This process of a multiple-method approach helps to minimise the limitations of a single method (as noted throughout section 2.2).

Given the example above, the process of triangulation also represents a mixed method, and with that (e.g. 1 represents a literature review, 2 represents a quantitative online survey and 3 represents a qualitative focus group) a separate range of limitations can be overcome. For example, there is concern within the literature that quantitative research can produce a static view of a phenomenon – a snapshot (Bryman and Bell, 2007), whereas qualitative research is more reflective of a process (of change over time) (Fox et al., 2014). Each has a place within the social sciences and each can add value to and provide insight into a phenomenon being studied, but they each come with specific advantages and limitations, which may reduce the validity of the data and then the ability to generalise about and transfer knowledge from one individual, business or organisation to another. However, if both methods are undertaken in a well-planned, structured and strategic way, both the static view and the process can be understood.

2.4 Summary

This chapter has reviewed a number of complex terms and philosophies associated with the simple premise of 'collecting data' and 'doing research'. Through the identification of the research POEM, it has been acknowledged that different perspectives exist and that the researcher themselves is in a position to influence the nature and type of data for their investigation. It is a case of identifying the most appropriate POEM for the individual research project and not believing that one process fits all methodological decisions that need to be made by the researcher. There are different research paradigms, ontologies, epistemologies and methodologies to consider and to determine the most appropriate discourse. From positivism to interpretivism, inductive to deductive and qualitative to quantitative dichotomies, all stages of the POEM can be distinguished between and judged on their level of suitability. Research is not as simple as it first seems!

Within the THE industry, a range of methods are commonly used and each chosen methodology comes with a range of advantages and limitations, which can guide the researcher in the process of determining the most suitable method for them, personally. These benefits and concerns are highlighted to offer insight into the methods themselves and to provide you with food for thought when considering how to design your project. More detailed consideration is given in subsequent chapters.

Exercises

1. What are the main attributes of the inductive and deductive dichotomy?
2. What is the principal difference between qualitative and quantitative research?
3. For the following methods of data collection, give a definition and suggest a suitable research project within THE where you might expect the method to be used:

   a) In-depth interview
   b) Focus group

c) Personal interview
d) Site survey
e) Telephone survey
f) Postal survey

4. Based on your examples provided for question 3, evaluate the main challenges of these approaches to THE research.

Further reading

Brunt, P. and Brophy, K. (2006). Gay Tourist Victimisation. *International Review of Victimology.* 13 (3): 1–25. This article offers an insight into an inductive approach to data collection.

Brunt, P., Mawby, R. and Hambly, Z. (2000). Case Study: Tourist victimisation and the fear of crime on holiday. *Tourism Management.* 21 (4): 417–42. This article offers an insight into a deductive approach to data collection.

Font, X., Walmsley, A., Coggoti, S., McCombes, L. and Hausler, N. (2012). Corporate Social Responsibility: The disclosure–performance gap. *Tourism Management.* 33 (6): 1544–53. This article utilises secondary data to inform the debate of the academics and acts as a good source of further information as to how secondary data are of value to a researcher.

Fox, D., Gouthro, M.B., Morakabati, Y. and Brackstone, J. (2014). *Doing Events Research: From theory to practice.* London: Routledge. Chapter 5 of this book offers an event perspective on research design through the discussion of specific approaches.

Guba, E.G. and Lincoln, Y.S. (1994). Competing Paradigms in Qualitative Research. In N.K. Denzin and Y.S. Lincoln (eds). *Handbook of Qualitative Research.* Thousand Oaks, CA: Sage. This chapter will deepen your understanding of POEM and offer you implications for choosing each paradigm.

Mason, J. (2002). *Qualitative Researching.* 2nd edition. London: Sage. This book will deepen your understanding of ontology and epistemology from a qualitative perspective.

Veal, A.J. (2011). *Research Methods for Leisure and Tourism: A practical guide.* 4th edition. Harlow: Prentice Hall. This book offers a brief insight into the numerous dichotomies that have been highlighted throughout this chapter, from a leisure and tourism perspective.

References

Agarwal, S. and Brunt, P. (2006). Social Exclusion and English Seaside Resorts. *Tourism Management.* 27 (4): 654–70.

Bailey, K.D. (1987). *Methods of Social Science Research.* London: The Free Press.

Bales, R.F. (1950). A Set of Categories for the Analysis of Small Group Interaction. *American Sociological Review.* 15 (2): 257–63.

Barton, A. and James, Z. (2003). Run to the Sun: Policing contested perceptions of risk. *Policing and Society.* 13 (3): 259–70.

Brunt, P. (1997). *Market Research in Travel and Tourism.* Oxford: Butterworth-Heinemann.

Brunt, P. and Courtney, P. (1999). Host Perceptions of Sociocultural Impacts. *Annals of Tourism Research.* 26 (3): 493–515.

Bryman, A. and Bell, E. (2007). *Business Research Methods.* 2nd edition. Oxford: Oxford University Press.

Burgess, R.G. (1984). *In the Field: An introduction to field research*. London: Allen & Unwin.

Creswell, J.W. (2009). *Qualitative, Quantitative, and Mixed Methods Approaches*. 3rd edition. Thousand Oaks, CA: Sage.

Font, X., Walmsley, A., Coggoti, S., McCombes, L. and Hausler, N. (2012). Corporate Social Responsibility: The disclosure–performance gap. *Tourism Management*. 33 (6): 1544–53.

Fox, D., Gouthro, M.B., Morakabati, Y. and Brackstone, J. (2014). *Doing Events Research: From theory to practice*. London: Routledge.

Gjerald, O. (2005). Sociocultural Impacts of Tourism: A case study from Norway. *Journal of Tourism and Cultural Change*. 3 (1): 36–58.

Guba, E.G. (1990). *The Paradigm Dialog*. Thousand Oaks, CA: Sage.

Guba, E.G. and Lincoln, Y.S. (1994). Competing Paradigms in Qualitative Research. In N.K. Denzin and Y.S. Lincoln (eds). *Handbook of Qualitative Research*. Thousand Oaks, CA: Sage.

Lawson, R.W., Williams, J., Young, T. and Cossens, J. (1998). A Comparison of Residents' Attitudes towards Tourism in 10 New Zealand Destinations. *Tourism Management*. 19 (3): 247–56.

McGehee, N.G. and Meares, A.C. (1998). A Case Study of Three Tourism-related Craft Marketing Cooperatives in Appalachia: Contributions to community. *Journal of Sustainable Tourism*. 6 (1): 4–26.

Marshall, C. and Rossman, G.B. (1999). *Designing Qualitative Research*. 3rd edition. London: Sage.

Mason, J. (2002). *Qualitative Researching*. 2nd edition. London: Sage.

Nachmias, C. and Nachmias, D. (1981). *Research Methods in the Social Sciences*. 2nd edition. London: Edward Arnold.

Office of National Statistics (ONS). (2016). *Internet users in the UK*. Available at: www.ons.gov. uk/businessindustryandtrade/itandinternetindustry/bulletins/internetusers/2016 (accessed 1 November 2016).

Ohmann, S., Jones, I. and Wilkes, K. (2006). The Perceived Social Impacts of the 2006 Football World Cup on Munich Residents. *Journal of Sport & Tourism*. 11 (2): 129–52.

Pernecky, T. (2007). Immersing in Ontology and the Research Process: Constructivism the foundation for exploring the (in)credible OBE? In I. Ateljevic, A. Pritchard and N. Morgan (eds). *The Critical Turn in Tourism Studies*. Advances in Tourism Research series. Oxford: Elsevier.

Savin-Baden, M. and Howell Major, C. (2013). *Qualitative Research: The essential guide to theory and practice*. London: Routledge.

Tarlow, P.E. and Muehsam, M.J. (1992). Wide Horizons: Travel and tourism in the coming decades. *The Futurist*. 26 (5): 28–33.

Veal, A.J. (2011). *Research Methods for Leisure and Tourism: A practical guide*. 4th edition. London: Prentice Hall.

Wahyuni, D. (2012). The Research Design Maze: Understanding paradigms, cases, methods and methodologies. *Journal of Applied Management Accounting Research*. 10 (1): 69–80.

Walmsley, A. (2011). *Report on Hospitality, Leisure, Sport and Tourism Higher Education in the UK*. Oxford: Higher Education Academy's Hospitality, Leisure, Sport and Tourism Network.

Walmsley, A. (2012). Decent Work and Tourism Wages: An international comparison. *Progress in Responsible Tourism*. 2 (1): 90–99.

Webb, S. and Webb, B. (1932). *Methods of Social Study*. London: Longman, Green and Co.

Wickens, E. (2002). The Sacred and the Profane: A tourist typology. *Annals of Tourism Research*. 29 (3): 834–51.

Yin, R.R. (1993). *Applications of Case Study Research*. London: Sage.

PLANNING A PROJECT

3.1 Why is it being done?

At university, the most common research project you will be required to undertake is an academic research project, for instance an undergraduate dissertation. An academic research project is an example of pure research which differs in purpose to other forms of research. Table 3.1 demonstrates that research of this nature seeks to make a contribution to knowledge, in a specific area or discipline, rather than to solve a commercial problem.

Table 3.1   Comparison of research purposes for common forms of research

Type of research	Pure research	Action research/ Market research	Consultancy research
Example	Dissertation PhD Academic journal article	Market research	Contracted research
Who determines focus of research	Researcher	Employer	Organisation which has contracted the researcher
Purpose	Contribute new knowledge	Establish market condition	Dependent on contract, usually industrial or commercial

Pure research is not governed by a wide agenda as with market research or consultancy research. These forms of research will be conducted with a specific purpose and application in mind. Although some pure research may have practical implications, this is not the primary focus in conducting the research. A pure research project will advance knowledge by exploring new ideas or building on the research of others within a certain field. Pure research can be used to test existing theories and to create new theories.

As the purpose of pure research is to contribute new knowledge, it is important that the researcher demonstrates full understanding of the subject area. In order to achieve this, a greater focus is placed on reviewing research that has already been conducted in this area. Conclusions will be drawn from the research to identify the contribution that the project has made.

3.2 Overview of the planning stages

There are a wide variety of models suggested by authors regarding the stages of a research project. Veal (2011) identifies 10 key stages in planning a research project, seven preparatory stages, one investigatory stage and one analysis stage. However, he, as do others, acknowledges that each project may require a different approach. Pure research is clearly distinct from a consultancy contract where objectives may be solely determined by the client. The following overview represents a synthesis of various sources, together with the authors' own experiences.

3.2.1 Planning a research project

Stage 1   Definition of the problem and development of research questions

Stage 2   Identification of information needs, to include:

- literature review
- review of secondary sources
- primary data requirements
- data collection methods
- sampling frame
- fieldwork arrangements
- analysis requirements
- budget implications.

Stage 3   Redefinition of the problem, the question and information needs (often in the light of budget and time constraints)

Stage 4   Statement of aims and objectives

Stage 5   Development of a research programme

Stage 6   The pilot stage

Stage 7   Data collection

Stage 8   Data coding and analysis

Stage 9   Report and presentation preparation

Each of these stages will now be considered in more detail.

3.3 The stages explained

3.3.1 Stage 1: Definition of the problem and developing research questions

Before a research project can begin, a topic area must be chosen. In the case of pure research, the project will usually come about from the researcher's own interests. In some instances, the researcher may have to work within a specified topic area. Negotiation may be necessary in order to finalise the topic. This may take place between a student and their supervisor, or between a team of researchers working on the same project. At the outset of planning a research project, the researcher should begin by familiarising themself with the topic they wish to explore. The likelihood is that this will involve finding out what has been done before in the same or similar topic areas. Once a thorough understanding of the topic area has been gained, the researcher can identify a research problem to help guide the project.

The type of thinking necessary at this stage (and throughout the initial stages) will be developed in the following hypothetical example (Illustration 3.1).

Illustration 3.1   Winter sports tourism research project

A tourism management student was required to write a dissertation on a topic of their choice during the final year of their degree. Due to a personal interest in winter sports, and an academic interest in consumer behaviour, the student chose to explore the motivations of UK residents who participate in winter sports tourism.
Initially, to gain an understanding of the topic the student needed to establish:

- the size of the winter sports market in the UK
- behavioural trends of British skiers
- trends in the global ski industry
- motivations for participating in winter sports.

After initial work in defining the problem, it was possible to develop some research questions – that is, to turn the initial statements or topics into the form of questions or research. In the case study, this might conceivably include:

> Initial statement: To explore the motivations of UK residents who participate in winter sports tourism.

> Research questions:

> 1. Is motivation commonly used to segment tourists?
> 2. Why do people participate in sport tourism and winter sports tourism?
> 3. What are the reasons for non-participation in winter sports?
> 4. What factors influence the choice of ski resort and other consumer behaviour?

Hence, the general statement has begun to be broken down into smaller, more achievable, parts or research questions.

3.3.2 Stage 2: Identification of information needs

The second stage of the project overlaps with the first in as much as the definition of the problem will inevitably involve some identification of material that will be used in the later stages. However, what distinguishes this stage of the project is the move away from 'what the project is about' to 'how it might be carried out'. Depending on the nature of the project, there are several aspects which would warrant some consideration.

(a) Literature review

As already mentioned in Chapter 2, a review of the relevant literature is an essential stage. The researcher may gain ideas about the sorts of questions which should be addressed or tips on successful methods of data collection and analysis. Similarly, ideas about how a research project could be organised can be usefully gained by looking at the work of others.

A literature review would involve reading articles in academic journals, textbooks, magazines, trade journals and newspapers. When scanning an article, it is always worthwhile seeing who the author has referred to and following up on these references. Academic and public libraries allow you to search electronically for relevant books and articles. Academic libraries will usually have a number of subscriptions to discipline-specific journals and ebooks which can be accessed electronically. In addition to works published by authors writing about the topic, or their own research findings, other types of sources may provide valuable tips. Examples of brochures or other forms of printed information could be investigated. This is developed further with the case study.

Illustration 3.2   Winter sports tourism research project – literature search

Sources investigated include articles from journals such as:

- *Annals of Tourism Research*
- *European Sport Management Quarterly*
- *Journal of Sustainable Tourism*
- *International Journal of Tourism Research*
- *Journal of Hospitality and Tourism Research*
- *Journal of Leisure Research*
- *Journal of Sport Management*
- *Journal of Sport Tourism*
- *Journal of Travel and Tourism Marketing*
- *Journal of Travel Research*
- *Journal of Vacation Marketing*
- *Scandinavian Journal of Hospitality and Tourism Research*
- *Tourism Management.*

For all of these sources, back issues would be scoured for anything on the same or similar topics.

(b) Secondary sources of data

The difference between items in a literature review and sources of secondary data relate to how the information will be used. As previously explained, the purpose of the literature review is to gain knowledge of the subject, pick up tips and perhaps use references in a report to help justify or compare. Secondary sources of data form part of the actual data collection. The 'secondary' element indicates that the data have already been collected for another purpose. Sources of secondary data can be categorised in a number of ways; one example follows.

Internal secondary sources

These are sources of data available from within an organisation. They include:

- minutes of meetings
- reports from sales representatives and the like
- financial records
- internal reports.

External secondary sources

There are a variety of external sources of secondary data which can be further sub-divided:

(i) Official statistics

Government departments and other public sector agencies in the UK undertake surveys for all sorts of purposes. In the tourism field, some of the main examples include:

- Office for National Statistics:
  - monthly overseas travel and tourism
  - Social Trends

- UK Government:
  - National Travel Survey
  - control of immigration statistics

- Visit Britain:
  - inbound tourism performance
  - International Passenger Survey

- Visit England:
  - GB Tourism Survey
  - the value of tourism in England

- ○ GB Day Visits Survey
- ○ Tourism Business Monitor
- ○ Trip Tracker
- ○ Beyond Staycation
- ○ Annual Survey of Visits to Visitor Attractions
- ○ England Occupancy Survey.

The above is a small part of the wide variety of official statistics available, often free of charge. In addition, international sources of statistical information are available from organisations such as Eurostat, the World Tourism Organization (WTO) and the Organisation for Economic Co-operation and Development (OECD).

(ii) Commercial Sources

There are some commercial organisations who undertake surveys which researchers can subscribe to or purchase reports on. Organisations which do this sort of work include Mintel, the Economist Intelligence Unit (EIU), Keynote, BMI Research, Euromonitor International and Plunkett Research Ltd.

As an example, Mintel produced a report entitled 'Snowsports UK' (2014), which researchers can purchase at http://reports.mintel.com/display/679944. The use of this type of information depends on the nature of the project and it is always wise to consider the purpose of the data when it was originally collected to ascertain whether the report will be useful.

Illustration 3.3   Winter sports tourism research project – secondary sources

In this case, no internal sources were utilised as the research project was not focusing on a specific business, instead a range of external sources were used. In order to understand the tourism market in the UK, the 'British National Travel Survey', conducted by the UK Government, and the 'Monthly Overseas Travel and Tourism Report', produced by the Office for National Statistics, were used. Although these reports presented trends in tourism amongst UK residents, more information was needed relating to the UK ski market. In order to fill this gap, Mintel reports, focusing on the ski industry and mountain tourism, were referred to. Commercial reports were also used to this end. Companies such as Crystal Ski produce an annual report on the UK ski market. Such reports identify trends in consumer behaviour such as destination choice, length of stay and resort considerations. In this project, external sources were used to understand existing trends in UK outbound tourism and the ski industry more specifically.

(c) Primary data requirements

Having scoured the literature and become aware of the range of secondary data sources available, the next decision is to consider what will still have to be found out. Thus, remaining gaps will require specific methods of data collection for the purpose of the research project.

Illustration 3.4   Winter sports tourism research project – primary data

Secondary sources of information were used to provide an understanding of the existing market for winter sports, however if the British winter sports market was to be segmented, the collection of primary data would be necessary. Primary data collection allows the researcher to identify the motivations of people participating in winter sports, their decision making to select a certain resort, their socio-demographic characteristics and their characteristics as a skier.

(d) Data collection methods

Once the necessity of primary data has been established, the methods of data collection require consideration. As outlined in Chapter 2, a decision will have to be made as to a quantitative or qualitative approach, or a mixture of both. The pros and cons of the individual methods will have to be evaluated and limitations recognised. Unfortunately, there is often no right or wrong answer in the selection but time and financial constraints may often be a determining factor. Clearly, the nature of the project in terms of the level of precision required from the results will have a significant bearing on the methods of data collection. What is required from descriptive research (such as in a position statement) is different from the methods needed to facilitate financial forecasting.

Illustration 3.5   Winter sports tourism research project – data collection methods

To establish primary information on the characteristics, motivations and behaviour of British skiers, a self-completion questionnaire was constructed and distributed online through UK ski clubs. This method of data collection provided quantitative information about British skiers and allowed the questionnaire to be completed by a wide range of skiers. Additionally, a series of in-depth personal interviews was carried out with a sample of British ski club members to provide qualitative information on characteristics, motivations and behaviour.

(e) Sampling frame

This aspect will be discussed more fully in the following chapter. At this stage in the planning process, decisions need to be made regarding how many people to question or interview, where and when to question or interview, and the length of the survey period. Again, the nature of the survey will determine sample size, for example, as well as the expected response rate for the data collection method and available resources.

Illustration 3.6   Winter sports tourism research project – sampling frame

As a relatively small proportion of the UK population participate in skiing, it is unviable to collect data from a representative sample. Instead, a convenience sample will be used to collect data from those known to have an interest in skiing.

The online self-completion questionnaire will be distributed to members of 12 British ski clubs via email. As these 12 ski clubs have a combined total of 4000 members, the population size for this study is 4000. The sample itself is likely to be much smaller due to non-responses. It is unlikely that all members of the population can be reached by an online self-completion questionnaire. Some members may not have supplied the ski club with their email address, or their contact details may not be up to date. Many of those who are emailed the questionnaire may not wish to participate in the research. In the case of the interviews, interviewees were sought from ski clubs in the UK.

(Continued)

(Continued)

Response rates for online surveys tend to be much lower than those of paper-based surveys. The opinion, on what an acceptable response rate is, varies between researchers. It is agreed, however, that when the response rate is greater, the research will have a greater ability to represent the whole population. In total, 1200 skiers completed the questionnaire, a response rate of 30%. Although a response rate of 30% may not be able to fully represent all ski club members, a sample of 1200 responses was more than adequate to conduct the required statistical tests. In the case of the interviews, a smaller sample was required as the data generated is more detailed. The researcher determined, after 25 interviews, that no new information was being generated.

(f) Fieldwork arrangements

Depending on the nature of the project and the methods of data collection selected, there will be a variety of fieldwork to organise. At this stage in the planning process, it is a case of preliminary identification of what will be required. This may well include:

- arranging permission to interview at a site
- gaining access to the names and addresses of potential respondents
- getting quotes for the printing of paper-based questionnaires or the cost of online surveys
- identifying any equipment that is required, for instance voice-recording technology
- establishing the training requirements of staff, or the need for the recruitment of staff
- obtaining ethical approval from your university before research can take place.

Illustration 3.7   Winter sports tourism research project – fieldwork arrangements

Permission to contact ski club members will be essential for the success of this research. At this stage, consideration is given as to which clubs would be approached to distribute the questionnaire. Once this decision is made, the clubs and forums will be contacted and briefed on the project before permission can be granted and the questionnaire made avaliable to their members. In order to get ethical approval, from the university, for the research to commence all respondents and interviewees must be over the age of 18. Permission to use the data must also be obtained from each participant so consent forms need to be drafted. The qualitative interviews require a trained interviewer. Identification of a suitable person will be necessary if the researcher is not going to conduct the interviews. Clerical assistance may also be required in the coding of questionnaires and transcription of the interviews.

(g) Analysis requirements

Before any data are collected, it is worth considering how the data will be analysed in terms of what computer package will be used and what statistical techniques will be performed. Statistical tests could include:

- Chi-square test
- Mann Whitney
- Spearmans Rank
- Pearsons Correlation
- T-tests
- ANOVA
- Multiple regression analysis
- Principal component analysis
- Importance performance analysis.

Further discussion of these tests can be found in Chapter 7.

At this stage, it is necessary to reflect on how the research questions posed might be answered when analysing the data. If this is by means of statistics, the requirements of the proposed statistical test must be considered. Some tests require a minimum number of responses to be reliable, whilst others require questions to be formatted in a specific way. For instance, it is often more useful to ask a respondent to rank variables, rather than select all that apply, when it comes to data analysis.

Illustration 3.8   Winter sports tourism research project – analysis requirements

The quantitative survey will be analysed using statistical techniques to determine the socio-demographic characteristics of the respondents and their characteristics as skiers, their motivations and behaviour. Independent variables such as age, sport, group type and level of experience will be cross-tabulated against dependent variables such as the choice of destination, equipment-buying behaviour, importance of resort features and motivations. Chi-square tests will be used to establish the significance of the variables (this is more fully explained in Chapter 7). The likely response rate is sufficiently large for variation amongst the respondents to be established by this technique. Due to the number of responses and the statistical tests required, quantitative analysis software, IBM SPSS, will be used. The qualitative interviews will be analysed, using content analysis to identify key themes and areas of contradiction and agreement within the transcripts. QSR NVivo will be used to organise, code and visualise the data.

(h) Budget implications

It is highly unlikely that financial implications have not already been considered by this point in the planning process. For research projects at undergraduate level, it is most likely that the budget will be determined by the researcher. Expenses will vary dependent on the nature of the project but may include travel to and from the fieldwork site, accommodation at the fieldwork site, printing of questionnaires, postage and subscription fees for online survey sites (note that many of these sites offer a limited number of questions free of charge). In some instances, incentives or payments are offered to respondents to encourage their participation. Cost may determine the data collection method chosen and the sampling frame.

Illustration 3.9   Winter sports tourism research project – budget implications

Costs of the fieldwork, including hosting a survey online, travelling to interviews and transcription costs need to be assessed at this point. It is anticipated that enough ski club members will be interested in interviews that participation will not need to be incentivised.

3.3.3 Stage 3: Redefinition of the problem

This is perhaps one of the most awkward stages in the research process. The researcher has undertaken literature searches, identified a range of secondary data sources, thought about the primary data requirements, methods of data collection, fieldwork, analysis and prepared a budget. It is now necessary for the researcher to determine whether the project is viable. The possible outcomes at this stage may well include the following:

1. Everything is fine and the research may progress.
2. Further clarification is needed.
3. The project is too costly and a less expensive option is needed, perhaps concentrating on the secondary sources alone or a smaller sample size.

Points 2 and 3, requiring clarification or modification, are common outcomes and therefore require a process of redefinition before the project can continue. The danger here, though, is that delays may ultimately result in a postponement because of missing, or not being prepared for, the survey period. In surveys of a travel and tourism nature, there may be a precise season when data collection must take place, otherwise few tourists are available for interview.

> **Illustration 3.10   Winter sports tourism research project – redefinition of the problem**
>
> The student, in discussion with their supervisor, establishes that the research is ready to go ahead.

3.3.4 Stage 4: Statement of aims and objectives

Following any necessary changes and redefinition, the project is ready to begin. At this point, it may be useful to reiterate the aims and objectives. In the case of an academic research project, these may have changed whilst the literature review was undertaken. If the aims and objectives are to be altered, negotiation will take place between the researcher and their supervisor, or amongst all researchers collaborating on the project, at this stage. This ensures that everyone involved in the project is clear on its aims and objectives.

Illustration 3.11   Winter sports tourism – aims and objectives

Whilst exploring the academic literature surrounding winter sports tourism, it is identified that no research has been undertaken which explores the differences in motivation between skiers and snowboarders. This becomes the research problem.

A clear aim is established: to develop a typology of British winter sports tourists through the identification and analysis of different trends in skier behavioural characteristics.

Four objectives are identified in order to achieve the aim:

1   To analyse the relevant literature to determine key factors influencing the British winter sports market.
2   To undertake data collection of key stakeholders involved in British winter sports tourism, including ski clubs and independent travellers.
3   To analyse data, relating findings to the key literature to enable the structure of a typology.
4   To analyse differences in characteristics between the participants of skiing and of snowboarding.

3.3.5 Stage 5: Development of a research programme

The preliminary work of stage 2, if largely unchanged, will be developed at this stage. This entails:

1.   Further reviews of literature
2.   Acquisition of secondary sources
3.   Confirmation of primary data requirements and methods of data collection
4.   The development of a sampling frame
5.   The design of questionnaires and observation recording sheets (if appropriate)
6.   Specification of the fieldwork arrangements
7.   Specification of the analysis requirements.

Overall, this stage represents the tidying up of loose ends before the project starts to 'roll'.

Illustration 3.12   Winter sports tourism research project – develop a research programme

At this stage, the student will develop a research programme and undertake the preliminary work that is necessary before data collection can begin. This will include reviewing literature and consulting secondary sources to determine what information needs to be gathered through primary data collection. Changes will be made to the initial plans if any new information is found. A suitable sampling frame will be established, a questionnaire designed and set up online, an interview schedule written and ethical approval for data collection obtained. Permissions, from selected ski clubs, will be gained, and interviews will be arranged with ski club members. The student will ensure, at this stage, that the questions asked in both the quantitative and qualitative research will meet the requirements for analysis.

3.3.6 Stage 6: The pilot stage

Having designed the necessary questionnaires, it is vital to test them out before the final launch into the data collection. The researcher, having put such effort into the project to date, may easily believe that the whole world is as interested in the topic as he/she has become. It is then easy to lose sight of how respondents will react and what level of understanding they might have. Therefore, it is necessary to see how things might work out. Thus, questionnaires, interviews or observations should be carried out on a small number of potential respondents first. This is called a pilot survey, which highlights:

- problems with questionnaires (wording, layout etc.) causing misunderstanding
- problems with interviewers not fully conversant with their requirements
- an indication of the likely response rate
- an indication of the range of responses to the questions which can be suggestive of the likely results.

From the pilot survey, modifications may have to be made and re-tested if necessary. If there are few or no changes to be made, it may be tempting to include the results of the pilot survey within the main data collection. However, before this dangerous course of action is undertaken, consideration should be given to what effects this extension of the survey period (to include the pilot stage) might have.

Moreover, what differences might the respondents of the pilot have against respondents of the main survey? Were they contacted by interviewers in the same way as will respondents in the main survey? Few authors comment on this point, perhaps assuming that the results of the pilot will affect the main survey in such a way that the inclusion of pilot data is never contemplated. In the opinion of the authors, this practice is setting a dangerous precedent. Having set out with a research programme geared to the successful completion of the project, to change it in this way now appears unscrupulous.

Illustration 3.13   Winter sports tourism research project – the pilot stage

The student will pilot the questionnaire and interview schedule to test that the questions and formatting make sense to respondents. Due to the terminology used, the questionnaire will be piloted by a small group of people who participate in winter sports. The problems that are highlighted during the pilot stage will be rectified before the data collection continues.

3.3.7 Stage 7: Data collection

This stage is either dreaded most or comes as a welcome relief. All the planning has been completed and the survey begins. If personal interviews or face-to-face questionnaires are being used, the project begins to 'run itself' in terms of actually doing the fieldwork and travelling to the site or people's homes. With self-completion questionnaires, there can be a brief lull in the proceedings. Having distributed the questionnaires, there may be a delay before they start being returned.

Whilst the data collection is under way, there is much that the researcher can be getting on with, assuming that they are not directly involved in interviewing or conducting face-to-face questionnaires. As the early interviews are completed, or questionnaires returned, the initial coding work and transcription can be started ahead of analysis. For an undergraduate research project, it is most likely that the student will be conducting the research themselves. Where interviewers are employed, however, checks should be made on their progress to ensure that all questions are being asked in the way that was intended and that their completion of the forms is up to standard. If interviewers are being employed by the completion rate, this aspect is of particular importance, as their interest in the project is likely to be much less than their interest in being paid! On this latter point, prompt payment can go far in maintaining the quality of an interviewer's work. Further information on the mechanics of data collection is given in Chapter 6.

Illustration 3.14   Winter sports tourism research project – data collection

The student will distribute the online questionnaire and wait for responses to be returned. During this period, the student will be directly involved in interviewing the ski club members, which may involve some travel. To stay on top of the work that needs to be done, before analysis can commence, the student will transcribe the interviews as they go.

3.3.8 Stage 8: Data coding and analysis

In the preparatory stages of the project, the type of analysis should have been specified in general terms and reinforced following the pilot stage. The requirements of the software package used for analysis will have been taken into account in the questionnaire design. A number of software packages are available for both quantitative and qualitative data analysis. IBM SPSS, Minitab, Stata and Statistica are popular software packages for analysing, managing and visualising quantitative data. QSR NVivo, ATLAS.ti and MAXQDA are packages for qualitative data analysis, which offer tools for aggregating, coding and visualising data. As a student, your choice of data analysis software may be determined by the licenses of your institution.

Coding, of the questionnaires and interview transcripts into the software, will be undertaken before statistical analysis can take place. Paper-based questionnaires will need to be coded into this software manually. If questionnaires are distributed online, the results can often be downloaded into an appropriate software package. The researcher will still need to code this data. Despite advances in analysis software, coding remains a distinct stage before the statistical analysis can begin.

When it comes to the analysis, many of the software packages avaliable offer greater sophistication in terms of the tests that can be run. These packages do, however, require the sample to be relatively large. For smaller surveys, where the sample size is perhaps less than 100 respondents and the purpose is largely descriptive, the researcher should question whether such packages are necessary. In such instances, familiar spreadsheet software, such as Microsoft Excel, may meet the data analysis requirements. This aspect, though, should have been established earlier in the planning process, rather than, having collected the data, the researcher now wondering how to analyse it.

Having loaded the appropriate information into the programme, the analysis of the data is performed and results appear for the first time. This can be one of the most exciting stages in the research process. Whilst you may have a feel for the data, having conducted the interviews and undertaken the coding, the first appearances of frequency tables on the computer screen can be quite gripping. The data have truly become information. Inevitably, some results will not have been anticipated and are surprising or give a different slant to what was expected, and this adds to the exhilaration. Following this initial stage, the data must be analysed and statistical tests performed in a systematic way. This is more fully explained in Chapter 7.

Illustration 3.15   Winter sports tourism research project – data coding and analysis

Once data have been collected, they will be coded into the appropriate software and analysis will be conducted using the planned methods, in this instance Chi-square tests on the quanititative data and thematic content analysis on the qualitative data. It is important that plenty of time is allowed to explore the data.

3.3.9 Stage 9: Report and presentation preparation

The final stage for the researcher is often writing a report of the research findings and providing recommendations for future research. As part of a pure research project, it is unlikely that a presentation of the research will have to be given. Findings may be reported in a journal article or written up in a thesis and are therefore publicly available. The techniques for report writing and presentation are developed in Chapter 8.

Illustration 3.16   Winter sports tourism research project – report and presentation preparation

The final stage is to write up the findings of the study. As this project is an undergraduate dissertation, the findings will be presented in a report.

3.4 Writing tenders for consultancy projects

Commissioning consultants to undertake research is common practice both within and outside the tourism industry. Tender documents for consultancy projects involve the researcher/consultant outlining how they would plan to do the project and what he/she will charge if they are awarded the contract. It can be seen, therefore, that for this type of research project consultants need to be able to demonstrate the ability to plan projects clearly before any data collection takes place in anticipation of what the client will require. This is normally done in the form of a written statement called a tender document or proposal. Consultants tender for all kinds of research work and, as such, the nature of tender proposals varies accordingly. In the context of this book, where some kind of survey research may be specified, a typical proposal would normally have to demonstrate:

- an understanding of the problem
- an explanation of the methods to be used in collecting the data
- an explanation of how the data will be analysed
- details of who will be carrying out the work and of their credentials
- the number of client meetings and the nature of interim reports
- the presentation of results – a presentation, a report or perhaps a management plan
- a clear schedule of the programme of work for the project
- that the consultant has all the necessary facilities to run the project (e.g. computing equipment)
- if a subcontractor is to be used, what credentials and experience are available (the proposal must provide information about the subcontractor on other aspects in as much depth as you would expect from a proposal to be completed solely in-house)
- that the consultant's resources are not over-committed
- the costs to be paid by the client
- the fees to be paid to the consultant.

On these last aspects, that of costs/fees for the project, it is often the case that the available budget is only known to the client or contracting agency. Some contracting agencies will stipulate a maximum budget in the invitation to tender whilst others may be unsure of what their project should cost, and some may specifically decide not to indicate any financial information at all. To a certain extent, the decision to do this depends on the nature of the project and the experience of the contracting agency. If a budget is indicated in the tender, then it is unlikely that consultants will strive to offer a lower amount (assuming the budget indicated is acceptable). However, if the contracting agency does not outline what the maximum budget is, consultants may state a low fee in the hope of receiving further work from the client or a high fee as an 'off-chance'. In the opinion of the authors, it is preferable for clients to indicate clearly what the maximum budget for a given project is. Then consultants decide whether or not they are interested in the project and can detail what they will provide for the given price. As such, the client will receive proposals that are better considered as the consultant must win the contract on the strength of their proposals, methods of data collection and analysis rather than the price.

3.5 Considerations for market research

Market research differs significantly from academic research in terms of purpose, working relationships involved and the conducting of research. The following considerations will be discussed below:

- the purpose of the market research
- working with an employer
- conducting market research.

3.5.1 Purpose of the research

When developing a market research project, it is important to recognise why the project is being undertaken. Market research is conducted in order to establish the market conditions, however there will be a further agenda prompting the research. For instance, market research is often conducted when a company is considering entering into a new market or developing a new product. Another situation which occasionally arises is that market research is carried out when the organisation is in a crisis as market research can be used to aid management decisions.

It is important that the research requested can meet the purpose for which it is meant. In some situations, it is unrealistic to expect that the results of a market research exercise can provide the answers desired. For a research budget to be justifiably allocated, there must be initial confidence in the validity of the research that has been requested and this requires communication between the employer and the researcher.

3.5.2 Working with an employer

In market research, the researcher will be working closely with an employer in order to conduct the research they require. Considerable negotiation will take place between the researcher and whoever is commissioning the research in order to define the research problem. Time spent on this stage avoids awkward comments in the final presentation such as 'we knew that' or (even worse) 'that wasn't what we wanted'. Such comments cannot always be considered the sole fault of the researcher.

During the research process, there may be a number of briefing meetings between the employer and the researcher. For the employer, these meetings are used to ensure that the research is successfully completed and that a suitable researcher is recruited. The researcher must use these meetings as an opportunity to gain a full understanding of the project requirements and to convince the employer that they are suitable and competent. Thus, the researcher must ask questions in the briefing meeting that lead to a thorough understanding of the project requirements on both sides. Pertinent questions in briefing meetings also enable the researcher to establish whether there is a 'hidden agenda' at play. For instance, the researcher may identify that the market research is being used to disguise and facilitate a particular course of action that has already been determined.

3.5.3 Conducting market research

Initially, the researcher should begin by familiarising themself with the topic of the enquiry. This will involve finding out what research has previously been conducted in the same or similar topic areas. Unlike an academic research project, less knowledge will be drawn from academic literature and a greater focus will be placed on secondary data sources and existing market research. Having reviewed these sources, the researcher will plan their primary data requirements by identifying gaps in their knowledge of the market.

In market research, the budget is fundamental in determining the scope of a project. A budget will usually be pre-determined and the researcher will have to bear this in mind in the early planning stages. This will govern the methods used in primary data collection and the resources avaliable to the researcher in terms of time, people and software. The budget will also impact the scale of the project. Market research is generally conducted on a larger scale than academic research, therefore, with a sizable budget, the researcher may employ researchers to conduct and transcribe interviews or code questionnaire data. The researcher will have a fundamental role in managing the researchers employed to ensure consistency in their work.

Once the findings have been analysed, a report on the research findings will be required. Often, the researcher will also need to give a presentation of these findings to their employer and key figures within an organisation. In market research, the report is often required to identify recommendations for a suitable course of action or outline the implications of the research.

3.6 Summary

The process of planning a research project is presented in this chapter and a case study example is provided to illustrate the process of writing an undergraduate dissertation. This chapter also considers other types of research, identifying the considerations for pure research and those for market research and consultancy. It is established that the purpose of the research will influence the requirements of the project and thus the planning process.

Inevitably, all research projects differ and the emphasis of different stages in the research process will similarly vary. For instance, a project which essentially comes from an academic background may have a much greater focus on a review of literature than would be the case for a consultancy project. In all research, identifying the information that is required and how this is to be collected is of crucial importance. Reviewing literature and secondary sources fully can save considerable time and expense. Of great importance in the planning process is the pilot stage. This is often neglected or considered a nuisance but can reveal important elements which will help shape the overall design of the project.

Planning is essential in conducting research that is fit for purpose. If the planning stages are overlooked, a number of negative situations may arise. For instance, data may be collected from an inappropriate sample, too little data could be collected, the results may not permit the intended method of analysis to be applied or, worst case scenario, the initial research question could not be answered. The planning stages, discussed in this chapter, are able to guide new researchers through the research process and provide a necessary level of knowledge to enable thorough research to be conducted.

Exercises

1. Identify the different purposes of pure research, action research and consultancy research and then list the different considerations that will need to be made for each form of research.
2. Explain why the time spent reviewing literature and searching for secondary data sources is worthwhile.
3. Identify the two different types of external secondary data sources and provide an example for each.
4. Select four different types of survey methodology and identify the necessary fieldwork arrangements.
5. Discuss the implications of an inappropriate sample for the outcome of a research project.
6. Examine why it is necessary to consider data analysis requirements prior to data collection.

Further reading

Altinay, L. and Paraskevas, A. (2011). *Planning Research in Tourism and Hospitality*. 2nd edition. Oxon: Routledge.
This book provides clear guidance on planning a research project in the context of tourism and hospitality. This book is particularly applicable to students undertaking a research project covering the literature review, research design, fieldwork and analysis.

O'Leary, Z. (2004). *The Essential Guide to Doing Research*. London: Sage.
This book is aimed at undergraduate and post-graduate students. Although it does not have a chapter dedicateded to planning a research project, the chapters on working with literature, methodological design and exploring populations provide useful insight into planning a project.

Veal, A.J. (2011). *Research Methods for Leisure and Tourism: A practical guide*. 4th edition.
Harlow: Pearson Education.
The third chapter of Veal's book is dedicated to planning a research project in this field. The explanation covers the whole of the research project and includes reference to the tendering process for consultancy-type projects.

References

Mintel (2014). *Snowsports UK: April 2014*. London: Mintel.
Veal, A.J. (2011). *Research Methods for Leisure and Tourism: A practical guide*. 4th edition.
Harlow: Pearson Education.

4

SELECTING A SAMPLE

LEARNING OBJECTIVES

From reading this chapter, you should be able to:

- understand the need for sampling
- understand how to determine a sampling unit and construct an appropriate sampling frame
- show awareness of the range of different types of sampling and know where it is appropriate to use them
- appreciate the necessary criteria when deciding the size of a sample.

4.1 Overview

Research in tourism, hospitality and events is undertaken by students to answer research questions. This is usually in the form of a final-year project or dissertation, or may be in the form of an applied consultancy project for a sector contact. This could be an organisation that you have already worked for on a part-time basis or as part of an industrial placement or internship. If this is the case, the answers you are about to find may or may not be used to inform management decisions. For instance, a tour operator may want to know what trust people have in their brochures or what types of recreational activities their customers are looking for whilst on a short break to a luxury hotel in the countryside. They may ask you to do this research on their behalf because they are interested or too busy to do it themselves!

Research for organisations that uses surveys or interviews often includes general statements about respondents' feelings and opinions that the organisation is keen to know about. However, in finding answers to these sorts of questions the researcher is faced not only with the difficulty of selecting suitable methods of data collection and survey design, but also with deciding whom to ask. When research focuses on attitudes to existing products, current customers could be asked to comment, unless there are proposals which will dramatically change the customer profile. However, if the research is associated with establishing new products, whom should you ask? And if the research involves talking to managers about their opinions, then who should be asked and why? And will you get access to these respondents?

In addition to whom to ask, how many people's views are needed? Often, it is not feasible to ask everybody who could be in the sample, for example those people who have purchased a holiday, but asking too few people may not provide a sufficient amount of reliable data on which to base your research findings, or may not help to make a management decision in a practical organisation. The aim of this chapter is to address these issues in a practical and pragmatic way, and to give you examples of practical sampling that have been completed by real students during their research.

4.2 What is sampling?

When you are planning to do research in the sector, it is unlikely that you will be able to ask all the individuals in the sample. Let us imagine that you want to find out the views of individuals who have experienced an event such as Glastonbury. There is a wide range of individuals who attend this event and it will be impossible to ask all their opinions, especially if you are doing the research yourself or you have a small team of researchers. You will therefore have to select a sample of attendees using a chosen method of sampling. You could select the respondents purely at random as they leave the site at the end of the event. Or you could decide just to select attendees from a particular age group at random. You could use convenience sampling and only ask attendees that you know personally.

All of these different methods of sampling will have their own advantages and disadvantages and will influence whether or not you will be able to analyse your results using statistical techniques. The method of sampling will also influence the claims you can make in your results and conclusions. This chapter will consider the different methods of sampling that you can use and highlight the advantages and disadvantages of the different approaches.

4.3 Selecting a sample

Research in hospitality, tourism and events is undertaken by students like you to answer research questions. One of the most important things to tackle is the issue of access to your chosen sample. You might be selecting a sample of respondents at an event or a tourist site, in which case as long as you have permission and the time you will not have a problem. If, however, as it often happens, you want to talk to customers, guests or managers in organisations as part of your sample, you will have to make sure that you have access to the relevant documents and to those respondents that you have identified in your sample frame. Illustration 4.1 shows some of the issues that can arise when this is part of your plan.

Illustration 4.1　Issues of access

Saunders et al. (2000) identify that first-time researchers often have problems with access which can make the research flawed. Research often requires that you have access to individuals or ideas and you may have issues with your status, ethical considerations and just plain access. Student research often takes place over a very short duration and you may underestimate how much time it takes to get the correct sample.

Buchanan et al. (1988) advocate an opportunistic approach and offer the following advice:

- Allow sufficient time to gain access.
- Use friends and relatives where possible.
- Use non-threatening language to explain the aims of the research.
- Deal with respondents in a positive manner.
- Offer a copy of your findings.

Gatekeepers are usually crucial players in gaining permission and often it is difficult to identify who these are so you must seek help from your supervisor about this. If the individuals that you want to cooperate in the sample do not go along with you, then you will have no study and you will have to seek out alternative respondents, or else your research will be over.

Personal experience – Susan Horner

I supervised a postgraduate dissertation when I was working at César Ritz Hotel School in Switzerland. The student had planned to go to India to interview a sample

of key managers in a 4* hotel that he had already gained permission from. When he got there (at his own expense) and had arrived at the hotel, the managers refused to see him, giving the excuse that their director had overruled them on company participation. Luckily, the student had a back-up hotel to talk to and the research proceeded, although a comparative study that he had planned was no longer possible within the time frame.

The lesson here is always send your aims and objectives, the details of your study and your questions in advance of the research and get *written permission* from the sample respondents and their managers, even if they are your friends. Do not use your friends as respondents unless you have gained permission from their managers or directors!

There are undoubtedly examples of studies where insufficient attention is given to these considerations and worthless information is produced from 'biased samples' (that is, those samples which differ in a fundamental way from the population from which they are drawn). However, it should be remembered that although sampling is often referred to as a problematical area in research, it is not the only area where bias or error can occur. In the preceding chapters, errors in the selection of methods of data collection and poor planning were shown to produce poor results. In the following chapters, it will be demonstrated that weaknesses in questionnaire and data analysis can also result in useless information being produced.

There are some good examples of dramatically biased samples. Perhaps the best known of these is the public opinion poll of the 1936 presidential election in the United States (Young, 1966; Moser and Kalton, 1993; Frankfort-Nachmias and Nachmias, 1996). Here, an incorrect result was predicted because of a major error in the sampling frame. Ten million people were identified from sources such as telephone directories. In 1936 few poor people had telephones and hence these voters were excluded from the survey. On election day, whilst the prediction had suggested a victory for Landon, the poor individual voted for Roosevelt. Hence, the sample was not representative of the voting population. Similar issues were observed with the opinion polls that were carried during the 2015 General Election in the UK, as you can see in Illustration 4.2. For a number of reasons, the polls did not predict the correct outcome. A similar phenomenon happened at the recent EU referendum, in June 2016, when opinion polls seemed to suggest a remain result, whilst the majority of citizens voted for the UK to leave the EU (for 'Brexit').

Illustration 4.2   The polls were wrong!

When the exit poll dropped at 10 pm, the numbers seemed unbelievable. A few hours later and that forecast was looking overly cautious.

The initial figures, which predicted the Tories would win 316 seats, ended up underestimating the party. David Cameron won an overall majority – an outcome deemed near impossible based on pre-election polling.

It is clear that the polls and, as sure as night follows day, the forecasts modelled on polling, had a bad election. The question is: why did the polls get it wrong?

In the end, the debate over whether online or phone polls are better, and discussions about different methodologies to weight undecided voters and filter for certainty to vote, all proved irrelevant. Although phone polls during the course of the campaign had shown several Tory leads, the final crop of polls were roughly anticipating a tie.

Across the polls, there appear to have been at least three errors:

1   Labour significantly underperformed compared with expectations set by the polls. Support for Miliband's party averaged 34% in the final polls, 3.5 points above the actual result. The figures for UKIP (12.5%), the Lib Dems (8%) and the Greens (4%) were within the polls' margins of error. Although the Conservatives' average in the final pre-election polls (34%) was also roughly three and a half points shy of the party's actual result, several companies – including Ipsos Mori, Opinium and ComRes – had the party's share at 35–36%.

2   The Lib Dems' result was catastrophic, even in their strongholds. The party held on to only eight of their 57 seats, which is in stark contrast to the snapshots provided by constituency polling.

3   Although turnout saw a one-point increase on 2010, the level (66%) was significantly lower than that implied in most polls, meaning that the opinion of non-voters weighed on polling numbers.

The net effect of these trends was that Labour only gained 10 seats from the Tories, a quarter less than expected, and even lost eight constituencies to Cameron's party.

The collapse of the Lib Dems, which lost 26 seats to the Tories (more than double the expected number) and 12 to Labour (which, on the other hand, was in line with expectations), provided the Conservatives with the final push they needed to get over the line.

Source: Adapted from The Guardian online, 9 May 2015

In analysing the reasons for the errors, it is true that a time component is applicable to any survey and external factors may change the result. For example, a holiday company may have strongly favourable results for a new product, but a change in exchange rates, terrorism, pollution or some other external factor not easily predicted could reverse this. The fact that people may have lied is something which is perhaps a researcher's worst nightmare. However, as previously mentioned, a range of different methods of data collection and careful questioning can reduce this problem. For opinion pollsters to be guilty of sampling error would appear surprising given the reputations of the organisations involved. What this example stresses is the need to select a representative sample from a population of an appropriate size which is not biased; how this ideal can be achieved will now be considered.

4.3.1 Sampling unit

When you contemplate undertaking a sample survey, it is important for you to define what is termed the sampling unit. This relates to a single member of the survey population. Within the field of market research, this is commonly an individual who possesses certain characteristics which are important to the objectives of the survey. For example, your sampling unit could be defined as people of a particular age and socio-economic group. However, as mentioned in the previous section, a sampling unit may not always be a person. Sampling units can be drawn from destinations, events, types of holiday, and so on.

Illustration 4.3   A sampling unit

Graham Busby and Callum Haines, Plymouth University

Doc Martin and film tourism: the creation of destination image

Following a pilot study, the data collection comprised 302 face-to-face, full interviews with visitors to Port Isaac, over seven days in autumn 2011; the timing was entirely due to researcher availability. Tourism is less affected by seasonality compared with 20 years ago (Visit Cornwall, 2010), although it is accepted that restricting data collection to just the autumn may influence results. Furthermore, recent research highlights the presence of international visitors year-round (Busby, 2003).

By undertaking the pilot study, the location with the highest footfall was identified as the viewpoint across the harbour, near the seating area in Fore

(Continued)

(Continued)

Street which, therefore, became recognised as the most appropriate site to inter-cept visitors. The on-site visitor survey was administered using the next-to-pass non-probability sampling technique recommended by the Tourism and Recreation Research Unit (1983). Additionally, the total number of people passing by whilst interviewing respondents was recorded across all seven days of research (see Table 4.1).

Table 4.1   Number of people passing by whilst interviewing respondents

Date of visit	Tally	Running total
04/11/2011	68	68
07/11/2011	84	152
08/11/2011	112	264
10/11/2011	129	393
12/11/2011	98	491
15/11/2011	77	568
22/11/2011	73	641

Through analysing the five most perceived images pertaining to Port Isaac gath-ered from the 302 survey respondents, quantitative content analysis (Holsti, 1969) of *Doc Martin* was undertaken as an alternative, secondary form of data collection. This took the form of numerical content analysis of the first, third and concluding episodes for each of the five *Doc Martin* series produced by using a systematic quota sampling technique (Neuendorf, 2002). Every series has been included for consistency purposes. The systematic quota sampling method is favourable as the five most referred to images, pertaining to Port Isaac, had already been identified from the results of the street survey.

Source: Busby and Haines (2013: 109)

4.3.2 Types of population

The population from which a sample is drawn can have one of two important characteristics: it may be finite or infinite. A finite population is one where the whole population is known and can be counted. For example, the population of tourists undertaking a particular type of holiday with a company is likely to be known as their names and addresses will have been stored by the company on a database and can be easily accessed. Alternatively, there may be situations where the population is not easily defined, hence the term infinite population. An example of this can occur at tourist attractions or events where no charge is made for entry. The staff of the site or the event organisers may be unaware of exactly how many visitors they receive each year. Moreover, there may be little or no information about the characteristics of visitors or visits (finding this out may be the objective of the survey). Under these conditions, deciding who and how to sample is clearly more problematic. There may also be situations faced by researchers between these two extremes. For instance, the total number of visitors to a site may be known, but there may be little known about when visits take place or the socio-demographic makeup of the visitors. Dealing with this situation is no easy matter and what is presented in the following sections represents a pragmatic solution to try and compensate for the inherent bias which may occur when selecting a sample of individuals for inclusion in your survey.

4.3.3 Sampling frame

A sampling frame is a list of the sampling units together with other information which enables a fair sample to be drawn. The main requirement here is that each of the sampling units must have an equal chance of being part of the survey. This is achievable in the situation where the names and addresses of all customers are known, in that the total number is known and checks can be made to ensure that no name is duplicated or omitted. However, as mentioned in the previous section, there are often situations where it is not possible to construct a truly complete sampling frame. It is worth considering why this may be the case before some solutions as to how to cope with the problem are put forward.

Errors in sampling frames

The following are some of the main errors which are commonly found with sampling frames. The details presented below have been developed from the work of Moser and Kalton (1993) and Frankfort-Nachmias and Nachmias (1996):

1.   The information is incorrect.

This can occur because mistakes were made in entering names and addresses when the list was written. Often, lists of names and addresses are compiled for purposes other than the needs of a future survey. Moreover, such lists quickly become out of date, with people moving away.

2.   The information is incomplete.

This commonly occurs because the need for a sampling frame was never envisaged. Many tourist attractions or event organisers are unlikely to know who visits their site or their event. Similarly, transport carriers may have some information where travel tickets are posted to an address or via an agent, but not about travellers who purchase at a rail or coach station. It is unlikely that a restaurant will have all the details of every customer who purchases a meal and individuals may visit in a group which means that the information will be incomplete.

3.   The information is duplicated.

This occurs when lists are combined to develop a sampling frame. For example, a tour operator or hotelier may wish to send postal questionnaires to a sample of customers who have purchased a holiday or hotel room from the company in the last five years. Although the names and addresses are known for all the customers, some will have purchased a holiday or hotel room more than once and therefore may appear on the same sample frame several times. As such, the sample drawn from this list may be biased as some holidaymakers or guests will have a greater chance of being included in the sample. If you assume that frequent purchasers are more favourable towards the company, then such a biased sample may ultimately produce results that are not truly representative. In this example, this is on top of the potential problem that going back five years will undoubtedly produce names and addresses that are out of date, so the sample may be biased in terms of a higher response rate from those who used the company more recently and have not moved house.

4.   The information is clustered.

The problem here is that perhaps several people live at a single address but the purpose of the survey is to interview a particular member of that household. Thus, the precise definition of sampling units (particular individuals in this case) is not possible from the sampling frame available. Another instance where this type of problem can occur is at tourist attractions where there is information known that a certain proportion of visitors come from within a 5-mile radius, a 10-mile radius or from particular towns and cities. As the survey focuses on individual visitors, this information is helpful in gaining an opinion about the proportions of those who should be interviewed from these locations, but not about who the visitors are or their characteristics.

5.   The information includes aspects not applicable.

A similar problem is that names and addresses may well still be valid but only certain types of individual are required for the survey. The survey may need to contact individuals of a particular gender, age or some other aspect, such as those holiday-makers who went on a particular excursion as part of their holiday. Hence, the list includes information which is not applicable but may not include the extra information needed to identify the particular sampling units (in this case certain holidaymakers) which are required for the survey.

Methods of coping where sampling frames are incomplete

Thus, there may be many instances where you are faced with the problem that developing a sampling frame, and hence selecting a true and reliable sample from it, is fraught with difficulties. It is easy at this point to fall into the trap of assuming that it is possible to compensate for all the potential errors in a sampling frame by simply increasing the sample size. Whilst it is true that, other things being equal, a larger sample stands a better chance of being more representative of the population than a smaller sample, a sample that is fundamentally flawed remains biased.

Where sampling frames are not available, complete or are otherwise suspect, additional aspects of the population can be considered to develop a procedure to assist in the better selection of a sample. These steps can be considered before and after the data collection.

To illustrate the types of problem here, consider the situation you face if you want to undertake a site visitor survey at a tourist attraction. This example shows the problems that exist with sampling and that will also occur if you want to undertake a guest survey in a hotel or to discover individual perceptions of events.

We can assume in this case that the site manager is unaware of who the visitors are (in terms of age, gender, type of group, etc.), where they have come from or their attitudes towards certain aspects of the site. In the main, answers to these questions are the objectives of your survey. The method of data collection for at least a part of the survey has been decided as a face-to-face interview with users of the site. This type of scenario is quite common in this area and the development of a suitable sampling frame requires careful consideration. The following steps represent a pragmatic way that you can approach this type of problem:

Step 1: Who to ask

Perhaps the first step is to determine who to ask. In the situation outlined above, any person visiting the tourist attraction for recreational purposes is eligible to be included in the survey. One aspect which should be considered is at what age visitors become suitable. Clearly, the responses, attitudes, decision making and purchasing requirements of young children may well be different to those of adults. Extreme care should be taken when contemplating interviews with children, and only ever with the full cooperation of parents (see ethical considerations in Chapter 1). In situations where the opinions of children are important, it may be preferable to design a separate survey (possibly with some comparable questions to an adult survey). In this sense, it could be much easier to train interviewers in the particular requirements of the survey, to gain permission and inform the local police of the aims and methods of the survey.

Although site surveys at tourist attractions with face-to-face interviews can achieve a high response rate, some people will refuse to cooperate. In the literature, those taking part in a survey are called 'respondents' and hence a response rate of 90% would indicate that 90% of those approached for interview agreed to and satisfactorily completed the interview. Thus, in order to be able to report the response rate, it is important to keep a record of non-respondents. If the response rate is very low, then a judgement may have to be made as to the reliability of the results.

Step 2: When should data be collected?

In deciding on what days to interview, consideration should be given to the patterns of visits at the tourist attraction over the season. For example, the number of visits made to the attraction is likely to be different at the beginning and end of the season than in the middle or following a significant advertising campaign. Moreover, there may be particular days when the usage of the site is untypical when compared to the rest of the year. Special events and visits by celebrities or public holidays could easily distort a sample drawn where the number of days allocated for interviewing included a high proportion of days when the site was unusually overcrowded.

In addition, variations in site usage can occur on a daily and weekly basis. At informal recreation sites such as country parks, dog walkers may visit the site on a very regular basis, perhaps early in the morning. Later in the day, the site might attract groups of people who visit the site less frequently than the dog walkers but make more use of the facilities provided. Furthermore, on weekdays, there may be a higher proportion of retired people than on weekend days when more families are likely to visit. At many tourist attractions, there will be differences between the number and type of people within and outside the main school holiday periods over and above seasonal variations.

In deciding when to interview, an awareness of the sorts of variations on different types of day is important. Ideally, the number of days selected should reflect these variations. The number of days needed will be related to the sample size, length of interview, number of interviewers and characteristics of the site. Interviewing should take place on at least three days of a similar type.

Step 3: When to interview in relation to the visit

For the majority of surveys, the end of the visit is normally the best time to approach people for an interview. In this sense, visitors to the tourist attraction will have had chance to make use of all the site facilities. If interviewing takes place during the visit, respondents may not be able to answer all the questions because they may not have had the opportunity to gain an opinion about facilities they have yet to make use of.

An exception to this was undertaken by Brunt (1990). Site surveys were used as one of several methods in establishing why visitors had selected certain tourist attractions for their day trips. In this particular instance, it was found, after the pilot stage, that interviewing people as they arrived at the site provided the best results. This was because some respondents found that the experience of the visit (whether positive or negative) caused difficulty in remembering why they had decided to visit the site in the first place. A typical response to an open question of 'why did you decide to visit this site today?' was 'I am not sure, but we are certainly not coming back'. Hence, interviewing people at the end of their visit proved unsatisfactory. However, most site surveys at tourist attractions require respondents to indicate what they feel about specific aspects of the site they have just visited. Thus, the most practical time to interview is at the end of the visit.

Step 4: Where on the site to interview

Given that it is advisable to interview at the end of the visit, it is necessary to find a suitable point near to the site exit. Ideally, if there is a location where all visitors pass on their way out of the site, then all would have an equal chance of being included in the survey. As equal chance is a crucial aim in developing a fair sample, effort should be made in establishing a suitable interview point.

There may be some sites, such as those in open countryside, where there is no single exit. Here, careful and systematic observations can be used to determine the main 'natural' exit points. Then, either an interviewer can be placed at each exit or a single interviewer could visit each in rotation.

Step 5: Whom to approach

As every person visiting the tourist attraction on a survey day has been deemed to be eligible for interview, then each should, as far as possible, have the same chance of being part of the survey. In the example, which has been developed here, the population of the visitors to the site is not known, and interviewing say every tenth person to exit may leave interviewers with little to do during parts of the day. However, instructing interviewers to decide for themselves whom to approach is likely to introduce bias. This is because some interviewers will naturally select certain types of people who they feel are more approachable and likely to agree to an interview. In a similar sense, individuals who present themselves for interview should not be permitted to be included. This is because self-selection may introduce bias in the form of producing results with a disproportionately high number of respondents who had 'something to say'.

The Tourism and Recreation Research Unit (1983) recommends that the 'next-to-pass' technique be adopted in these circumstances. In short, the interviewer is suitably located and the first person to pass this point is approached for interview. When this interview is completed (if agreement to take part is reached), the next person to pass is similarly approached. Obviously, if somebody passes whilst an interview is in progress then they are not chased after or required to wait! With a fair number of survey days, interview points and well-trained interviewers, this technique should yield satisfactory results. The interviewer has no control over when a visitor decides to leave the site and pass the interview point and hence this removes interviewer bias in the selection of respondents.

Step 6: What about groups?

Inevitably, at tourist attractions people are highly likely to visit in groups, either as a family, group of friends or some other combination. It is preferable if the interview is undertaken by a single respondent. Often, this occurs naturally if the interviewer truly selects the first person in the group to pass and addresses the questions directly to this individual. However, occasionally there can be a problem with respondents conferring with other members of the group or even disagreements being caused by the questions. Trained interviewers may have to be permitted to exercise a certain amount of practical judgement in such situations.

Step 7: Weighting

Observations made at the site to help develop a sampling frame and define the sampling unit will have established times of the day when the site has most of its visitors. Unfortunately, it may not be possible to increase the number of interviewers to account for this. Thus, by using the next-to-pass technique there may be certain times when many more people are passing the interview point and leaving the site because the interviewer is occupied. For example, it could be found that half of those interviewed on a particular day had travelled to the site by coach, whilst observations had shown that a higher proportion of visitors had arrived by car. Some account should be made of this to allow for possible errors in the results. Thus, some replies in the analysis stage could be adjusted or 'weighted' to allow for the higher numbers of coach trippers interviewed than were actually present on the site.

4.3.4 Summary: selecting a sample

When selecting a sample for the situation outlined in the preceding section, it has been shown that the construction of a sampling frame depends on factors which include:

- awareness of the population
- definition of the sampling unit
- patterns of use at the site, event or organisation
- type of survey method.

In many instances in tourism, hospitality and events, developing a sampling frame can be difficult to achieve. Awareness of the possible limitations is important and must be fairly reported. Whilst all surveys aim to provide the best possible sampling frame from which to select a sample, the purpose and requirements of the survey should be borne in mind. Clearly, the accuracy required from a survey, where the results will prompt important decisions, is higher than in an exploratory, descriptive study. If there is a mismatch between the level of precision and accuracy required of the results and the ability to construct a suitable sampling frame, then the only recourse is to extend the range of methods of data collection. Moreover, any limitations known in relation to the sampling frame must be fairly discussed in your report so that subsequent management decisions are appropriately informed.

4.4 Types of sampling

Previous sections have stressed the importance of every eligible member of a survey population having an equal chance of selection in a sample. This is an important principle within sampling, and, as far as possible, the market researcher must try to ensure that this is the case if the results are to be viable. At a general level, there are two basic types of sampling which follow this condition, which can then be sub-divided into a number of particular types. The two basic types of sampling where the 'equal chance' principle applies are probability sampling and random sampling. Before defining these, it should be remembered that often the types of sampling procedures used are not mutually exclusive, but overlap with each other to a certain extent. For a specific research project, it is common to find several sampling techniques being adopted.

4.4.1 Probability sampling

In situations where the extent of the survey population is known, an individual sampling unit (often in tourism, hospitality or events, an individual person) has a known chance of being included in the survey. For example, if a company in the industry has developed an accurate sampling frame of its customer base, then the potential population is known. If this is, say, 200,000 individual customers and a sample size of 2,000, then each customer must have a 1 in 100 chance of being included in the sample. The calculation of the probability in this instance is behind the concept of probability sampling. However, of equal importance is that the actual selection of the 2,000 individual respondents must be done on a random basis. Methods of selecting a sample randomly will be discussed shortly, but first it is necessary to define what we mean by random sampling.

4.4.2 Random sampling

Random sampling is almost the same as probability sampling with one slight exception, which is pertinent to the topic of this book. As has been shown, there may be situations where the population in a survey is not known. With the case of informal recreation sites or events, which are admission-free, this is often the case, with the total number of visitors from year to year being estimated rather than calculated. Hence, true probability sampling is not possible. The principle of random selection can still apply, but the probability of inclusion in a survey cannot, as the population size is unknown. Take, for example, interviewing, on a next-to-pass basis, 200 people leaving a beach. They are selected on a random basis but it is not known whether the 200 interviewed are from a population of 1,000, 1,500 or 5,000 beach-goers on that day or over a season. Awareness of the limitations this may cause in terms of the inability to predict from these 200 the attitudes of all visitors to the beach is clear. However, this should not suggest that such a survey would be worthless, as descriptive studies or 'straw polls' can be of much value in certain situations where predictions and generalisations about the rest of the population are not necessary.

Nevertheless, probability sampling, where a population is known, can be seen as preferable wherever it is possible. This is because statistical techniques can be used to suggest the amount of 'error' between the sample and its representativeness of the rest of the population. This specific aspect will be investigated in a later section.

Returning to the different types of sampling, it can be seen that probability sampling and random sampling share many characteristics. Both methods involve the random selection of sampling units in a survey. Because they are so similar in many respects, the specific difference is often ignored and either the term 'probability sampling' is loosely used to include 'random sampling' or vice versa. Having defined the starting point, it is now possible to look in more detail at some more specific types of sampling methods which are based on the principles of equal chance and random selection.

Simple and systematic random sampling

Simple random sampling is a method which is similar to a lottery. In the case of a known list of customers of, say, 100,000 names, a sample of 1,000 could be drawn by placing all the names on paper, placing them in a very large hat and drawing 1,000 from it. Such a method in practice would be somewhat cumbersome and computers are able to generate random numbers to achieve the same goal. In a survey, it would be necessary to draw 1,000 different names, thus once a name had been selected it would not be eligible for selection again. In theoretical terms, statisticians would start to complain about this as the second name drawn from that hat would have a 1 in 99,999 chance of being drawn unless the first name was replaced in the hat. However, in surveys it is not practical or desirable to interview the same person more than once. Obviously, some common sense and judgement are necessary to be fair yet pragmatic.

If random numbers are used, then the next random number selected should suffice if duplication occurs.

To overcome some of the potential pitfalls with simple random sampling, the selection of respondents can be carried out in a more systematic way. Taking the same scenario, where the population is known, if a sample of 1,000 is required from the list of 100,000 names, then every 100th name could be taken. The starting point could be determined randomly and then every 100th name selected from this point.

Simple and systematic samples are used where the members of a population are similar or homogeneous. No account is made of any particular characteristic of the population and every member of the population is given an equal chance of inclusion in the survey. As we have already seen, in tourism, hospitality and events, full knowledge of the population may not be possible or it may not be homogenous. If the latter aspect is the case, then the following method of sampling may be more appropriate.

Stratified random sampling

Where information about the population of a survey is known, it is possible to divide that population into smaller sub-samples or 'strata'. It is common in our field for this to be done on the basis of socio-demographic characteristics such as gender, age, socio-economic group or a categorisation of previous purchasing behaviour. A particular sampling unit such as a potential individual respondent can be placed in the sub-sample only once. After each sub-sample has been determined, the individual sampling units are randomly selected from each sub-sample.

In effect, this process is similar to probability sampling where every member of a population has an equal chance of inclusion in the survey and selection is conducted randomly. Here, the population is divided into strata, and within each stratum every member has an equal chance of inclusion and the selection is random.

The main purpose of this method of sampling is to achieve a more reliable sample. However, a great deal of knowledge about the population is required, over and above the extent of the population, if stratification is to be workable. If, for example, within a survey population there are clearly identifiable groups where there is a high level of similarity (homogeneity) within the groups and there are many differences (heterogeneity) between the groups, then stratification may be worthwhile. This may particularly be the case if the distinct groups vary in size. For instance, if a company has a small minority who complain about their product, then they may not be sufficiently recognised in a large survey. If, however, they are characterised as a group by several easily identifiable factors, then the problem could be much greater than is apparent. This could, for example, be a group of holidaymakers who are identified by their age or social class, or those who stayed at a specific resort.

There remains the problem, though, of whether such groups can be identified 'prior' to the main survey to enable this type of sampling method to be performed.

Computer analysis of survey results allows for such groups to be selected out from the sample and to be analysed specifically and separately from the rest. Thus, prior selection and stratification, as well as not often being achievable (lack of prior knowledge), are not always necessary.

Perhaps the main use of this type of sampling method in the field of tourism, hospitality or events is where the residence of individuals is known and can be stratified. To demonstrate this, take, for instance, a survey of season ticket holders to and from an island for a ferry operator. Season tickets are purchased by commuters to the island and to the mainland. Prior to the survey, the population of all season ticket holders was found to be 20,000. Of these, 15,000 live on the mainland and 5,000 live on the island. If it is decided that a sample of 1,000 should be interviewed, then appropriate proportions could easily be calculated, i.e. 750 mainlanders and 250 islanders.

Illustration 4.4   An example of stratified random sampling from an undergraduate dissertation

'The transformational leadership style: an assessment of the application of emotional contagion and its impacts on employee motivation and performance' by Chloe Locke, BSc Events Management, supervised by Richard Parkman and Steven Jakes, Plymouth University.

Aim

An assessment of emotional contagion within gender groups and preferred leadership style within service sector, business sector and manual labour occupations.

Objectives

- To identify which gender groups are most susceptible to emotional contagion
- To identify which occupational group experiences the highest levels of emotional contagion
- To understand the attributes employees associate with an effective leader
- To recognise the preferred leadership style within occupational groups.

Sample

A random stratified sample (Brotherton, 2015) was used for the purpose of the study, whereby individuals were identified from three distinct, defined occupational groups – business, service and labour industries – and the specific gender groups of male and female. This sampling method was used due to the research design of the study, which required the population to be divided into subpopulation groups. Random stratified sampling was used to ensure the sample population best represented the entire population being studied. Additionally, the sampling method meant precision of the data was obtained, due to reduced sampling bias; finally, this method of sampling was used due to its administrative convenience (Das, 2009). The sample consisted of 360 respondents, comprising of 120 individuals from each of the three industries, containing 193 males and 167 females who were employees from companies within the UK. The minimum age of participants in the sample was 17 and the maximum age was 64. The descriptive statistics show that the mean age was 33.75. The sampling method used in the current study decreased sampling bias, which reduced the sampling error. This suggests that the sample in the current study is representative of the population. To further support this, the age range of the sample indicates diversity and a wide range of understanding of variation amongst the groups; therefore, the findings are considered generalisable.

4.4.3 Cluster sampling

Where surveys cover very large areas, such as whole countries, the types of sampling methods described to this point may not be very cost-effective. Consider, for example, a company wishing to conduct a nationwide survey of a sample of its customers using personal interviews. Random sampling may well yield a list of potential respondents spread widely across the country but thinly in some areas, thus interviewers may have to travel very long distances to conduct a small number of interviews. To overcome this type of problem, the researcher identifies groupings or clusters of respondents in a particular area. A range of clusters are selected randomly and then, within each cluster, respondents are again selected on a random basis. This method of sampling is called 'cluster sampling' (some older texts may refer to this as area sampling). This method can also be useful where the extent of the survey population is not fully known, as shown in the following example.

Example: travel agent services

Background

A branch of a travel agency has been established for the first time in a town. A survey is decided to ascertain the awareness of this venture amongst the resident population of the surrounding area, but no complete list of all residents is available.

Stages

1. A map is used to define the boundary of potential users of the shop.
2. The area within this boundary is divided into segments, reflecting all areas, both residential and non-residential.
3. Each segment is numbered.
4. A sample of segments is selected on a simple random or systematic basis.
5. Within the segments, actual residences are numbered.
6. Systematic or simple random samples of residences are selected.
7. Individuals within the selected residences are contacted for interview.

In this example, two clusters are used: segments within the defined boundary and residences within each segment. In some surveys, it may be necessary for several stages of clustering to take place in this way. Where this occurs, the process is sometimes referred to as 'multi-stage sampling'.

A variation on this theme can be found with what is termed 'multi-phase sampling'; the difference between 'multi-stage' and 'multi-phase' often relates to the latter using a follow-up survey. In our example, a first 'phase' might be to investigate the awareness of the new travel agency outlet. From the results of this, a second 'phase' could be to develop a follow-up survey amongst those respondents who answered a particular question in a specific way. For example, further details could be sought from those who have indicated that they are planning to book a holiday in the next six months, or those who have asked to be informed of special offers. Thus, multi-phase sampling could be used to first gain a general picture and then to follow up with more detailed (and longer) interviews in a subsequent phase with particular sub-sets of respondents. In all phases, the respondents are always selected randomly.

4.4.4 Summary: Probability sampling methods

Simple random, systematic random, stratified random, cluster sampling and its variants are the main methods of probability sampling. All methods are similar in that the probability of a sampling unit within a survey population being included in the sample is known and the selection of sampling units is conducted randomly. It is now worth considering, briefly, what the opposite of this is. When you are designing research, especially if you intend to target young adults, it is tempting to construct your sample using non-random sampling and to invite your contacts to participate in the research, especially if time is limited. This approach will make your sample non-representative but it will give you some ideas that can be worked on in your findings. The findings, however, will not be generalisable. An example of an undergraduate dissertation that used focus groups in this way, at Plymouth University, is shown below. This was a qualitative piece of research using convenience sampling and focus groups. The results were not statistically valid but gave a number of interesting insights into the views of Generation Y on the colour of brands in the events sector.

Illustration 4.5   Sampling technique using non-random methods

'The significance of brand design and colour on event purchase and participation amongst Generation Y' by Emma Macphie, supervised by Susan Horner, Plymouth University, 2016.

Aim

To critically analyse the significance of brand design and colour on event purchase and participation amongst Generation Y.

Objectives

1   To analyse the underlying literature to this research, including consumer behaviour and branding strategies within the events sector
2   To investigate perceptions and attitudes towards persuasive branding and the impact of repeat purchase using content analysis
3   To measure the influence of design and colour in branding on Generation Y using a qualitative data method of research
4   To put forward recommendations for further research within the events sector and make practical recommendations for branding within the events sector.

Sample

In order to gain rich data, a sample of willing individuals is required to complete the study. The sample is chosen to reflect those segments of the population which provide the most meaningful information in relation to the project objectives. The study requires no specific gender as it is focused on consumers that attend events, thus the study requires all participants to have attended an event at any time. Due to time constraints and access to an ample sample, the sample will be conducted using University of Plymouth students. The probability of being chosen was

(Continued)

(Continued)

unknown and relies on the researcher's discretion (Zikmund, 2013). Due to the nature of events, using a sample of Generation Y would allow the researcher to understand how consumers of this generation see branding. Unlike previous peer groups, they have grown up alongside smartphones and tablets and have been the most eager adopters as new technologies are released. With this in mind, this sample of the population (Generation Y) will be shaping the events market in the coming years, thus understanding what influences them to purchase events is key to selling events in the future. It is clear that some participants have specific expertise or experiences within the events sector that can help the researcher. Creswell (2014) notes that it is up to the researcher to decide on whether or not the participants need to be knowledgeable in the subject area. However, in order to make sure that everyone is aware of the research, questions will be emailed to each participant prior to the focus group.

4.4.5 Non-probability/non-random sampling

In situations where the population is not known or there is insufficient time to build a sampling frame, some researchers may turn to non-probability sampling methods. The most commonly used (and criticised) method is called 'quota sampling'. For example, in street surveys interviewers may be required to question certain types of people and are given a 'quota' to complete of each type. The population may be divided in terms of apparent age, social class or other controlling variables upon which the interviewers must make a subjective judgement in the selection of potential respondents. In the opinion of the authors, this leaves too much discretion to the interviewer, enabling a significant amount of bias to enter the sample.

4.5 Sample size

Moser (1958) stated that anyone who ever has to advise on sample designs will know that the first question he is asked is – how big a sample do I need? Many years later, this statement remains true. However, often the question being asked could be more accurately re-phrased as 'what is the minimum number I can get away with?' Selecting the size of the sample is clearly an important question in the design of any survey.

All surveys where a sample of the population is used, will involve a level of 'sampling error'. This is the difference between what has been found in the results based on the sample and the actual values that would have been found out if everybody in the population had been included in the survey.

It is tempting to assume that by simply enlarging the sample size, problems of error will disappear. However, any sample which is biased in its sampling methods or selection of respondents will remain biased whatever its size. Furthermore, until the sample size becomes a high proportion of the population (say, over 20%), the actual size of the sample is more important than the sample's proportion of the population. Clearly though, an increase in sample size in a survey where the sample is drawn by fair means will reduce the level of sampling error. Thus, the sample size often represents a compromise between what is achievable in a pragmatic sense and what is desirable statistically in relation to the concept of sampling error. These two sides of determining sample size will now be evaluated in turn.

Illustration 4.6   Sampling extract from an undergraduate dissertation

'Tourist satisfaction: the mythology of King Arthur's Tintagel' by Danielle Chapman, supervised by Natalie Semley, Plymouth University, July 2016.

Aims and objectives of the research

The aim of this research project is:

- To determine the factors responsible for tourist satisfaction in Tintagel by exploring the requirements, expectations and overall satisfaction of tourists on-site.

In order to achieve the research aim, the following objectives need to be met:

- Investigate factors contributing to tourist satisfaction
- Investigate the role of motivations as a contributor to satisfaction
- Investigate the impact of on-site experiences on tourist satisfaction.

Specifically, to Tintagel:

- Determine if tourist satisfaction is influenced by historic myth and legend.

(Continued)

(Continued)

Sampling is a cost-effective way of gaining information on a section of the public that can be used to draw conclusions about the larger population (Brunt, 1997). The sample population for this study was composed of visitors to Tintagel in February 2016, including tourists, locals and day trippers (Veal, 1997): 300 questionnaires were printed and taken to Tintagel over the February half-term, and 242 were completed by respondents; 2 were excluded due to missing or incomplete data, which left a total of 240 questionnaires to be used for analysis. Table 4.2 outlines the number of questionnaires completed throughout the data collection period, which was influenced by researcher availability, weather conditions and destination footfall.

Self-completed questionnaires were distributed by several trained research assistants, who approached respondents with a brief overview of the purpose of the study, before asking respondents if they would like to complete the questionnaire. The research assistants were able to give help in completing the questionnaires, as required by respondents (Veal, 1997). As the population was unknown, random sampling was used, and research assistants used the next-to-pass technique to ensure bias was removed from the sampling process (Brunt, 1997).

Table 4.2   Data collection schedule

Date	Time	Researchers	Location	Responses
13-02-2016	13:30–15:00	2	Near Tintagel Castle	28
			Near Tintagel Castle	15
14-02-2016	12:15–15:00	2	Near The Old Post Office	13
			At the bottom of the street	43
15-02-2016	12:45–15:45	2	Near Tintagel Castle	71
			At the bottom of the street	22
18-02-2016	13:00–15:00	1	Near Tintagel Castle	50

4.5.1 Pragmatic determination of sample size

At several points in this book, we have returned to the question 'what is the purpose of the survey?' and in deciding on sample size this should again be borne in mind.

Where a high level of accuracy is required from the results, and forecasting or other generalisations are required from the sample about the rest of the population, then the size of the sample becomes crucial. However, in more descriptive studies, if 350 people out of 500 interviewed requested extra refreshment facilities at a tourist attraction, then a management decision might reasonably be based on this alone. Thus, the need for complicated, predictive statistics requiring large samples may be unnecessary. Perhaps the first question to ask is the level of accuracy required from the results in relation to the survey objectives.

At a second level, the researcher should consider what statistical tests will be performed on the data. Here again, there is a relationship with the objectives of the survey. In Chapter 7, we will look at analysing results from surveys and this will show that some statistical tests require a minimum number of responses on which the test can be satisfactorily executed. If an objective of the survey is to investigate how age affects the reaction to a product, then the results might be tabulated as seen in Table 4.3.

In Table 4.3, there are 20 cells (5 columns of opinion scores multiplied by 4 rows relating to age category). For there to be a possible relationship between age and opinion to be tested, the sample size needs to be sufficiently large for there to be responses in each cell. The pilot stage in a survey is useful in showing whether the classification of categories is appropriate.

A third level of questioning which helps to determine sample size is the amount of resources the researcher has available. There will be a finite budget in terms of the time available and the cost of the project. The larger the sample, the greater the resources required. Larger sizes may therefore result in the need for more staff and an increased number of survey days for interviews. Hence, sample size is often influenced by the constraints on the resources available.

At a fourth and final level, the researcher must consider the anticipated response rate shown by the pilot stage. This is particularly applicable to postal or online surveys. If the requirements of the survey in terms of the accuracy and statistical analysis call for 1,000 completed questionnaires and a response rate of 50% are anticipated, then clearly 2,000 questionnaires would be distributed.

Table 4.3   Cross-tabulation table of age and opinion of product

Age	Opinion of product (1 = Excellent, 5 = Very poor)				
	1	2	3	4	5
16–30					
31–45					
46–60					
61 & over					

To summarise, to determine sample size in a pragmatic way, the researcher should consider:

- the accuracy required of the results in relation to the objectives of the survey
- the requirements of statistical tests in the analysis stage
- the available resources for the project
- the anticipated response rate.

Illustration 4.7   A sampling excerpt from an undergraduate dissertation

'Determining the level of consumer-based brand equity (CBBE) in the airline industry' by Lauren Polhill, supervised by Andreas Walmsley, Plymouth University, 2016.

Purpose

The purpose of this study is to provide a framework to determine a level of consumer-based brand equity (CBBE) in the airline industry, through assessing brand knowledge amongst consumers and quantifying the results, in particular drawing on existing studies by Keller (1993), Aaker (1996) and Yoo and Donthu (2001), and their approaches to measuring CBBE. Despite CBBE being widely researched, there is no consensus for quantifying it, which this study aims to do for Emirates, British Airways and American Airlines.

Methodology/Approach

The primary research in this study combined use of a face-to-face questionnaire and of an online questionnaire in order to reach its population. A total of 270 responses were collected.

Sample

An appropriate sampling technique had to be decided that would represent the relevant population and its relationship to airlines (Frankfort-Nachmias and Nachmias, 1996). The target population of this study was those in the general public who have used an airline. Reaching the population was important and involved selecting an appropriate sampling method for the research; a successful sample is one where, if the study was repeated elsewhere, the findings should not vary considerably (Frankfort-Nachmias and Nachmias, 1996). Probability sampling was relied on in the face-to-face surveys; this assumes the sample selected represents the larger population (Berg, 2001).

A systematic sampling strategy was used in the face-to-face street surveys to select the sample (Frankfort-Nachmias and Nachmias, 1996), where every 8th person that walked past was selected; most people were willing once the purpose of the survey was explained. Usually in systematic sampling, the interval between respondents is decided by dividing the population by the desired number of questionnaire responses, however Plymouth's population is 261,546 (Plymouth City Council, 2016/17) and only 54 face-to-face responses were needed, which would involve approaching every 4,670 person, something not feasible given the time constraints. A systematic sampling method was adopted as it was appropriate for use on a large population where a printed list of the population is unavailable (Frankfort-Nachmias and Nachmias, 1996; Berg, 2001).

The online sample consisted of a convenience sample or availability sample where potential respondents were close and accessible via the internet (Berg, 2001). Through convenience sampling, the questionnaire was circulated via email through a personal database, as well as by online forums that were accessible. The use of convenience sampling over the internet gave a total of 216 responses. Although convenience sampling is criticised (Berg, 2001), in the circumstances of this study and given the time constraints, this technique, in addition to the systematic sampling, provided an inexpensive way to reach a larger sample, making the research more relevant and representative (Berg, 2001).

4.5.2 Sample size and the calculation of sampling error

Where samples are selected on a random basis, the range of sampling error can be calculated according to the laws of probability and statistical theory. For a full discussion of the formulae to perform this calculation, the reader is referred to Moser and Kalton (1993). The formula produces margins of error in percentages in relation to the proportions of respondents answering in a particular way for a given sample size, as indicated in Table 4.4.

To understand Table 4.4, consider that in a survey of visitors to a tourist attraction 50% were found to be local residents and 50% tourists. If the sample of a known population was 30 people, the actual amount for the whole population could be expected to be between 30 and 70% of this result (that is, plus or minus

Table 4.4   Sampling errors in percentages

Percentage found		Sample size				
in sample	30	50	100	500	1000	3000
50	19.6	14.9	10.3	4.5	3.2	1.8
40 or 60	*	14.6	10.1	4.4	3.1	1.8
30 or 70	*	*	9.5	4.1	2.9	1.7
20 or 80	*	*	*	3.6	2.5	1.5
10 or 90	*	*	*	2.6	1.9	1.1

Note: * Shows that the sampling error percentage is greater than the original size

N.B. The percentages in this table are calculated to the 95% level. This means that there is a 95 per cent probability that the percentages found in a survey lie within a range equal to the percentage found, plus or minus the percentage shown in the table. The table shows the range of sampling error for the results of simple random surveys with samples of varying sizes.

19.6% of the result found in the survey). If the sample size is increased to 3,000 people, the actual value for the whole population (for a similar 50% result) could be expected to be between 48% and 53% (plus or minus 1.8% of the result found in the survey). As the proportions of people answering a question in a particular way change, then so does the sampling error. For example, if it was found in a survey of 3,000 people that 90% were in favour of providing an additional facility and 10% were against it, then the real value for the survey population could be expected to be plus or minus 1.1% of this figure.

A problem arises: on which question in a survey do we focus the sampling error to inform the sample size? Clearly, a practical solution is to set the standard of accuracy at the most crucial question or issue in the survey. If, for example, the main objective of the survey is to test the different reactions to the tourist attraction by residence of the respondents, then this is the best question to set sample size against. If a survey has several objectives of equal importance, then the subject where there is most disagreement or variation should be taken as the basis on which to inform sample size.

This method assumes some knowledge of the population and furthermore stresses the need for carefully conducted pilot surveys. What has not been mentioned in this context is the influence of response rates on these calculations. Clearly, the accuracy of sampling error calculations becomes increasingly suspect if non-response rates are very high.

4.6 Summary

In the field of research in travel and tourism, where we are often concerned with the attitudes of customers to the quality of products, sample surveys are vital and hence it is important to understand the nature of sampling. This chapter has introduced some of the basic concepts of sampling theory applicable to the readership of this book. The reasons why a sample survey is chosen are often down to considerations of cost and access to respondents. In many instances, it may not be possible to define a population and construct a sampling frame and the chapter has demonstrated compensatory strategies where this occurs.

The selection of sampling units needs to be random and fair if the results are to be assumed to be unbiased and precise. This aspect is at the heart of sampling theory. However, practical techniques, such as those involved with stratification, provide the researcher with an opportunity to select a sample which will give maximum utility and cost-effectiveness to the research project.

Exercises

1. Outline the salient factors to ensure that a sample is representative in the following types of survey:

    (a) a household survey
    (b) a site survey
    (c) a postal survey.

2. Justify the main criteria for determining sample size.
3. Attempt the below sampling challenge by Steven Jakes.

This is a challenge that Steve uses in his classes to help students to understand different types of sampling. It may be undertaken when working in small groups, a whole

Image 4.1   **Beads**

group, individually or in pairs. If the challenge is undertaken in small groups or as a whole group, the tutor will need to purchase a quantity of beads or different coloured sweets and place these in a large glass jar, whereas if undertaken individually you will need to buy a packet of beads or different coloured sweets.

In either case, the challenge requires you to consider the definitions of some probability and non-probability sampling techniques before outlining:

i) how you would apply it to obtaining a sample of, say, five beads or sweets
ii) how representative your sample of five sweets is in relation to your whole packet of beads or sweets
iii) the advantages (e.g. degree of sample representativeness, extent to which you have been able to eliminate sampling bias) and disadvantages (e.g. implications for time, effort and money) of each technique and when you would use it (e.g. need sampling frame).

You should populate Table 4.5 with your responses before checking the answers with your tutor. The sheet can then be used for revision purposes at a later date.

Table 4.5   Sampling techniques

Sampling technique	Definition	How do you use the technique to get a sample of five beads or sweets?	Does the technique produce a representative sample? Why?	Advantages and disadvantages of the technique. When would it be best to use this method? Why?
Random	Every member of the target population has an equal and independent chance of being selected for inclusion in the sample.			
Systematic	Population members are ordered in a particular way before a random-start-and-fixed-interval procedure is employed to select every 'x'th element from the sampling frame.			
Stratified	Population is divided into groups and then subjects are randomly selected from these subgroups in proportion to their numbers in the target population.			
Snowball	Existing population members recruit future participants from among their acquaintances.			

Sampling technique	Definition	How do you use the technique to get a sample of five beads or sweets?	Does the technique produce a representative sample? Why?	Advantages and disadvantages of the technique. When would it be best to use this method? Why?
Purposive	The researcher has a clear idea of the sample they want; they will pick participants that meet their criteria.			
Quota	The researcher has a clear number of people they need to include in their sample based on certain characteristics.			

Further reading

Aaker, D. (2010). *Building Strong Brands*. London: Simon and Schuster.

I'Anson, R.A. and Smith, K.A. (2004). Undergraduate Research Projects and Dissertations: Issues of Topic Selection, Access, and Data Collections amongst Tourism Management Students. *Journal of Hospitality, Leisure, Sport and Tourism Education*. 3 (1): 19–32.

References

Aaker, D.A. (1996). Measuring Brand Equity across Products and Markets. *California Management Review*. 38 (Spring): 102–20.

Berg, B. (2001). *Qualitative Research Methods for the Social Sciences*. 4th edition. Boston: Allyn and Bacon.

Brotherton, B.M. (2015). *Researching Hospitality and Tourism*. 2nd edition. New York: Sage.

Brunt, P.R. (1990). Tourism trip decision making at the sub-regional level: with special reference to Southern England. Unpublished PhD thesis, University of Bournemouth.

Brunt, P. (1997). *Market Research in Travel and Tourism*. Oxford: Butterworth-Heinemann.

Buchanan, D., Boddy, D. and McCalman, J. (1998). Getting In, Getting Out, and Getting Back. In A. Bryman (ed.). *Doing Research in Organisations*. London: Routledge, pp. 53–67.

Busby, G. (2003). 'A True Cornish Treasure': Gunwalloe and the Cornish Church as Visitor Attraction. In P. Payton (ed.). *Cornish Studies Eleven*. Exeter: University of Exeter Press, pp. 168–91.

Busby, G. and Haines, C. (2013). Doc Martin and Film Tourism: The Creation of Destination Image. *Tourism Preliminary Communication*. 61 (2): 105–20.

Creswell, J.W. (2014). *Research Design: Qualitative, quantitative, and mixed methods approaches*. 4th edition. London: Sage.

Das, N.G. (2009). *Statistical Methods*. 2nd edition. New Delhi: Tata McGraw-Hill.

Frankfort-Nachmias, C. and Nachmias, D. (1996). *Research Methods in the Social Sciences*. 5th edition. London: Edward Arnold.

Holsti, O.R. (1969). *Content Analysis for the Social Sciences and Humanities*. Reading, MA: Addison-Wesley.

Keller, K. (1993). Conceptualizing, Measuring, and Managing Customer-based Brand Equity. *Marketing*. 57: 1–22.

Moser, C.A. (1958). *Survey Methods in Social Investigation*. London: Heinemann.

Moser, C.A. and Kalton, G. (1993). *Survey Methods in Social Investigation*. 2nd edition. London: Edward Arnold.

Neuendorf, K.A. (2002). *The Content Analysis Guidebook*. Thousand Oaks, CA: Sage.

Plymouth City Council. (2016/17). *Annual Report 2016/2017*. Available at: www.plymouth.gov.uk/aboutcouncil/annualreport (accessed 13 March 2017).

Saunders, P., Lewis, P. and Thornhill, A. (2000). *Research Methods for Business Students*. 2nd edition. London: Pitman Publishing.

Tourism and Recreation Research Unit. (1983). *Recreation Site Survey Manual: Methods and techniques for conducting visitor surveys*. London: E.D. & F.N. Spon.

Veal, A.J. (1997). *Research Methods for Leisure and Tourism: A practical guide*. 2nd edition. Harlow: Pearson Education.

Visit Cornwall. (2010). *Cornwall Visitor Survey 2010 Report*. Available at: www.visitcornwall.com/sites/default/files/generic_files/Cornwall%20Visitor%20Survey%202010%20-%20Report1.pdf (accessed 9 April 2012).

Yoo, B. and Donthu, N. (2001). Developing and Validating a Multidimensional Consumer-based Brand Equity Scale. *Journal of Business Research*. 31 (1): 656–61.

Young, P. (1966). *Scientific Social Surveys and Research*. London: Prentice Hall.

Zikmund, W.G. (2013). *Business Research Methods*. 2nd edition. Mason, OH: South Western Cengage Learning.

5

QUANTITATIVE DATA COLLECTION METHODS

LEARNING OBJECTIVES

From reading this chapter, you should be able to:

- provide a summary of quantitative methods, their advantages and disadvantages and when they should be used
- explore initial thoughts on questionnaire design and links to the literature review
- design workable questionnaires
- understand the different types of questions
- understand potential errors in the design of questions
- explore different types of measurement scales
- understand ethical issues with quantitative methods.

5.1 Introduction

During the length of a project, fieldwork is carried out at various times. The nature of the fieldwork you use depends on the type of project and your chosen methods of data collection. If a survey is to be carried out at a tourist attraction, then it will be necessary to first gain an overview of the site, decide on suitable interviewing points and talk to staff to gain an understanding of the patterns of site use. There may also be fieldwork involved in observations of visitors either as part of the data collection process or to assist in developing a sampling frame.

When it comes to the actual data collection itself, there is a variety of aspects which need to be planned. This chapter considers the quantitative approach to research in some depth and considers how the techniques can be designed, and administered including the use of online surveys. In the next chapter, we will consider the qualitative approach to research in some depth.

5.2 Understanding the value of quantitative methods

There is a wide variety of different types of questionnaire used in hospitality, tourism and events for both academic research and industry application. Structured questionnaires are those which ask precise, concrete questions prepared in advance to facilitate quantitative analysis. Unstructured questionnaires, sometimes referred to as interview guides, also aim at precision and contain topic areas where respondents are less restricted in their answers. This latter type is common within in-depth interviews and focus groups.

5.3 Research design and the literature review

The literature review provides the framework for the design of the research method. It is very useful to try to link the review to the questions that are to be asked in your survey or interview. You can see one example of this below where the student wanted to carry out research with small entrepreneurial hotel and restaurant companies in Germany to see whether they thought that the Slow Food movement and label could offer them any competitive advantage. The student framed the questions around the literature and produced a chart to summarise the issue that he was interested in finding out about, and the relevant authors. This allowed him to return to the literature review later on during the analysis stage and to test whether his research matched the views of the authors in the literature review or not. This can be referred to as 'threading the literature' through the whole research process.

Illustration 5.1   Linking the literature to the questions

Table 5.1   Linking the literature to the questions – Slow Food

1.	Do you know about Slow Food?	Yes – proceed	
2.	How long have you been involved with the Slow Food movement?	To analyse the experience and expertise of the respondent	
3.	How are you involved with Slow Food?	To be able to understand the personal interest of the respondent in relation to Slow Food	Slowfood.com (2010)
4.	To what extent do your personal values and beliefs match those of Slow Food?	To monitor how important personal engagement is in relation to the credibility of the Slow Food movement	Enz (2009) suggests that engagement and dedication are necessary to successfully implement ideas and market effectively
5.	Have you seen any marketing campaigns of hospitality organisations featuring Slow Food? And can you provide examples?	To evaluate how often Slow Food is used in the marketing campaigns of hospitality organisations	Heding et al. (2009) suggest that a brand image can help to position a company in the market
6.	Is the Slow Food market financially attractive from your point of view?	To evaluate the overall attractiveness of Slow Food consumers as a market	Slowfood.com (2010) suggest that the Slow Food brand can add value
7.	Is Slow Food in your eyes a quality symbol representing sustainability?	To evaluate the perception of Slow Food and the original intentions	Font and Buckley (2008) suggest that sustainability can provide competitive advantage
8.	What is the current development in the market in terms of Slow Food?	To evaluate how Slow Food marketing is achieved	Slowfood.com (2010) suggest that the movement is still in its infancy
9.	What strategic opportunities does Slow Food provide and how are they used in your point of view?	To evaluate the understanding of the full potential of what Slow Food offers	Enz (2009) outlines different opportunities that can shape competitive strategy
10.	Does Slow Food exclude certain market segments through its philosophy, values and beliefs?	To determine whether Slow Food can be used as a differentiation strategy for bigger market segments or only for niche markets, while evaluating the overall attractiveness of the Slow Food attributes	Porter (2004) suggests that differentiation can exist in a niche market as well as in the global market, depending on the attractiveness of the attribute

(Continued)

(Continued)

11.	Does Slow Food mean more expensive prices?	To evaluate how Slow Food is perceived in relation to value for money and willingness to pay price premiums	Parnell (2006) suggests that a differentiation strategy can lead to higher value and prices
12.	Does Slow Food provide superior resources and possibilities for superior competitive strategies?	To evaluate the understanding and usage of Slow Food to gain a competitive advantage	Enz (2009) suggests that superior resources and superior strategies (Porter, 2004) can provide a competitive edge
13.	What attributes do you relate to the Slow Food label and what attributes do you want to be related to the label?	To evaluate the perception and potential of the Slow Food brand	Heding et al. (2009) suggest that a brand image can provide competitive edge
14.	Is Slow Food still an innovation and trend? If yes, what are the strategic risks related to the increasing awareness of Slow Food?	To identify if Slow Food is seen as a trend or a growing market and to evaluate whether the industry and the Slow Food movement are aware of the 'negative' aspects that may arise due to the globalisation of Slow Food	Porter (2004) suggests that niche strategies target small market segments
15.	Does the Slow Food network offer possibilities to exchange knowledge and increase product awareness within the Slow Food community?	To identify whether an information flow within Slow Food exists and to understand whether individual Slow Food organisations see each other as a network or as competitors	Enz (2009) suggests that superior linkages offer the possibility to gain competitive edge
16.	What defines high quality in relation to the Slow Food movement?	To evaluate the values related to a product and define what quality means in the eyes of the Slow Food market	Peter and Olson (1993) state that functionality, value satisfaction and physical condition define quality
17.	Does Slow Food have the ability to function as a quality label?	To find out how the Slow Food symbol is seen and to evaluate how easy it is to use the symbol to enter the market	Enz (2009) suggests that high entry barriers can help to sustain competitive advantage
18.	Are you aware of other brands or labels associated with similar values? If yes, please list and describe your perception of those	To evaluate the uniqueness of Slow Food in comparison to other movements with similar perceived values	Porter (2004) says that uniqueness can provide competitive advantage

Note: The example citations in the final column are not included in the References, as these are for illustration purposes only

Source: 'The potential of using Slow Food for gaining strategic marketing advantage in small hospitality organizations' by Julius Anders, supervised by Susan Horner, César Ritz Colleges, Switzerland.

When Julian produced his first version of the chart (Illustration 5.1), I encouraged him to widen his literature review further so that other authors could be incorporated in each box, and so that he could consider research that had been carried out in relation to sustainability in hospitality as well as by general management commentators. This allowed him to get a deeper and fuller picture. In this way, the linking of the literature to the methodology was developed and refined until he was happy with the final version of the questions. He could also check whether he had the correct authors in the literature review.

Consider another example of a chart that was used to develop the questions for an online survey that was carried out by Luke to try to discover the perceptions of local food in the Devon area (Illustration 5.2). A quantitative approach was used to both collect and analyse data from 175 respondents who were asked 16 questions; 100 responses were collected through random sampling across different locations in South Devon and 75 responses were obtained online through the Qualtrics package (2013). We consider the Qualtrics package later in the chapter. A series of filter questions were included within the survey to ensure analysis was only completed on respondents fitting each hypothesis, and all questions were closed.

Illustration 5.2   Linking the literature to the questions in the survey

Table 5.2   Linking the literature to the questions in the survey

Questions (in order of asking)	Reason	Theoretical base
Are you aware of the term 'local food produce'?	To measure general and regional awareness of LFP	LFC (2006)
When visiting a food establishment, would you expect local food produce to be sourced within a set distance from the place you are eating?	To determine a food mileage acceptance value within South Devon	Weatherell et al. (2003)
If yes, would you expect this food to be sourced within: 5, 15, 30, 45, 60, 75, 76+ (miles)?	To determine a food mileage acceptance value within South Devon	Weatherell et al. (2003); DEFRA (2005)
If you have stayed in a boutique hotel, was there local food produce on the menu?	To determine BH awareness of the demand of LFP	Balekjan and Sarheim (2011)

(Continued)

(Continued)

Questions (in order of asking)	Reason	Theoretical base
Would you expect local food produce to be available at a boutique hotel?	To determine demand for LFP at BH	Sloan (2007)
Would you be prepared to pay more for locally sourced produce?	To test existing research stating that BH users are more likely to purchase LFP due to higher disposable incomes	Pretty et al. (2005)

Note: The example citations in the final column are not included in the References, as these are for illustration purposes only

Source: 'Consumer attitudes to local food produce in boutique hotels' by Luke Slater, supervised by Christina Kelly, Plymouth University.

5.4 Designing workable questionnaires

5.4.1 Question types: closed and open questions

Broadly speaking, all questions are either **closed** (structured) or **open** (free-response) that you can use.

Closed questions

A closed question is one in which the respondent is offered a choice of replies. He/she may be asked to tick a box in a self-completion questionnaire, or the answers may be read out to him/her or shown on a prompt card. Questions of this kind may offer simple alternatives such as yes or no, a simple list or something more complex. For example:

1. Have you visited this site before?   Yes   No
2. How did you travel to this site?

   Car   Service bus   Coach

   Walk   Bicycle   Other

3. If it is proven that bracken at recreation sites affects human health, with which of these statements would you agree most?

A programme of bracken removal/control should be implemented.

People should be made aware of the health risks, but the bracken should not be removed.

I do not think there is anything to worry about.

Other types of questions that are essentially closed include ranking and rating scales. Below are some examples:

1. Look at the following card and rank the reasons why you decided to visit this attraction:

   (Interviewer to assist respondent with ranking as necessary)

   Near to accommodation/home

   Cheaper than other local attractions

   More choice of rides

   Easy parking

   Less walking

2. Look at this card and use the scale provided to answer the following question (a score of 5 indicates you believe it to be of great importance and a score of 1 that you believe it to have no importance): When you decided to stay at this resort, how important was the cost?

   5   Great importance

   4

   3

   2

   1   No importance

3. Indicate which of the following applies to you:

   When deciding on a holiday, the type of accommodation is the most important consideration:

   Strongly agree

   Agree

   Uncertain

   Disagree

   Strongly disagree

4.   Indicate which of the following applies to you:

How satisfied are you with the helpfulness of staff at this hotel?

Very satisfied

Satisfied

Dissatisfied

Very dissatisfied

Reference to the literature will show that there is much debate on the length of the various scoring systems and whether to have an odd or even number of categories. Note here that I have not included a 'don't know' category. In the next section, this is discussed more fully.

Thus, closed questions can be attitudinal as well as factual. In the last example, if left to their own thoughts, some respondents may have come up with their own proposals. Here, the list of alternatives has been derived after careful piloting to ensure that the categories do cover the majority of opinion.

Advantages of closed questions:

1.   Easier and quicker to answer.
2.   No writing.
3.   Quantification and coding easier.
4.   More questions possible in terms of time/money available.

Disadvantages of closed questions:

1.   Loss of spontaneity and expressiveness (will never know what the respondent would have said if left to their own devices).
2.   Bias, in forcing a particular set of answers that might not have occurred to the respondent.
3.   Closed questions are often simpler and less subtle as no probing is possible.
4.   Loss of rapport with interviewer – some respondents may become irritated because they feel that their real opinions are not represented in the set of alternatives.
5.   It is easier for the respondent to cheat.

Open questions

Open questions are not usually followed by any kind of choice. Answers are recorded in full. In the case of a self-completion questionnaire, the amount of space made available will help to determine the length and fullness of the responses obtained. There are several types which are best demonstrated using examples:

1. Open

   Why did you decide to go on a day trip today? (Record answer.)

2. Open – with clarification:

   In the following questions, I am going to focus on day trips. This is defined as a journey away from home lasting longer than three hours but not including an overnight stay. Why did you decide to go on a day trip today?

3. Open – with probing:

   Why did you decide to go on a day trip today? (This is followed by probing either from a checklist or left up to the interviewer.)

Advantages of open questions:

1. Freedom on the part of the respondent in giving an answer.
2. Spontaneous.

Disadvantages of open questions:

1. Difficult to code.
2. Hard to analyse quantitatively.
3. Interviewer bias.

Overall, there are obviously pros and cons with both question types. In order to offset the disadvantages, it may be useful to ask the same question topic both ways. With open questions, whilst the answer may be valuable, the interpretation and comparison between respondents may be difficult. With closed questions, you cannot be sure that an impromptu sketch contains all the factors that are important.

5.4.2 Some worked examples illustrating how to decide which type of question system to use

For each of the following scenarios, consider whether it is appropriate to use an open or closed type of question system.

1. You want to find out how many people read the *Daily Mirror* yesterday.

Answer: Closed question system. This is a straightforward head count, thus the answer is yes or no. There may be potential problems with the word 'read' being ambiguous.

2. In your survey, you aim to ask each head of household what his/her job is.

Answer: If your main 'aim' is to find out precisely what their job is, then an open question system will be required. It is not possible to list all jobs so the question will be open. However, sometimes the interviewer (if present) may need to probe or seek clarification of the response. An answer such as 'engineer' may require the interviewer to ask for more detail. In other surveys where this is not the main 'aim', often job categories are listed and respondents decide for themselves which is most suited to their situation. In a postal survey, closed questions would have to be used.

3. You want to find out how many people agree with different views about their holiday to the Seychelles, but you do not know what these views are.

Answer: To do this properly, two surveys are required. To begin with, you need to find out what views people have about the Seychelles. Because you do not know what views people have, open questions where interviewers probe for as much information as possible is probably the best method. Then, after analysing the results of this survey, closed questions can be constructed. These can then be used to count the number of people who endorse or reject those views about the Seychelles.

4. A product of your company is not selling well to your target market. You only have a few vague suspicions as to why this is so and you want to explore in an empirical way the nature of the problem.

Answer: Here your purpose is exploratory. You cannot design closed questions if you only have vague suspicions as to why the product is not selling well. Therefore, open questions are required to explore the nature of the problem.

5. You have a list of, say, 30 different characteristics of management in a travel firm. You would like to find out, for each of these characteristics, how many employed persons say it is true of their firm. However, you are worried about offering more than 10 characteristics on a show card because you feel your respondents would not properly consider more than that on a single card.

Answer: In this case, you are trying to find out what opinions people have of the 30 characteristics of management you are studying, rather than asking them to describe the characteristics of their firm for themselves. Thus, the answer is that a closed question system is used to count the number of people who say that a given characteristic is true or untrue. Fears about presenting a long list relate to the wording and layout of the questionnaire. These aspects are investigated in the next section.

5.4.3 Wording questions and laying out a questionnaire

The content of your questionnaire is obviously governed by the nature of the survey, but there are many potential problems in the communication of the questions. These types of problem apply to all surveys.

Illustration 5.3   An example of a questionnaire used for a street survey

'How is consumer behaviour towards discount promotions affecting restaurant organisations?' by Lauren Read, BSc (Hons) International Hospitality Management, supervised by Christina Kelly, Plymouth University.

Method

The method chosen for data collection for this research was questionnaires, as seen in appendix A. Questionnaires were chosen as this was in likeness to the method used in the majority of the secondary data researched as part of the literature review and can be seen in research conducted by Lee and Lee (2012), Ong (2015) and Santini et al. (2015). The questionnaire was designed with the questions linking in with the literature review, theory and concepts. It is said that to measure the concepts of the research, 'it is necessary to have an indicator or indicators that will stand for the concept' (Bryman and Bell, 2015: 164). This can be done through questions as part of a self-completion questionnaire and the questions could be related to the respondent's description of an attitude or their behaviour (Bryman and Bell, 2015).

The questionnaire's introduction informed respondents that their data would be confidential, this being in line with ethical research. The questionnaire was devised with 17 questions with a mixture of closed and open types and in line with previous secondary research conducted. The questions which related to dining out and the use of discount promotions were asked as a generalisation around dining out and not about a particular restaurant. It is suggested that 'if an existing restaurant is used to measure perceived value, it is difficult to determine whether the measurement accurately reflects perceived value' (Lee and Lee, 2012: 449). Similarly to the research conducted by Ong (2015), participants were asked if they had purchased a discount promotion and, if so, which product or service category they had purchased in. Participants were also asked which product or service category they would engage in. Other questions also related to previous research conducted, in that the questionnaire 'included questions related to respondents' demographic information and dining behaviour'.

The questionnaire was designed and piloted four times to a general and varied selection of respondents. Each gave feedback which included errors with the language used, the sequence of questions and the options available for answers. All feedback

(Continued)

(Continued)

was processed and amendments were made in accordance with recommendations. The fifth pilot took place in the style of a street survey focusing on method of delivery. Here, feedback was similar to the previous pilot and further adjustments to the sequence of questions and available answers were made. During this final pilot, every nth person was asked, so as to deter from bias. This was seen to be ineffective as some participants were asked in couples and not every nth person would want to participate. This meant that the next available person would then be asked, this being due to the need for the sample size to be met within a certain time constraint.

Differently to the methods used in secondary research, this research did not use web-based surveys as there was no available access to a large enough source of data which was needed to meet the sample. This led to street surveys being the chosen method for collecting the data. All respondents that were stopped were asked for their consent to participate in answering the questionnaire so that the research conducted was ethical. Street surveying was chosen because of its advantages, which include being able to reach out to a large sample and being able to generate a high response rate due to face-to-face contact with respondents and being able to engage a small team to help with data collection. The online questionnaire follows.

Image 5.1   Succeed with Plymouth University

Use of discount promotions in the hospitality industry

As a final-year student studying at Plymouth University, I am conducting research surrounding the use of discount promotions in the hospitality industry. This questionnaire is a vital part of the process which will help me to gain the information I need to complete my research.

Your responses are anonymous and the confidentiality of respondents will be respected; any of the raw data collected will be shared only with the supervisory team at Plymouth University, if necessary.

If you could please take the time to complete this questionnaire, it would be greatly appreciated, and if you have any questions about the questionnaire do not hesitate to ask.

1   Do you live in Plymouth?

(Please select one answer)

○ Yes   ○ No

2   Have you eaten out in the past six months?

(Please select one answer)

○ Yes   ○ No

If you answered 'No' to the previous two questions, please do not continue with the questionnaire. Thank you very much for your time.

3   Do you eat out in casual dining restaurants?

(For example, Nandos, Café Rouge and Giraffe are all casual dining restaurants.)

(Please select one answer)

○ Yes   ○ No

4   Do you use discount promotions when eating out?

(Discount promotions offer a lower or discounted price on a product or service; this is in comparison with the original price of the product or service that is being offered. Some examples of discount promotions include: voucher codes, e-mail and newsletter subscription offers, seasonal discount offers and loyalty card rewards.)

(Please select one answer)

○ Yes   ○ No

5   If yes, how often do you use discount promotions when eating out?

(Please select one answer)

(Continued)

(Continued)

- ○ Every day
- ○ Once a week
- ○ Twice a week
- ○ Once every two weeks
- ○ Once a month
- ○ Once every three months

6   Which type of discount promotion would you use?

(Please select all that apply)

- ○ Groupon
- ○ Wowcher
- ○ Voucher code mobile phone applications
- ○ Voucher codes obtained directly through company website
- ○ Voucher codes obtained via e-mail
- ○ Voucher codes obtained from social media page
- ○ Loyalty card rewards

7   Please read the following statements and circle the probability, on the 4-point scale, which you are most in agreement with:

Highly unlikely	Unlikely	Likely	Highly likely
1	2	3	4

a)   I will select a restaurant to eat in because it offers a discount promotion.
1 2 3 4

b)   I will visit a restaurant more regularly than others, if they offer me a discount. 1 2 3 4

c)   If a restaurant does not provide me with future discounts, I will not return. 1 2 3 4

d)   Discount offers make me feel like a valued customer and I will return to a restaurant because of this. 1 2 3 4

e) I am loyal to a particular brand, however if a different brand offers a better discount promotion than my regular restaurant, I will choose to eat in the restaurant offering what I perceive to be the better discount. **1 2 3 4**

f) If the brand I am loyal to retracts a discount promotion, I will not use this brand again. **1 2 3 4**

8 Do you feel that discount promotions give you added value?

(Please tick one answer)

○ Yes   ○ No

9 Please highlight the extent to which you agree with the following statements by circling the appropriate number on the 5-point scale:

Strongly disagree	Disagree	Neither agree nor disagree	Agree	Strongly agree
1	2	3	4	5

a) I am value-conscious and compare prices to make sure I am getting the best deal. **1 2 3 4 5**

b) I use discount promotions regardless of the saving. **1 2 3 4 5**

c) I know I will be getting the same quality meal and service despite using a discount promotion. **1 2 3 4 5**

d) There is a limited option for discount promotion users. **1 2 3 4 5**

e) I prefer getting a discount off my bill as opposed to reward points and bonuses. **1 2 3 4 5**

f) If I am satisfied with my experience when using a discount promotion, I feel the discount was of value and that this would attract me to future discount promotions. **1 2 3 4 5**

10 Do you expect to be satisfied with the overall dining experience when using discount promotions?

(Please select one answer)

○ Yes   ○ No

(Continued)

(Continued)

If no, please select a reason why from the options below:

(Please select one answer)

- ○ Discount promotions are used because the company wants to sell excess inventory.
- ○ The quality of the food will be below the normal set of standards.
- ○ I do not trust large discounts.
- ○ The restaurant is not successful enough to draw customers in without using discount promotions; therefore the business is not one that I want to go to.

11   Do you write reviews about your dining experiences?

    ○ Yes   ○ No

If yes, where do you write your reviews?

(Please specify)

....

12   Do you look at reviews for restaurants via hospitality services' websites, social media or mobile phone apps?

(Please select all that apply)

- ○ Hospitality services websites
- ○ Social media
- ○ Mobile phone apps
- ○ I do not look at reviews for restaurants

13   Is it important to you that a website is easy to navigate, accessible and useful?

(Please select one answer)

    ○ Yes   ○ No

If yes, if a website was not easy to navigate, accessible and useful, would this deter you from returning to that website?

(Please select one answer)

    ○ Yes   ○ No

14 Do you have a positive or negative opinion on your data being obtained by companies who offer discount promotions in return?

(Please select one answer)

○ Positive

○ Negative

15 Would you be more willing to provide companies with your personal data if they could provide you with a more customised dining experience?

(Please select one answer)

○ Yes   ○ No

16 Are you?

(Please select one answer)

○ Male   ○ Female   ○ Other

17 What is your age?

(Please specify)

....

18 What is your yearly income?

(Please select one answer)

○ Below 10,000

○ 10,001–20,000

○ 20,001–30,000

○ 30,000 +

○ I would rather not say

Thank you for taking the time to complete this questionnaire.

(Continued)

(Continued)

References

Bryman, A. and Bell, E. (2015). *Business Research Methods*. 4th edition. Oxford: Oxford University Press.

Lee, I. and Lee, K. (2012). Social Shopping Promotions from a Social Merchant's Perspective. *Business Horizons*. 55 (5): 441–51.

Ong, B. (2015). Attitudes, Perceptions, and Responses of Purchasers versus Subscribers-only for Daily Deals on Hospitality Products. *Journal of Hospitality Marketing & Management*. 24 (2): 180–201.

Santini, F., Sampaio, C., Perin, M., Espartel, L. and Ladeira, W. (2015). Moderating Effects of Sales Promotion Types. *Brazilian Administration Review*. 12 (3): 169–89.

5.4.4 Language and translation

The language used in the wording of questions is of critical importance. You should give careful thought to how the question will be interpreted by the respondent. There are two salient points to remember when you begin to write your questions:

1. Be clear and concise. Keep questions short, as long sentences which require respondents to concentrate will not be answered accurately.
2. Avoid using jargon. The vocabulary should be simple everyday language (unless aimed at a particular technical audience).

Familiar words

As a rule, you should always use familiar, simple words. However, occasionally some words are too vague – for example, 'how often', 'how much' and 'how far' may result in answers that are not comparable. Asking 'How much do you drink?' in an open sense is likely to result in a set of replies that either overstate or understate a true reply! In addition, words such as 'good', 'bad' and 'regularly', which are not enumerated precisely, do not lend themselves to quantitative analysis.

Technical terms

Technical words should only be used if the survey is aimed at a specific group of respondents to whom the language is common. Words and phrases such as 'sympathetic planning', 'green tourism', 'sustainable tourism', 'national tourism organisation' and 'tour operators' are likely to mean different things to different people. Some may have a genuine and accurate grasp of what is meant by the term, whilst others may respond favourably to stereotyped concepts. The solution here is to ask questions that can be easily understood by all respondents. Technical terms which have to be used may need to be defined or respondents asked to explain what they understand by them.

Ambiguous questions

Whilst previous sections have suggested that simple, everyday language should be used in the wording of questions, sometimes this can lead to ambiguity. Consider posing the question to different groups of students, 'What kind of course are you on?' This could be answered in terms of degree/HND, sandwich, good, bad, well organised, interesting, difficult, etc. The likelihood is that a range of replies that had no relationship to each other would be produced. If answers cannot be compared, then it becomes impossible to express the data in quantifiable terms. This aspect reinforces the need for all surveys to have a pilot stage to test the usefulness of your questions and thus avoid ambiguity during the main data collection.

Leading questions

A leading question is one in which the respondent is guided to give a particular answer by the nature of the question. This is clearly unacceptable and leads to the validity of the whole survey being brought into question. For example, 'Most people like to holiday abroad nowadays; would you?' This is a leading question because it is more difficult to answer no than yes. To answer no implies that you are different to 'most' people. These types of questions essentially put words into the mouth of the respondent. It should not be easier to reply 'yes' than to say 'no' or vice versa.

The don't know problem

This issue is a difficult one, as there will always be some answers which will fall between yes and no, or between agree and disagree. Sometimes questionnaires include a category of 'don't know' or 'no opinion'. However, you should bear in mind that respondents may reply 'don't know' for several reasons. These have been developed from the work of Gardner (1978):

1. Interview failure

Perhaps the question was not heard or understood. The interviewer may not have waited long enough for a reply. Maybe the respondent hesitated – 'Well, I don't know' (down goes the answer). 'Yes, I suppose I would' – but it is too late; the interviewer is already asking the next question.

2. Ignorance

This can occur in two ways. Either the information was not available or the information was available but it was not understood. Preliminary questions will help to sort out those who are not aware of it or who have not had time to consider it. Again, the pilot survey would help to sort things out here.

3. Indecision

Having considered the matter, the respondent can come to no definite view either way. This is a genuine response and you should allow for this. However, it could be argued that a response of 'no opinion' is better than a 'don't know'.

4. Indifference

This response relates to respondents who have heard about the issue but do not feel that they need to bother themselves with it. A series of preliminary questions could cover for this, for instance:

(i)   Have you heard about our latest Frequent Traveller Benefits Scheme?
(ii)   Have you had time to consider it?
(iii) Do you think it matters whether it goes ahead or not?
(iv)   Do you think the scheme should go ahead?

After a negative response to (i) or (ii), there is no need to proceed with the rest.

Sequence of questions

The sequence of questions is important and is one of the advantages that interviews have over self-completion questionnaires. In interviews, the interviewer has control over the sequence of questions, whereas with self-completion there is very little control over this aspect. The respondent can look ahead and see what is coming. For both methods, there are some general guidelines:

> *Introduction*: whether written or spoken, this must create interest and motivate the respondent to cooperate. Confidentiality should again be assured. Some of the introduction may come in the form of a covering letter.

> *First questions*: these should be interesting, simple and related to the topic you have outlined in your introduction. That way the respondent is assured that he is neither going to be bored nor floored.

Sequence: as far as possible, the sequence of questions should follow a natural order. To avoid sudden jumps from one topic to another, insert suitable bridging passages.

'Crux' questions: these should come in the body of the interview, about or just after midway, when rapport is strongest and before boredom or impatience sets in.

Personal questions: the general convention is to put these at the end of the questionnaire, perhaps with a reminder of confidentiality and an explanation that they are for comparative purposes.

General to specific: it should not be possible for answers to be influenced by previous questions. If a respondent is forced to take a stand on one issue, it is much harder for him to modify his position later when other questions suggest different possibilities or require different sorts of comparisons. Once a train of thought has been narrowed to a particular aspect, it becomes difficult to put this in proper perspective when broader issues are involved.

Illustration 5.4   Emotional Contagion Scale Questionnaire

Aim

An assessment of emotional contagion within gender groups and preferred leadership style within service sector, business sector and manual labour occupations.

Objectives

- To identify which gender groups are most susceptible to emotional contagion
- To identify which occupational group experiences the highest levels of emotional contagion
- To understand the attributes employees associate with an effective leader
- To recognise the preferred leadership style within occupational groups.

Questionnaire

Hello Sir/Madam, my name is Chloe and I am collecting data for my dissertation study; this survey is going to ask you questions in regards to your emotions. Please be honest in your responses and be assured that all the information you provide will be kept anonymous and *completely confidential*. If you wish to continue, please start the questionnaire below:

(Continued)

(Continued)

Age..

Gender..

Ethnicity...

Occupation..

(If you are student with a job, please state you are a student and the job role you have.)

The following questions represent a scale that measures a variety of feelings and behaviours in various situations. There are no right or wrong answers, so try very hard to be completely honest in your answers. Read each question and indicate the answer that best applies to you using the following key: **4** – Always; **3** – Often; **2** – Rarely; **1** – Never.

1　If someone I'm talking with begins to cry, I get teary-eyed..............
2　Being with a happy person picks me up when I'm feeling down.........
3　When someone smiles warmly at me, I smile back and feel warm inside..........
4　I get filled with sorrow when people talk about the death of their loved ones..........
5　I clench my jaws and my shoulders get tight when I see the angry faces on the news.........
6　When I look into the eyes of the one I love, my mind is filled with thoughts of romance........
7　It irritates me to be around angry people.........
8　Watching the fearful faces of victims on the news makes me try to imagine how they might be feeling...............
9　I melt when the one I love holds me close...........
10　I tense when overhearing an angry quarrel..........
11　Being around happy people fills my mind with happy thoughts......
12　I sense my body responding when the one I love touches me.......
13　I notice myself getting tense when I'm around people who are stressed out........
14　I cry at sad movies...........
15　Listening to the shrill screams of a terrified child in a dentist's waiting room makes me feel nervous

Finally, please could you write, in the box below, any characteristics you would identify with an effective leader:

Thank you for your time.

Source: 'The transformational leadership style: an assessment of the application of emotional contagion and its impacts on employee motivation and performance' by Chloe Locke, BSc Events Management, supervised by Richard Parkman, Plymouth University.

You can see here that Chloe placed the personal questions about the respondents at the beginning of the questionnaire and it worked well for her, but it is interesting to note that evidence suggests that these are best placed at the end of the questionnaire.

Checklists and prompt cards

Prompt cards can be used to suggest a wide range of possible answers. They indicate the appropriate frame of reference and help the respondent to think of other possibilities. This may sound like coercion, and indeed an interviewer may unknowingly put stress or a pleasant intonation on some items if she has to read out the list. However, prompt cards can be handed to the respondent with a question such as:

Please look at this list. Which of the activities mentioned have you undertaken today?

Nature trail

Guided walk

Self-guided walk

Bird hide

Thus, prompt cards are meant as reminders and not arm-twisters.

When compiling a checklist, only use comparable items. Clear instructions should say if only one item or all relevant items can be recorded. Furthermore, you must be consistent as to whether the interviewer or the respondent reads the list.

Some worked examples in the choice of answer system

For each example, state everything you think is wrong with the choice of answer system offered.

1. Which of these apply to you?

	Married	1
PASS CARD TO RESPONDENT SHOWING:	Single	2
MARRIED, SINGLE, WIDOWED, DIVORCED,	Widowed	3
SEPARATED	Divorced	4
	Separated	4

CODE REPLIES

Criticisms include the following: Does married mean married 'now'? What about unmarried couple/partners? All could apply but the question is unclear in this respect – why distinguish between widowed, divorced and separated? Code numbers suggest the categories are somehow ranked, with the same code number for divorced and separated suggesting they are the same. Clearly, the need for a question such as this will depend on the survey topic.

2. Generally speaking, how much trust do you have in the claims made about holiday products in television advertising?   SHOW CARD AND CODE REPLIES

1	2	3	4	5	6	7	8	9	10

NONE AT ALL   A GREAT DEAL

NUMBER..................

Criticisms include the following: There is no explanation of how to use the answer system. It is unclear whether 1, 2 and 3 refer to 'none at all'. What if the respondent is unsure or undecided? It could be argued that the scale is too wide.

3. What is your opinion of the holiday brochure I left you to read?

READ OUT THE SIX CHOICES TO THE RESPONDENT; REVERSE THE ORDER OF CHOICES FOR EVERY OTHER RESPONDENT

Extremely good	1
Very good	2
Fairly good	3

Not so good	4
Pretty poor	5
Awful	6
No opinion	7

Criticisms include the following: The respondent may not be able to hold all seven options in mind whilst making a choice. The scale is biased. The interviewer may be tempted to use the scale as a running prompt (i.e. reading out the scale slowly and stopping after the respondent indicates a suitable choice). As it may not be possible to rely on an interviewer to alternate (if this is deemed important – which in itself is questionable), different questionnaires should be provided.

4. Last week, did you work………?

CALL OUT THE FOLLOWING, CODING AS YOU GO:

For an employer for wages, salary, payment in kind, etc.	1
In your own business with employees	2
In your own business with no employees	3
Without pay in a family business	4

Criticisms include the following: The choices offered may not fit all categories. What does 'etc.' mean? The respondent may not have worked last week but be in employment.

5.5 Data collection methods

5.5.1 Postal and other self-completion surveys

In Chapter 2, the various advantages of self-completion surveys were discussed. Assuming that a postal survey has been decided on, consideration needs to be given to how the survey will be conducted to achieve the best possible response rate. When sending out questionnaires by post, attention should be paid to:

1. The covering letter

Often, a letter accompanies the questionnaire and aims to get the recipient to take part in the survey. If possible, the more 'personal' this can be the better. An individual's name rather than 'Dear Sir/Madam' (or, even worse, 'The Occupier') is more likely to catch attention. The letter should introduce the purpose of the survey and stress the confidentiality of the respondents.

The covering letter should also explain who is sponsoring the research. In my experience, students explaining that their research is properly supervised and endorsed by their tutor can achieve high response rates. This is because well-written covering letters explaining, truthfully, that the project will help with the student's educational advancement can go far in appealing to the respondent's altruistic sentiments.

2.   The questionnaire

As mentioned previously, self-completion surveys may be seen to have the particular disadvantage that no interviewer is present to explain and prompt. Thus, the questionnaire layout and presentation require greater consideration than for surveys where an interviewer conducts the data collection. In this latter case, interviewers can be trained and can practise using the questionnaire; not so for respondents on their own. Research has been undertaken to test what types of format, fonts, colour and length are best. Clearly, the nature of the project and available budget may determine these factors. The main consideration is that the questionnaire must be clear, easy to understand and as professionally laid out and printed as the budget permits.

3.   Method of postage

One of the largest costs of postal surveys is the postage – for sending surveys to respondents and where a posted reply envelope is provided. Pre-paid (freepost) labels are a satisfactory method as only those returned are chargeable. However, there is some suggestion (Frankfort-Nachmias and Nachmias, 1996) that such business-reply envelopes achieve slightly lower response rates than those with a normal stamp attached.

4.   Reminders

After the first distribution of questionnaires, reminders are often required to boost the response rates. Obviously, extra cost is involved here and sending reminders requires the researcher to be able to identify which respondents have not replied. When contemplating this method of data collection, the time involved in following up late responders should be anticipated as it can lengthen the whole data collection period. Some researchers include a gift or entry into a free draw as an inducement to participate. However, care should be taken not to offend particular respondents who would be willing to take part anyway because of the value of the survey. Monetary or other inducements perhaps suggest that a low response rate is already anticipated.

Overall, the various stages involved in the data collection of postal surveys are as follows:

(i)	Questionnaire preparation	– presentation
		– layout
		– printing
(ii)	Covering letter	– presentation
		– layout
		– printing
(iii)	Postage preparation	– filling envelopes
		– addressing
(iv)	First reminder postage	– decision whether to include questionnaire and reply envelope or just letter
(v)	Subsequent reminders	– as necessary within time frame and budget

5.5.2 Online questionnaires using Qualtrics

The use of online questionnaires in tourism, hospitality and events is a growing area of interest. Businesses are increasingly using social networking sites to collect information about their consumers. Social networking sites such as Facebook are gaining in popularity for both individuals and organisations and it is interesting to debate how useful they are for data collection. The use of social networking sites to collect data is appealing because they are easy to access and you are able to target particular market segments such as the millennials who are very active in their use of systems. There are issues with online surveys because people may not trust them and it is easy to ignore them, so response rates may be low. You may want to consider conducting your survey or questionnaire both online and on paper so that you target a wider set of respondents.

Other organisations offer to design and conduct surveys on your behalf online, and these are becoming important in the research process. Companies such as Surveymonkey (www.surveymonkey.co.uk) and Qualtrics offer online and analytical tools to help you with the design and analysis of your questionnaire. At Plymouth University, we bought the Qualtrics package for our students in the business area and this is being increasingly used by them to conduct their research. We saw in Illustration 5.2, for example, that Luke employed an online survey using Qualtrics to research the consumer view of local food. A colleague at our university has become an expert in the use of Qualtrics and he provides his short guide to this in Illustration 5.5.

Illustration 5.5   Using the Qualtrics insight platform, by Rob Giles

Introduction

Data collection is a science combining elements of technology, psychology, statistics and data interpretation before conclusions can be suggested and tested for consistency.

Cloud-based survey builders have become an increasingly popular method for collecting quantitative data. There are many to choose from, however Qualtrics provides an illustration of how, with a user-friendly and highly flexibly interface, the focus for the research can be placed on the research objective rather than on technical restrictions.

Free questionnaire applications are likely to handicap your research and increase the time and effort required by the researcher. For serious researchers and professionals, it is not a question of how one might compromise from the ideal research solution but more a case of how an improved solution might be possible utilising some of the many advanced features that are available within the application.

The following is a brief explanation that highlights just some of the features regularly used by researchers to elicit the maximum response rate possible. Ensuring both the quality and appropriateness of the data collected will inevitably result in more rigorous hypothesis testing and generally improved outcome and recommendations.

Questionnaire design

A well-presented and engaging online survey is likely to increase the number of successful responses generated. With a 10% response rate thought to be a reasonable level of success within an already crowded market, well-thought-out questionnaire design cannot be underestimated.

Sub-branding

The Faculty of Business within Plymouth University obviously benefits from the quality and reassurance of the brand. A user intrinsically knows that a well-established university will have adopted a rigorous ethical approval process and is therefore more likely to take part in a survey conducted by a researcher from within the brand. Qualtrics allows sub-branding which is applied as a default logo image at the top of every survey generated. This can be added to or replaced by other branding options depending on the requirements of the researcher. Free applications, other than Qualtrics, often generate income through banner ads, however this will inevitably have a direct impact on credibility and therefore response rate.

Questionnaire design

The various question types are readily available within Qualtrics and a very thorough library of readymade resources is available to choose from. Questions can be easily copied and moved within a survey during development, and formatting options for editing text styles are also available. Adding pictures from your personal user library is easily achieved under the 'Look and Feel' menu and there are a number of additional options for customisation.

Any new questions created within Qualtrics are given an automatic question number, however I would recommend utilising the progress bar option rather than using question numbers for online surveys generally. Numbered questions can be confusing within an online survey, particularly when branching or survey flow control is being made use of.

Survey branching

The two most common types of branching tend to be 'Skip Logic' and 'Display Logic'. Skip Logic navigates the respondent to the next question based on their selection. This method would be utilised at the beginning of the survey when the respondent was asked if they were willing to participate, for instance. Display Logic, on the other hand, is placed on a question which is either displayed or not, depending on the responses already given. This can be more complex as the criteria assessed can be a combination of answers, i.e. the question might only be displayed if the user is: male *and* has an income of over £30,000 per year *and* drives a car *or* rides a motorcycle. In this example, a combination of data collected and an alternative are taken into account before the question is displayed.

Flexible question/answer options

The majority of the various question-style answers found in Qualtrics present the 'allow text entry option'. This is commonly used to provide the researcher with the option to utilise an 'other' selection within, for example, a list or a drag-and-drop menu. This is a very useful option to extend the possible selections in, for example, a list to include data not included by the researcher that could provide additional insight into the topic.

(Continued)

(Continued)

Another excellent feature found in Qualtrics is the piped text feature. A simple example of this might be if a user was asked to pick their favourite colour from a list or add their favourite colour through an additional 'allow text entry' option. That input can be 'piped' into a separate question, for instance 'Would you be more likely to buy a [piped text] "red" car'?

Survey flow

Larger questionnaires can be organised using the 'Block' feature to organise the questions. A standard type of use for this would be to organise questions related to a certain theme together, i.e. questions about holiday choices might be separated into those holidays taken in the respondent's home country and those taken abroad. Based on a respondent question selection, they might be automatically directed to either one or other of these blocks to answer the associated questions. Complex survey flow options can be set up in the survey flow menu within Qualtrics.

Distribution

The general guidance for survey distribution is split between anonymous and unspecific distribution and that specific to a particular respondent sample. The basic approaches to these two distribution options are quite different, as outlined below, however some aspects of the basic introduction do apply to both. The introductory message is often cited as one of the most important aspects of a survey based on indications that the majority of respondents make their decision on whether or not to respond at this stage. The university ethical approval process will advise the researcher about specific issues surrounding confidentiality, data security and storage, depending on the specifics of the research, however the generic key messages that need to be added to the introduction should include the following:

- who you are and who you represent (if applicable) and why you are administering the survey
- some reference to *privacy* – who will have access to the survey data; if the survey data will remain anonymous; and whether the respondents' privacy will be protected
- the offering of incentives, such as entry into a prize draw, which can increase response rates. In the case of anonymous surveys, however, incentives should be optional as they usually involve the respondent choosing to relinquish their

anonymity by providing some form of contact details. Incentive information should be clearly described and the user instructed about how and when they can opt to take part

- a guide to timing – generally, it is best practice to clearly but approximately state how long the survey will take to complete. Before you activate your survey, you will be able to see the estimated response time on the My Projects page. Timing yourself to complete your own survey will most likely lead to an under-estimated result due to an awareness of your own questions and the possible answers. Other issues could be: where branching has been used, respondents are likely to experience an unequal number of survey questions; and where open questions have been used, responses can vary significantly
- a request to confirm participation – ask the respondent to confirm that they are willing to participate. Make it clear that they must click the 'Continue', 'Accept' or 'Submit' button in order to confirm and participate in the online survey. This can be ensured by adding programming so that if a participant chooses not to complete your online survey, they can be automatically skipped to the end.

Anonymous link distribution

Anonymous link surveys, i.e. those that collect data without identifying personal information, can be distributed via email or social media options, such as Twitter or Facebook, and also by utilising the QR code option that can be added to leaflets or posters. There is an additional offline app available which would allow data to be collected by the researcher using a tablet or phone and uploaded later, however this is currently a purchased add-on facility. Where Wi-Fi is available, students can choose to allow multiple survey submissions from any device and open a new survey for each respondent to achieve the same result.

There are many online companies offering a purchase respondents' service in order to define the demographic. Qualtrics also offers Qualtrics Panels and Online Sample services to help you find your target demographic.

Panel distribution

Utilising the Contacts section of the Qualtrics Insights Platform allows researchers to distribute their surveys to a specific cohort of recipients, for example

(Continued)

(Continued)

Railtrack employees. This research technique is common for a situation where the researcher is employed to carry through an agreed research procedure including data collection, analysis and possible recommendations in a consultancy capacity. To technically achieve this, a contact list is required. The researcher creates the survey and uploads the Excel-style contact list for distribution utilising the Qualtrics email service. There is an option to define the email content when you distribute the survey and a unique survey link is generated for each recipient. The email can use piped text to utilise specific details from the contact list to appear more personal, i.e. 'Dear ${m://FirstName}' displays the first field from the contact list, i.e. 'Paul'.

Utilising a contact list has the additional benefit of scheduling the distribution and reminders that allow the survey to be resent only to contacts from the list who have not already taken the survey, and together with the personalised email should have a positive effect on the response rate.

Data and analysis

Qualtrics also includes options to collect open-question responses. These responses can be grouped together in different groups known as 'Topics' which can be useful for more qualitative-style analysis. All data collected can be analysed individually, together against all the responses or filtered to give an interesting range of options. Along with this, Qualtrics has now further improved the data analysis options for cross-tabulation to compare various data to create improved analysis without exporting the data. All data are available to be exported, however, in various formats including Excel and SPSS file formats which have been the most commonly used.

Report view and export

Finally, Qualtrics also allows for the ability to report on your data via the Reports module. This allows the researcher to create a comprehensive report based on the data collected and the analysis they might have carried out, i.e. various filters, cross-tabulations and even tests such as T-tests or Chi-square, for example. There are a variety of visualisation options available when generating the reports to display the data in the clearest fashion possible, including various types of charts and graphs generated as required. Reports can be exported in various formats including Word, pdf or PowerPoint, for instance.

Free account versus licence

Qualtrics does offer a free account; however, many of the features described here are not available with this option. The educational licence available through Qualtrics covers all staff and students for any non-commercial academic research and allows collaboration with other partners outside of the institution. Academically funded projects are covered; however, purchased research from independent businesses would require a separate licence negotiated with Qualtrics, with the price dependent on the scale of distribution and respondents. (For more information about purchasing an educational licence, visit www.qualtrics.com/higher-education.)

Summary

Qualtrics has proved to be very popular for many years, providing tremendous flexibility of the features described here and many more within the application. The clear and user-friendly design that this platform offers has resulted in Qualtrics being an essential tool for undergraduates, postgraduates and experienced researchers alike.

5.6 Conclusions

5.6.1 Practice examples – a real exercise to design a questionnaire for a piece of research on a visitor attraction

Brief

You have recently been employed by Leisure Consultants Ltd, who carry out consultancy in the leisure, recreation and tourism field. The company has just landed a contract to undertake market research for a conglomerate which has some interests in tourism facilities in the UK. One aspect of this contract (a fairly minor one) is to evaluate the future use of a zoo and wildlife park. There are several aspects to this contract, including a feasibility study and a visitor survey of current visitors. It is this latter aspect that your boss has delegated to you. The deadline is tight and without visiting the site, she (your boss) needs a report on how the company should go about undertaking the visitor survey. There is no time for you to visit the site, nor talk to anybody who has worked there. Thus, at this stage, she needs a report on what you feel would be a suitable method of undertaking a visitor survey, how long it should take and how much it would cost. To help (or hinder) you, your boss has given you a questionnaire from a similar survey which she conducted some years ago.

Facts

- The wildlife park is called Tiptree Zoo and is based in South Devon between Ashburton and Buckfastleigh.
- It currently has 35,000 visitors a year on a 250-acre site, with an adult charged £5 and children under 16, £2.50.
- On the site there are four main sections: Animals, Reptiles, Birds and Fish.
- In addition, there is a gift shop, a catering kiosk, a cafeteria, a children's play area, and interpretation provision. The latter consists of leaflets to guide visitors around the zoo itself, and of displays in a wildlife interpretation centre.

Objectives of your visitor survey

To establish:

1. The characteristics of current visitors: who they are, where they come from and any other variables you consider suitable for comparative purposes.
2. Their past and current day-trip activities.
3. Their use of Tiptree Zoo and their opinions on current aspects of it.

What you have to do

1. Criticise the existing questionnaire and state all that you consider to be wrong with it, both in terms of what is presented and the approach that was adopted. To this end, you may have to make deductions about aspects that are not immediately apparent.
2. Write a report indicating how you would satisfy the brief given. The report should include an identification of the necessary planning stages, and reference to the investigatory, analysis and write-up stages.

In short, you need to design a suitable approach and include aspects such as methods, sampling, population and sample identification, fieldwork, analysis requirements and proposed budget. On this latter point, no budget has been set and your boss has indicated that she would like you to prepare and justify what you need to do the job properly. If what you propose is not feasible within the context of the objectives, you can expect the supervision of the contract to be passed to your main competitor in the department and you will end up being an interviewer and doing the coding!

The following is the questionnaire designed by your boss for criticism. The method for this visitor survey was an on-site face-to-face method of data collection. No other techniques were used.

Wickham Zoo Survey 2013

Ensure you have the letter of authority from the zoo with you in case it is required.

Good morning/afternoon. I would like to ask you a few questions about the zoo. Could you help me complete this questionnaire?

Time ....   Date ....   Weather ....

Code No. ....

1 INTERVIEWER CODE GENDER   Male .... Female ....
2 Is this your first visit to Wickham Zoo ?   Yes.... No....
3 How many times have you visited the zoo in the last 10 years?
   Once ....   Twice ....   3–4 times ....   5 or over .....
4 Was your last visit in the past:
   3 months ....   6 months ....   1 year ....   Over 1 year ....
5 Have you been to another zoo or day-trip attraction in the last 5 years?
   Yes ....   No ....
6 How does Wickham Zoo compare to the last one you visited?

   Much better   Much worse

   1   2   3   4   5   6   7   8   9   10
7 Who have you come with today?
   INTERVIEWER TO ESTABLISH GROUP AND RECORD BELOW

   ....

8 How long have you spent at the zoo today?
   Up to 1 hour ....   1–2 hours ....   3–4 hours ....   Over 4 hours ....
9 When did you decide to come here today? READ OUT
   Today ....   In the past week ....   Longer ....   Don't know ....

   (Continued)

(Continued)

10 Why did you decide to come here today?

For educational purposes ....

For the children ....

To be entertained ....

11 How did you get to the site here today on your visit?

Foot ....   Car ....   Van ....   Motorbike ....

Bus ....   Bicycle ....   Coach ....   Train ....

12 Have you come from ...

Home?

Holiday accommodation in the Wickham area?

13 What accommodation are you staying in? RECORD ANSWER

....

14 How long did it take you to get here today? RECORD ANSWER

....

15 Many people come here on recommendation of their friends. How did you hear about the site? RECORD ANSWER

....

16 When you entered the zoo, did you pay the full price or the discounted price that is on offer today?

Full price ....   Discount ....

17 How would you rate the following aspects of the site:

Good   Average   Poor   Very poor   Don't know

Animals

Reptiles

Birds

Fish

Viewing arrangements

Car park

Toilets

Catering

Admission charges

Staff courtesy

18 Do you think that the facilities are adequate?

Yes ....   No ....

19 Do you think we should provide additional facilities?

Yes ....   No ....

20 Do you think additional facilities would spoil the look of the site?

Yes 1   2   3   4   5 No

21 (a)   Don't you think there should be more catering facilities and toilets?

Yes ....   No ....   Don't Know ....   Undecided ....

21 (b)   Why is that? RECORD BELOW

....

22 We find that most of our customers spend in excess of £10, not including the entrance charge. How much did you spend?

Up to £1   £1–5   £5–10   £10+

Catering

Shops

Kiosk

Total spent per person

23 (a) Are you satisfied with your purchases?

Yes ....   No ....   Don't Know ....   Undecided ....

23 (b) Why is that? RECORD BELOW

....

24 What did you like about the zoo least? RECORD BELOW

....

25 Most people like the animals most; what did you like? RECORD BELOW

....

26 Which category best describes your age?

12–15   16–20   21–25   26–34   35–44

45–64   65–74   75+

(Continued)

(Continued)

27 What is the occupational class of the head of the household?

    A   B   C1   C2   D   E   Unemployed   OTHER

28 Finally, what is your address?

    No. and street   ....

    Town   ....

    County   ....

5.7 Summary

Designing a questionnaire is clearly a crucial part of the market research process. Questionnaires are used in different types of survey, from the highly structured commonly used in-street and postal surveys to the informal, where interviewers may ask open questions requiring in-depth answers. Whatever the purpose of the survey, the main aims of the questionnaire are to:

- obtain accurate information from the respondent
- provide a structure and format to an interview
- facilitate data analysis.

The chapter has demonstrated important considerations to be remembered when framing questions and laying out the questionnaire. Of particular importance in asking questions is the need to be clear and simple and to avoid bias which occurs when questions are leading, hypothetical or ambiguous.

It should also be stressed that the testing of questions within pilot surveys is critical. This will show up problems of understanding and misinterpretation and give some indications of the likely results. On this latter point, it should be borne in mind that it is possible (and probable) that you will achieve different results when asking the same question but using open rather than closed techniques. For example, an open question asking 'What did you like about your last holiday?' would probably provide a wide range of answers which reflected that respondent's own particular circumstances and experiences. If, however, the question is asked in a closed way – such as 'The following list shows things which people often like about their holidays. Which are true about your last holiday?' – we may be trying to achieve the same objective but the responses will be quite dissimilar. The open question may provide a wider range but will be more difficult to analyse, whereas the closed question may provide a narrower range of responses (depending on how many items are on the list) but will be easier to analyse. What could be lost in the closed question are items that respondents would have stated were important but are not on the list. Equally, with the open question, respondents may not remember things which were important at the time (which a checklist might prompt) but are forgotten when interviewed.

Unfortunately for the researcher, there is necessarily no absolute right or wrong approach. The best solution, perhaps, is to reflect on the objectives of the survey and include more than one questioning technique for each specific research objective. This way the pros and cons of question types will be compensated for and a full response will be provided overall.

Further reading

Brace, I. (2008). *Questionnaire Design: How to plan, structure and write survey material for effective market research*. London; Philadelphia: Kogan Page.
Although this book is aimed at the general market researcher, you will find some helpful tips in here in terms of design wording and the planning of effective surveys.

Czaja, R. and Blair, J. (2005). *Designing Surveys: A guide to decisions and procedures*. Thousand Oaks, CA: Pine Forge Press.
This book provides a comprehensive guide to the planning, design and implementation of effective surveys. It will be helpful to you as a general text.

Oppenheim, A.N. (2000). *Questionnaire Design and Attitude Measurement*. New edition. London: Continuum.
The first edition of this book was published in 1996 and it has been in print since that time. It is a general book on questionnaire design and uses a wide-ranging set of examples from different fields. You will find some useful ideas in this book, including chapters devoted to the wording of questions, checklists, attitude questions and other types of questioning techniques.

Reference

Frankfort-Nachmias, C. and Nachmias, D. (1996). *Research Methods in the Social Sciences*. 5th edition. London: Edward Arnold.

6

QUALITATIVE DATA COLLECTION METHODS

LEARNING OBJECTIVES

From reading this chapter, you should be able to:

- provide a summary of qualitative methods and when they should be used
- review the links between the literature review and the data collection
- gain an understanding of the value of secondary data sources in qualitative research
- understand observation and participant observation
- explore the use of different types of interviews in qualitative research
- understand the value of focus groups as a research method
- explore the use of images as a data source
- gain an appreciation of the ethical issues associated with qualitative methods.

6.1 Introduction

During the length of a project, fieldwork is carried out at various times. The nature of the fieldwork depends on the type of project and the methods of data collection. If a survey is to be carried out at a tourist attraction, it will be necessary to first gain an overview of the site, decide on suitable interviewing points and talk to staff to gain an understanding of the patterns of site use. There may also be fieldwork involved in observations of visitors, either as part of the data collection process or to assist in developing a sampling frame.

When it comes to the actual data collection itself, there is a variety of aspects which need to be planned. This chapter is essentially divided into two parts. The first part will look at the arrangements which are required for data collection (sub-divided by the main methods of data collection). The second part focuses on the nature and practice of undertaking interviews. The chapter finishes with a review of the case study approach to illustrate how you can use a mixed-method approach in this type of study.

6.2 Understanding the value of qualitative methods

In the previous chapter, you saw the types of situation where it is more appropriate to conduct quantitative research in the form of surveys and questionnaires. This is the most appropriate approach when you are trying to prove or disprove a hypothesis and when you have large numbers of data to collect. Hotels, for example, collect information about guest satisfaction using surveys which are often placed in the room or, more recently, sent out via the internet to the guest's email address after checkout. When your research is about ideas or feelings, it is often more appropriate to use qualitative techniques such as interviews or focus groups.

There are many advantages of a qualitative approach which include the opportunity to investigate an issue in depth and to amend your questions during the research as a result of feedback from the respondent. The negative aspects of this type of research are that it is often more difficult to conduct and you need to have particular skills if you are to do the research successfully. It always takes more time to conduct the research and, because of this, when time is limited, it is difficult to statistically analyse your results, so the research often just gives you an indication of the situation rather than proving it one way or the other.

Qualitative research also has other issues associated with it, such as the possibility of researcher bias and often a much higher possibility that you might upset or disturb respondents. This is why you must have a well-thought-out ethical framework when you are using a qualitative approach, and you often have to get the organisation's permission before you may start the research.

Illustration 6.1 is an example of when the use of qualitative research is most appropriate. This student wanted to find out how managers in the Bulgarian hotel industry used emotional intelligence in their normal working environment to help them achieve their goals. It would have been nearly impossible to design a survey to investigate this issue and he thought that by doing in-depth interviews he would get a much 'richer picture'. It would also allow him to explain to the respondents what was meant by emotional intelligence before he started the interview. He did, of course, have to get the organisation's permission to conduct the research with their staff and he also had to explain issues of confidentiality and his approach to the individual respondents. By doing the research in this way, he was able to obtain some detailed information from a small group of respondents over a six-month period. If time had permitted, it would have been good to interview the respondents again at a later date to see if their attitude had changed, but, as with most student research, this was not possible because it was time-limited to one year of study.

Illustration 6.1   An example of a rationale for using a qualitative approach to research

Emotional intelligence theories have psychological underpinnings and they belong to the social sciences as they aim to explain human behaviour and actions (Brackett et al., 2011). In order to achieve a thorough understanding of such a complex phenomenon, the research approach used was of a qualitative nature, allowing the researcher to gain a deep insight into the topic by collecting rich data that captured the totality of the issue (Lugosi, 2009). It was also interpretive in nature so that an understanding of the participants was developed (Creswell, 2007).

This study used a purposive sampling technique and did not aim for statistical significance. The researcher selected the participants based on a specific set of criteria, which is often employed in qualitative hospitality research (Altinay and Paraskevas, 2008). The English-speaking participants in this study were departmental heads, division heads and general managers in full-time employment in four- or five-star properties located in Bulgaria, due to the high probability of exposure to emotionally intense situations in these hotels (Barrows et al., 2009), and with minimum managerial experience of 12 months. The sample was derived from hotel school alumni associations and national labour organisations. The goal of this research was to achieve a response rate of 12 participants who met the profile outlined above (Kwortnik, 2003).

The interview questions were, first, developed from a thorough literature review, then pre-tested and pilot-tested to enhance clarity, reliability and validity. Interpretative phenomenological analysis (IPA) was used to analyse the interview transcriptions, since it is favoured in social psychology studies (Eatough and Smith, 2006) and fits very well with the research topic of emotional intelligence (Brackett et al., 2011). This method is also recommended as a good match for qualitative studies using in-depth interviews because the objective is to explore the participant's views, experiences and understandings of a phenomenon (Smith et al., 2009). Direct quotations from the respondents' answers were also noted (Chapman and Smith, 2002).

References

Altinay, L. and Paraskevas, A. (2008). *Planning Research in Hospitality and Tourism*. Oxford: Elsevier Linacre House.

Barrows, C.W., Powers, T. and Reynolds, D. (2009). *Introduction to the Hospitality Industry*. 8th edition. Hoboken, NJ: John Wiley & Sons.

Brackett, M.A., Rivers, S.E. and Salovey, P. (2011). Emotional Intelligence: Implications for personal, social, academic, and workplace success. *Social and Personality Psychology Compass*. 5 (1): 88–103.

Carter, S.M. and Little, M. (2007). Justifying Knowledge, Justifying Method, Taking Action: Epistemologies, Methodologies, and Methods in Qualitative Research. Qualitative Health Research. 17 (10): 1316–28.

Chapman, E. and Smith, J.A. (2002). Interpretative Phenomenological Analysis and the New Genetics. *Journal of Health Psychology*. 7 (2): 125–30.

Creswell, J.W. (2007). *Qualitative Inquiry and Research Design: Choosing among five approaches*. Thousand Oaks, CA: Sage.

Eatough, V. and Smith, J.A. (2006). 'I was a Wild Wild Person': Understanding feelings of anger using interpretative phenomenological analysis. *British Journal of Psychology*. 97 (4): 483–98.

Kwortnik, R.J., Jr (2003). Clarifying 'Fuzzy' Hospitality-Management Problems with Depth Interviews and Qualitative Analysis. *Cornell Hotel and Restaurant Administration Quarterly*. 44 (2): 117–29.

Lugosi, P. (2009). Ethnography, Ethnographers and Hospitality Research: Communities, tensions and affiliations. *Tourism and Hospitality Planning & Development*. 6 (2): 95–107.

Smith, J.A., Flowers, P. and Larkin, M. (2009). *Interpretative Phenomenological Analysis: Theory, method and research*. Thousand Oaks, CA: Sage.

Source: 'Emotional intelligence of hotel managers in Bulgaria' by Susan Horner, Matthew Yap and Goran Yordanov; a conference paper presented at EuroCHRIE, 2013.

6.3 Qualitative methods and the literature review

We saw in the previous chapter that it is important for you to link the literature to the questions that you ask in a survey or questionnaire. It is equally important for you to carry out the same process when you use qualitative methods. This is particularly important so that you can focus your attention on the key authors that you have considered during the literature review process. You can even extend your thoughts to consider what you are going to ask and why and relate the question to the literature. A really good example of this type of thinking is shown in Table 6.1. Kimberley was trying to find out about status-seeking consumption behaviour amongst young females and she used focus groups conducted in London and Bournemouth to explore this. In Table 6.1, you can see how the questions she asked were linked to the literature and allowed her to see whether her research supported the existing literature or offered new insights.

Table 6.1   Design of the focus group questions based on the literature

Area of research/lit.	Question asking	Issue: Why is this being asked?	Author(s)
To assess what hospitality venues young professional females visit on a frequent basis	Q1. Interviewer: OK, so to begin with I just want to discuss what sort of hospitality venues you visit on a weekly or fortnightly basis?	To assess the sorts of places young professional females (YPFs) go to	Williams (2002)
Reference groups	Q2. Does the place you visit depend on who you are with?	To assess how the different reference groups that exist within their lives have an impact on the different venues that they choose	Blythe (2008); Solomon et al. (2010)
Self-concept	Q3. Do you believe that the hospitality venues that we visit portray an image of who we are?	To assess whether the respondents believe that material possessions etc. reflect the way they see people and how people see them	Dolfsma (1999); Solomon et al. (2010); Brekke et al. (2003); Starr (2008)
Exploration of the motives of conspicuous consumption and the role of consumer expertise as its key variable	Q4. I know we have answered this a little bit in previous questions but do you often talk with the people that you work with about the hospitality venues you visit?	This research is investigating status-seeking consumption among young professionals. Part of this is to explore how the people that they work with influence their consumption choices	Braun and Wicklund (1989); Starr (2008); Hoyer and McInnis (2007); Veblen (1994); Williams (2002); Blythe (2008); Mittal (2006)
How do the products people consume, their leisure activities, etc. affect the image that they portray to others?	Q5. Do you associate people who visit high-status hospitality venues with success?	To assess whether this segment believes that material possessions etc. reflect the way we see people and how people see them.	Dolfsma (1999); Solomon et al. (2010); Brekke et al. (2003); Williams (2002);
		High levels of consumption indicative of social success	Hoyer and McInnis (2007); Starr (2008); Holt (1995)

Area of research/lit.	Question asking	Issue: Why is this being asked?	Author(s)
General question to lead on to following questions about which celebrities are most admired by the group and why	Q6. Which celebrity (-ies) would you say you would aspire to be like?	Does celebrity endorsement affect the popularity of clubs and does celebrity consumption influence the consumption of the YPFs?	Solomon et al. (2010)
Does the media influence people's leisure decisions? Do they portray certain lifestyles that consumers seek to become a part of?	Q7. What are your favourite television programmes that are currently being shown or have been shown in the past?	To assess the impact of media on consumption choices in relation to leisure consumption	O' Gunn and Shrum (1997); Starr (2008); Solomon et al. (2010)
Influence of leisure activity on portraying a high status image within the media	Q8. Does the type of hospitality-related leisure activity the characters undertake help to form the image of the type of people they are?	To assess whether the ability for the leisure activities of characters in programmes to reflect their social status, is something used by YPFs to reflect their own social status	Holt (1995); Blythe (2008)
Social media and consumer behaviour	Q9. What social media do you use?	To assess whether social media has enhanced the use of conspicuous consumption through leisure activities	Kaplan and Haenlein (2010)
Portrayal of consumer behaviour through social networking	Q10. Do you ever update your status or tag yourself when you visit a hospitality venue?	To assess whether the YPFs use conspicuous consumption through social media to portray an image of how they wish to be seen	Mittal (2006)
Self-concept Role acquisition Symbolic interactionism Conspicuous consumption	Q11. Does seeing the type of venue a person goes to affect your perception of them?	To assess the extent to which YPFs believe a venue can imply something about social status	Starr (2008); Holt (1995); Blythe (2008)
Self-concept Management of image portrayed	Q12. Are you conscious of the image you portray of yourself online? Can writing about where you have been help to manage this?	To observe whether YPFs use social media to manage their image	Starr (2008)
Media and its influence on how venues are portrayed through celebrities	Q13. What magazines or newspapers do you read?	To understand the paper media consumed by YPFs	Solomon et al. (2010)

(Continued)

Table 6.1   (Continued)

Area of research/lit.	Question asking	Issue: Why is this being asked?	Author(s)
Celebrity endorsement and its effect on venue perception	Q14. Do you think that this sort of media has helped to expose the lifestyles of celebrities in relation to the types of hospitality venues that they visit?	To see how celebrities directly influence consumer perceptions of hospitality venues	Solomon et al. (2010); Starr (1998)
How the marketing of a venue can affect YPFs' perception of it	Q15. If a venue is described as glamorous, exclusive or for the discerning, would this encourage you to visit?	To understand how venues can market themselves to attract the YPF segment	Holt (1995); Williams (2002); Dolfsma (1999); O'Cass and McEwan (2004)
Marketing concepts in advertising and marketing hospitality venues to women	Q16. Does the branding of a venue affect your perception of it?	To assess the importance of branding in creating a high-status venue	O'Cass and McEwan (2004)
Self-concept	Q17. Does attending a venue that is seen as exclusive or classy make you feel good about yourself?	The overall impact of attending high-status venues on YPFs and their feelings and attitudes towards themselves	Starr (2008); Williams (2002); O'Gunn and Shrum (1997)

Source: 'Status-seeking consumer behaviour and its impact on the hospitality consumption of young professional females' by Kimberley Anne Kirk-Macaulay and Susan Horner; paper presented at EuroCHRIE, 2013.

Note: The example citations in the final column are not included in the References, as these are for illustration purposes only.

6.4 Data collection arrangements

6.4.1 Postal and other self-completion surveys

Section 5.5.1 has already given advice on distributing postal surveys. Please refer back to this.

The survey can also be sent out using email as an alternative to the post. We discussed this in some detail in Chapter 5 when we considered the Qualtrics package and the use of social networking sites as a vehicle for distribution.

6.4.2 Surveys with interviewers

With many surveys, staff are required to perform the data collection. This may be the actual interviews with respondents, undertaking observations or manually recording tourist numbers. Once the sampling frame has been developed and the questionnaire designed and tested, the precise staffing requirements can be calculated. Where interviewers are used to collect the data, several factors require thought, as follows:

1.   Recruitment of interviewers

Skillful interviewing is not within everyone's capabilities. Interviewers need to be able to probe answers, have administrative ability and be able to stay strictly within whatever sampling or interview instructions are required. In addition, interviewers must be able to approach all types of people and gain their cooperation. Perhaps the most important thing is that the potential interviewer should enjoy interviewing.

Depending on the nature and timing of the research, students are sometimes used because of their availability in the summer months. However, it is essential that younger people possess the right personality and confidence to interview older members of the public, particularly in relation to questions regarding income. Large organisations and market research companies often have a pool of experienced staff to whom they turn for interviewing. In the case of in-depth, qualitative interviews and focus groups, prior experience is essential.

2.   Training interviewers

All interviewers, whether new or experienced, should be briefed on the particular requirements of the project. The nature of the training may take a variety of forms, but commonly includes:

(a) An instruction manual – this outlines the purpose of the survey, interview techniques, questionnaire, sampling instructions and any other relevant guidelines.
(b) In-class training – interviewers are brought together for instruction on survey requirements.
(c) Field training – as above, but also including supervised training and practice in the field prior to the main survey.

Often, one of the interviewers is appointed as a supervisor. His or her particular responsibilities will involve dealing with problems that invariably occur on the first day, checking the quality of the interviews and ensuring that all information is accurately recorded. Overall, there are some general guidelines which interviewers must learn and adhere to (though variations may occur for particular surveys).

Things interviewers must *always do*:

1. Be courteous, confident and positive.
2. Follow all instructions closely.
3. Practise interviewing prior to data collection.

4. Make sure that all necessary materials are carried (prompt cards, identity card, questionnaires, pens, clip board, etc.).
5. Be smartly dressed.
6. Interview respondents on their own (unless couples or groups are specified).
7. Outline the introduction correctly (explaining the purpose of the survey, stating for whom by whom and assuring confidentiality).
8. Ask questions in the correct order.
9. Ask all the appropriate questions.
10. Record the answers fully and accurately.
11. Thank the respondent for their cooperation.

Things interviewers must *never do*:

1. Mislead respondents about the length of the interview.
2. Chat about other issues.
3. Pass on any opinion about respondents' answers.
4. Allow the respondent to see the questionnaire.
5. Interview people personally known (occasionally this may be unavoidable).
6. Interview people previously interviewed on another survey day.
7. Interview children without appropriate permission.
8. Interview as tourists or customers people who work at the site.

Payment of interviewers:

In the training of interviewers, time should be spent ensuring that the methods of payment (including travel and subsistence expenses) are thoroughly understood. This is especially the case where temporary staff are employed for the data collection. Clearly, the level of payment is determined by the budget or organisation but should reflect a level well above basic clerical staff and take account of the, sometimes, arduous working conditions. Payment should be made promptly, again particularly for temporary staff who may have limited funds to cope with legitimate expenses before their first payment is received.

6.4.3 Participant and non-participant observation

This type of research is particularly suitable when you are working in an organisation. You might be working part-time in a hotel, for example, or attending an event which you are interested in researching. Whilst you are working at or attending the event, you might observe what is happening either around you or in a situation in which you are not directly involved. You will have to keep notes of what is happening, either all the time or at a later time, say in the evening when you have finished work. This diary will then form the basis of your research. This type of research generally provides a great deal of interesting information that can be analysed later. If you do not reveal that you are doing the research, you will collect some 'real' information, but it could be regarded as unethical, particularly if the things you see are embarrassing or, in the extreme, harmful. You could, of course, tell people that you are doing the research, but it is important to remember that people quickly forget that you are doing this, particularly if the workplace is a stressful environment.

6.4.4 Content analysis

Another method of research that you can employ is content analysis. This is where you analyse documents or images for themes and ideas which you report on. This is often a useful thing to do before you engage in further research such as interviews. A good example of this that I supervised recently was an undergraduate student who was researching the talent management process at a case study hotel. He started the research by looking at all the published documents that the organisation had on the topic before he completed in-depth interviews with a sample of managers and staff at the second stage. The documents were analysed using the themes which had emerged in the literature review.

I also recently heard a research paper that was about the findings from a PhD study. The student in this case had analysed photographs that tourists had taken during their holidays in Scotland to explore the importance of certain features of the country through the eyes of the tourists. He then made comparisons between tourists with different demographic backgrounds. This research revealed new and interesting insights into the tourist view of the country and provided both academics and the destination marketing office with new and unique information.

6.5 Interviewing

This section is divided into four parts investigating the nature and practice of undertaking interviews. The first part discusses the different types of interview, followed by interview errors, telephone and group interviews.

6.5.1 Types of interview

When interviewing individual respondents, there are perhaps two broad types of interview method – structured and unstructured. The differences between them are revealed in Table 6.2.

Between these two extremes are a variety of other techniques which are more or less structured. For example, some interviews avoid a standardised questionnaire but answers are 'focused' around a series of open questions which gently guide the respondent. On the other side, where there is unsystematic questioning of respondents, only a topic area may be specified by the interviewer and the respondent is free to pursue their own particular line of thought.

Table 6.2 Comparison of interview types

Type	Structured interviews	Unstructured interviews
Other words to describe	Formal, guided, systematic	Informal, less or unguided, unsystematic
Interview questions	Determined prior to interview, often raised/covered on a questionnaire; and interviewer instructions strictly controlled	May have no set questions but standardised topics; sequence appropriate to respondent
Conversation	Very unlike a natural conversation as highly systematic	More like an informal conversation
Probing	Limited to open questions, geared to gaining full response to question	Respondent free to answer freely, probing used to develop understanding.
Advantages	Comparability of answers lends itself to quantitative analysis	'Rich' information, greater likelihood of respondents revealing more opinions/attitudes
Disadvantages	Loss of spontaneity/depth of response	Difficulty of comparison in quantitative terms

Whilst it may appear easy to be dismissive of unstructured interviews as a waste of time, the purpose of the two broad methods should be considered. Unstructured interviews may be used to 'discover' the attitudes and opinions of, say, a tourist or customer rather than to 'prove' or 'test' something. If the research objective is to test whether age or social class has an influence on tourist purchasing behaviour, then something more structured will be necessary. However, in doing so it may be first appropriate to discover the range of views with unstructured interviews so that a structured questionnaire and interviews can be designed and conducted. Hence, unstructured (or less structured) interviews may be useful in the preliminary stages in preparing for and informing more structured data collection. In Illustration 6.2, an example is given of the prompts that were used by a student using a semi-structured interview technique.

Illustration 6.2 Interview prompts used in a semi-structured interview

- Your role here at...
- Tell me about the business.
- Aware of the term culinary tourism?
- Your understanding?
- Untapped potential?
- What could be done to strengthen...?
- What challenges do you think Devon and Cornwall face...?
- What support do you receive?

- Do you receive enough?
- Opportunity to combat seasonality?
- Strategies to extend season?
- Marketing attempts.
- Successful?
- Important for business for culinary tourism to grow?
- Anything else to share?

Source: 'Culinary tourism in Devon and Cornwall: a supply-side perspective' by Rebecca Makepiece, final-year project, supervised by Craig Wight, Plymouth University, 2014.

Language and translation

Research that is carried out with respondents in another country has the risk of certain issues and potential problems. You must first of all decide whether the respondents will be able to understand the interview if you conduct it in English. If you decide that they will not understand the content, you will have to translate the questions into their language, conduct the interview in their language and then translate their answers back into English when you come to the analysis and writing-up stage. Translating an interview in this way has two major issues. First, you must be very careful that the translated version has the same meaning as the original English version, which is not always easy to ensure. Second, the interview process and transcription take even more time than normal and you must build this into your research time frame. Illustration 6.3 shows an example of an interview that was translated and conducted in Italian. The student found this process very time-consuming, although the results were extremely interesting.

Illustration 6.3   An example of research carried out in Italian

It is important to note that the research was conducted in Italian and that all data reported has, therefore, been translated into English by the author.

(Continued)

(Continued)

Interviews were conducted on a non-scheduled basis and depended on the availability of local residents, and fieldwork notes were taken of the responses given. Each participant was asked a total of nine questions, each worded in familiar terms to avoid complex and ambiguous language. The English transcript of the interview questions is presented below in English and Italian.

Host communities interview questions

1   Would you say tourism along the Via Francigena (VF) has increased/is increasing? Why? Is it thanks to government, public or private sector investment?
2   Would you say the VF generates a good form of tourism, respectful of host communities and the environment?
3   Do you think the local and national government is right in promoting this form of tourism?
4   Do you think the VF has the potential to stimulate economic growth in your area? Or do you think it has the potential to do this in the future?
5   Has any investment in the VF (infrastructure, roads, signs, walkways, public spaces, public toilets) improved/impacted your daily life and that of the local community?
6   Have you noticed any particular investment to valorise local culture and heritage?
7   Has there been community involvement in any stage of the development process of the VF? Were you consulted and/or included?
8   Do you think the VF promotes intercultural dialogue and understanding?
9   Do you think the VF reinforces the idea of a shared European culture and identity?

Host communities interview questions (in Italian)

1   Diresti che il turismo lungo la Via Francigena sta aumentando negli ultimi anni? Per quali motivi? E' grazie a investimenti pubblici o privati?
2   Secondo lei la Via Francigena genera una buona forma di turismo rispettoso delle comunità locali e dell'ambiente?
3   Pensi che il governo regionale e nazionale faccia bene a promuovere questa forma di turismo?
4   Pensi che la via Francigena abbia il potenziale di generare sviluppo economico nella tua zona? O credi che ne creerà nel futuro?

5   Gli investimenti fatti dal governo per migliorare il percorso, (sentieri, segnal-
    etica, infrastruttura, servizi pubblici) hanno avuto un impatto positive/
    negative sulla tua vita quotidiana, se alcuno?
6   Ha notato un investimento particolare nella valorizzazione del patrimonio
    culturale locale riconducibile alla Francigena?
7   C'e' stato il coinvolgimento dei residenti locali nello sviluppo del sentiero?
    Siete stati inclusi/consultati?
8   Pensi che la via Francigena promuova un dialogo interculturale?
9   Credi che la via francigena rinforzi il concetto di una Identita' e Cultura
    Europea condivisa?

Source: 'An evaluative enquiry into the social, cultural and economic impacts of the
Via Francigena, Cultural Route of the Council of Europe', Honours project by
Antonio Calogero Nobile, supervised by Derek Shepherd, Plymouth University, 2016.

Familiar words

It is important when you are conducting any form of qualitative research that you use
words that the respondents will be familiar with. It is easy to forget that many words
that appear in your literature review often involve jargon and terms that the woman or
man in the street will not recognise, and you will have to frame the questions in language that they understand. It is also dangerous to assume that managers understand
the academic terms associated with their jobs since this is not always the case, in my
experience. The key here is to pilot the interview questions before you go ahead.

Ambiguous questions

It is also important for you to avoid ambiguous questions for the same reasons as
above. Your questions should be straightforward and easy for the respondent to
understand. Again, piloting the interview before you go ahead will make sure that you
have not fallen into this trap.

Leading questions

It is very important during qualitative research that you do not lead the respondent
on. This is a particular danger for you if you have your own hypothesis about the

situation which you are trying to prove in the research. For example, say you believe that women are not given the same opportunities in the workplace as men and you are asking respondents about this – you could ask the question in two ways as follows:

1. Tell me about the roles of women and men in your organisation.
2. Women don't seem to do very well round here, do they?

The first question just asks the respondent to discuss the situation in an open way, whereas the second question asks them to confirm your view, which they are likely to do. You should adopt the first approach to avoid leading the respondent on. We can now consider common errors that occur in interviewing in more depth.

6.5.2 Common errors in interviews

Errors can occur throughout the survey process. Chapter 5 suggested how questions can be poorly written, which leads to error in terms of inaccurate or poor responses. Chapter 4 highlighted potential pitfalls with sampling, which again can lead to unrepresentative results occurring. Moreover, the correct selection of the method of data collection for the purpose of the market research is crucial to the success of the project. When it comes to interviewing, there are, again, several areas where errors can occur. These are now discussed.

1. Interviewer cheating

Perhaps the most dramatic of all interview errors is cheating by the interviewer. The worst form of this is the falsification of data – that is, making up the responses. Either fictitious respondents who were never interviewed are recorded or not all the interview was completed and the interviewer 'makes up' the gaps. In either case, the action is deliberate and dishonest. To control and discourage this, the research director must put in place a variety of checks on the interviewers. For site surveys at tourist attractions, for example, the interviewer can be observed periodically and his/her questionnaires checked throughout the day. For interviews in the respondent's home, where names and addresses are required, interviewers can explain that a small subsample of respondents will be contacted to verify that an interview took place. Such checks can avoid this type of problem arising.

2. Interviewer influence: Type 1

Occasionally, in an attempt to develop a rapport with the respondent, or because the interviewer is embarrassed asking certain questions, the interviewer will pass a personal opinion. Where this happens, bias may be introduced into the responses. A respondent may not wish to disagree with the interviewer or be uncertain about their own opinion and consequently 'side' with the interviewer. Such bias is clearly inappropriate and should be a focus of training in the survey requirements. Regardless of the nature of the research or interview technique, the interviewer must never pass their own opinion.

3. Interviewer influence: Type 2

Another type of interviewer bias occurs in relation to the appearance and unspoken manner of the interviewer when interacting with the respondent. Age, gender, apparent class, ethnic origin, personality, clothes and hairstyle may all have some influence on how respondents react. Similarly, the age, gender, etc., of the respondent may in turn affect the interviewer's approach. In western countries, women are often more successful as interviewers, particularly where it is necessary to gain entry into households to collect data. Day-time home-based interviews of females by male interviewers may inevitably suffer from low response rates. In very large surveys, these influences may be limited, but how a potential interviewer will be viewed by respondents should be given consideration in the selection procedure.

4. Errors when asking questions

Sometimes, quite unwittingly and with the best intentions, interviewers will change the wording of a question. This may be done to better fit the way the interviewer would ask such a question or be reworded, thinking it would elicit a better reply from the respondent. In structured interviews, such practice cannot be permitted, as considerable variability in the responses may occur. In the one of the authors' own experience (Brunt, 1990), where a face-to-face site survey of a tourist attraction was being undertaken, an open question required respondents to state where they had been on day trips in the previous four weeks. For speed of coding, a range of different types of day-trip site were printed on the questionnaire for the interviewers' own use. Because it was a difficult question, requiring recall, one interviewer speeded up the process by using the questionnaire as a prompt card and asked respondents to indicate yes or no to each of the categories printed on it. Consequently, the results from this interviewer were completely out of step with other interviewers who asked the question in the way intended. This type of problem, yet again, stresses the need for clear instructions and thorough training.

5. Problems probing

Even structured questionnaires often have a number of 'open' questions where interviewers must 'probe' for the fullest possible answer. However, where several interviewers are used to collect data there is a real possibility of inconsistency between them. Clearly, where the aim of the survey is to compare the responses to such questions and make judgements, inconsistent answers from variable probing are worthless. To cope with this type of problem, there are a variety of solutions, as listed below:

- extensive interviewer training
- a probing 'pro-forma', i.e. probing on strictly prescribed lines
- a mixture of question types: open questions followed by closed questions of the same topic to facilitate cross-checking
- no open questions at all
- a separate data collection method using unstructured interviews in support of structured ones.

6. Errors recording the answers

With closed questions where the interviewer is required to tick a box, errors here are down to carelessness. This of course assumes the interviewer understands how to complete the questionnaire. Other errors of this type occur in response to open questions where either the interviewer must write down what is said or interpret the open answer and allocate it to a particular box of pre-coded categories. The potential for error in the former case is due to carelessness, laziness in writing or trying to abbreviate the answer, and in doing so misses the point. In the latter case, the interpretation of replies and trying to make them 'fit' a particular category can cause bias. Wherever such circumstances arise, it is better for interviewers to record answers verbatim, as opposed to paraphrasing or only writing down what appears relevant. For interviewers to listen, interpret and then write an answer down in brief whilst maintaining rapport is difficult. Accuracy and consistency can easily be lost. It is much more preferable for interpretation to occur at a later stage. This solution further avoids potential problems by having a variability between interviewers in terms of their vocabulary and ability to summarise.

6.5.3 Telephone interviews

Telephones have become a part of everyday life and as such now provide the researcher with a convenient, cost-effective method of conducting an interview. This has not always been the case. In the 1950s and 1960s, fewer people owned or had access to a telephone and hence this method tended to result in a sample biased towards more affluent people. Nowadays, this is much less the case. Moreover, it could be argued that in the field of travel and tourism, very few respondents who are able to afford a holiday are unlikely not to own a telephone. The telephone is useful for arranging appointments for a personal interview, for checking that personal interviews have been carried out and for reminders with postal surveys.

The telephone interview has the advantage of reduced cost, with savings on travel for personal interviews being the main area. It also provides a speedy method of data collection. Interviewers can code and input the data directly into computers whilst the interview is progressing. In addition, the interview supervisor is able to listen to interviewers to ensure that questions are correctly asked and coded.

There are some disadvantages though. As an alternative to personal interviews, the telephone is more impersonal and respondents may break off the interview easily. The use of checklists and prompt cards is severely limited and thus the ability to gain detailed information is less than it is for personal interviews. In addition to the normal requirements, interviewers need to have a clear voice and an easy-to-understand accent.

Remote interviews using technology

We saw in the previous chapter how questionnaires can be sent out using email or via social networking sites. It is also possible to conduct interviews remotely using Skype technology or video-conferencing systems. This can open up new opportunities for you as a researcher because you can now conduct interviews in distant places without the need to physically go there, which means you can do research in remote areas and keep the cost down. This type of technology is particularly useful if you are conducting the research amongst people in organisations or with individuals who have access to Skype on their home computer. Conducting interviews remotely needs special training because it is not as simple as being face to face with a respondent and needs more patience.

6.5.4 Focus groups

Focus groups involve a recorded discussion of perhaps 5–10 people who share a common interest (such as having undertaken the same holiday). Open questions are asked of the group and the interviewer acts as a discussion leader. The main functions, other than those of the leader, are to ensure that the discussion does not stray from the topic in hand by occasionally prompting, and to ensure that all members have an equal opportunity to speak.

Focus groups are useful to gain an understanding of *why* particular behaviour occurred. In tourism, this can be most useful in finding out what motivates travel to particular destinations. Information collected in this way is often detailed and lengthy. Thus, focus groups interviews are particularly valuable in the exploratory stages of research or to provide qualitative information alongside a quantitative survey. When developing the focus group method, the following list provides some practical considerations:

1. *The leader* must have thorough training and experience.
2. *The location* must be appropriate for the respondents who will make up the group. Thus, a back room of a public house, hotel or church hall might be suitable for resort guest house owners, marketing managers of airlines and touring caravan owners, respectively. You can also use a room in your college or university to carry out focus groups.
3. *Number of respondents*: 5–10 is ideal as larger than this may be unmanageable in terms of letting everyone have an equal input.
4. *Timing*: to ensure a respectable response rate, select a time when respondents are most likely to be available.
5. *Recording*: tape recording is easiest but video recording may provide additional insights into the dynamics of the group. The main consideration is that the recording equipment must be quiet and unobtrusive.
6. *Respondent type*: respondents should share a common interest related to the topic of the research. There should be balance within the group in terms of gender, age or other characteristics (e.g. buying behaviour). Some groups may be made up of particular types (e.g. all male) but effort should be made to avoid a single individual differing significantly in some way from the rest of the group. If possible, respondents should not know each other or have had previous experience of this type of research.
7. *Refreshments*: when respondents arrive, they should be welcomed and helped to relax. Refreshments can be served and respondents can get to know each other informally.
8. *Questions*: the leader opens the discussion with some general questions and an explanation of how the discussion will be run. From this point on, the leader takes a 'back seat' role unless:

    - one person dominates the discussion (must be suppressed)
    - a respondent is not taking part (question should be specifically directed)
    - a respondent is aggressive/unhelpful (reason for aggression probed and encouraged to participate positively).

9. *Silences*: these can be embarrassing, but the leader should resist stepping in unless absolutely necessary. Pauses can prompt respondents to become involved with comments that have been carefully thought out.

Overall, focus groups can yield large amounts of valuable qualitative data. The results come not only from what was said by members of the group but also from the interaction within the group. Where it is important to investigate the reason for behaviour, group interviews can be most useful, especially in the exploratory stages of the project.

There are practical issues associated with conducting focus groups, particularly when the time set aside for the research is limited and respondents are difficult to find.

Emma, who conducted her undergraduate research last year into the effect of branding on the millennial event attendee, planned to do her research using focus groups of students at the university. We can see the issues that she had during her organisation of these sessions in Illustration 6.4. Despite these issues, the research was successfully completed and the findings were very interesting.

Illustration 6.4   Practical issues associated with the organisation of focus groups

The process of data collection was simple in nature and for the size of the sample it worked most effectively compared to other data collection processes. However, problems arose when trying to find participants to take part in the focus groups. Due to the time of year, students were very busy with exams and work, therefore many could not spare the time. Although an initial setback, the sample of participants that attended provided satisfying responses to the research question. Within each of the focus groups, there was always one person that was more vocal than the others (such as Lily, Harry, Alice, Ella, Hazel and Finn). Focus group 3 was particularly bad for participation and contribution, although this could be associated with the IT equipment failure early on, which meant that the running order of the session had to change slightly. However, the focus group lacked the momentum after the equipment was fixed, therefore it could be related to the participants in the group. This contradicts previous literature by Barrows (2000), who said that smaller focus groups allow you to drill deeper and attain more in-depth insights,

Table 6.3   Names of the attendees of the focus groups

Focus Group 1	Focus Group 2	Focus Group 3	Focus Group 4	Focus Group 5
Sophie	Harry	Ava	Chardonnay	Claire
Olivia	Charlie	Isla	Violet	Stella
Lily	Lucy	Ella	Rose	Luna
Emily	Annabel	Mia	Hazel	Finn
Amelia	Alice	Oliver	Nora	
Chloe	Elizabeth			
Isabelle				

Source: 'The significance of brand design and colour on event purchase and participation amongst Generation Y' by Emma Macphie, final-year project, supervised by Susan Horner, Plymouth University, 2016.

(Continued)

(Continued)

although this was only isolated to this group. From the results and the quality of data collected, a smaller group of four people (Focus group 5), rather than a large group (Focus group 1), allowed the participants to go into more detail about their experiences and opinions.

Another issue was finding male participants for the focus groups; however, the males that took part in the groups seemed to have similar views to the female participants, therefore the author questions whether the responses differ much between men and women. Table 6.3 indicates who attended each group and how many attended per group.

6.5.5 Case study

To illustrate the do's and don'ts of interviewing, the following is an example of some initial questions on a site visitor survey. Whilst the transcripts are clearly hypothetical, the questions are selected from a questionnaire which was used by one of the authors in a consultancy contract.

Interview A

Interviewer A	Good morning, Sir. I am carrying out a survey on behalf of Torbay Borough Council to find out your views of Cockington Country Park. Would you please help us by answering a few strictly confidential questions which will take no more than 10 minutes?
Respondent A	OK, you can ask me.
Question 1	*Where have you come from today?* (Instructions are to allow the respondent to answer and simply code within or outside Torbay)
Respondent A	I've come from Paignton today (within Torbay).
Question 2	*Is that your home or are you on holiday?*
Respondent A	I am on holiday at the moment with my family.
Question 3	*What is the purpose of your visit here today?* (Instructions to the interviewer are to allow the respondent to answer freely and probe for a full answer)

Respondent A   Well, as I said, we're on holiday and we decided to have a day away from the beach.

Interviewer A   Uh-huh.

Respondent A   Oh, and we saw this place advertised in the hotel, so we thought we'd give it a try.

Interviewer A   That's interesting; was there anything else which was important?

Respondent A   Well yes, the kids liked the idea of a horse and cart ride and we decided to have a family treat here with a picnic and ride back to the sea front.

Question 4a   *Have you ever been to Cockington before?* (This is a filter question: if the respondent indicates that they have been before, 4b asks how often they visit Cockington and a prompt card is issued showing categories, e.g. daily, weekly, fortnightly)

Respondent A   No, this is our first visit.

Interview continues successfully.

Interview B

Interviewer B   Hello folks, we're doing a survey. Can you answer a few questions?

Respondent B   Well we all liked our visit, didn't we, yes I suppose we can answer a few questions if it's not too long.

Question 1   *Where have you 'all' come from today?* (Instructions are to allow the respondent to answer and simply code within or outside Torbay)

Respondent B   We have all come from Paignton this morning.

Question 2   *Is that your home or are you on holiday?*

Respondent B   Well, my wife and I live there and this couple are our friends who are on holiday staying with us. We've been here lots of times but this is their first visit ... No it isn't we came years ago before it was all developed and you just had to walk across the fields ... Well it must have been before we were married, Frank, because I'm sure I've never been here before ... Well I'm sure I have, the cottages must have been there then though, but I don't remember seeing them ... yes, they're very pretty, but you can't go in them ... No it's a shame you can't look inside, is that because people live there … Yes … anyway we're not helping this nice young man what is your next question only you will have to be quick because I haven't much time left on the car park ticket and if we're going to get a good seat at the pub for lunch in Babbacombe we'll have to get a move on.

Interviewer B	I'll only be a couple of minutes, so you'll be OK in the car park; the traffic warden hasn't been around today. Look, I have to have one of you as my respondent or we'll get in a terrible muddle …
Respondent B	Well, you've been here the most George, you had better answer his questions.
Interviewer B	That's fine, so you have come from your home today.
Resp. B (George)	Yes, are there many more questions?
Interviewer B	No, just a few.
Question 3	*What is the purpose of your visit here today?* (Instructions to the interviewer are to allow the respondent to answer freely and probe for a full answer)
Resp. B (George)	Well, like we said, we had our visitors staying and decided to show them somewhere, where I thought they hadn't been before.
Interviewer B	Thanks; the next questions asks …
Resp. B (George)	Look, I'd better go and get the car; Frank can answer the rest of your questions and I'll pick you up when you're finished.
Question 4a	*Have you ever been to Cockington before?* (This is a filter question; if the respondent indicates that they have been before, 4b asks how often they visit Cockington and a prompt card is issued, showing categories, e.g. daily, weekly, fortnightly)
Resp. B (Frank)	Yes, though my wife thinks I haven't. George and Mary come here a lot, but then they live close by.
Interviewer B	Look at this card: which of the categories best explains how often you visit Cockington?
Resp. B (Frank)	Well, I just said I have been here once before, oh it must have been forty years ago. You don't really have a category for that – why don't I answer for George and Mary? I'm sure they must come here every week.

George and Mary arrive in the car and off they all go to Babbacombe for lunch. The interview was not completed. Interviewer B looks around to see if the supervisor was watching and thinks about filling in the rest of the questionnaire himself. To make matters worse, Interviewer A has finished for the day. B thinks, there must be an easier way to earn a living; perhaps I'll become a traffic warden.

Comments

Introduction

Interviewer A stated the introduction which was printed on the questionnaire. As such, she referred to the commissioning organisation which is good for public relations, and indicated that the responses would be confidential and how long the interview would take. B did not follow the instructions but made up his own introduction which, whilst he may have felt it was quicker and more chatty, left the potential respondent without appropriate information on the basis of which to decide whether to take part in the survey or not. Because it was not the same as A and deviated from the instructions, there may well have been differences in the response rates between A and B which could have a bearing on the sampling through interviewer bias.

Response to introduction

Whilst A gets a positive response immediately, B's respondent seems less sure, especially over how long it is going to take. Moreover, B should step in at this point and indicate that an individual respondent is required, as group responses may be confusing.

Questions 1 and 2

The responses to A's questions are easy to understand and code. B, however, has not realised the importance of having only one respondent because the group is split over whether they have come from home or are on a holiday. B has not taken control of the interview as the responses show that whilst the group members are trying to be helpful they are digressing from the questions. The way this is resolved is not particularly satisfactory as the group has self-selected its spokesperson. It is also clear that the respondent wants to get away and doesn't really have much time to answer the questions. This aspect would have been covered if B had read out the introduction properly so that the respondents may have politely declined if they were unable to answer questions for 10 minutes.

Question 3

Interviewer A asks the question properly. The first response is not complete so A makes a non-verbal response, gets some more information and then again encourages the respondent to develop the answer more fully. In the end, the purpose of the visit is clear. B, however, senses the irritation and urgency of the respondent and does not bother to probe. Furthermore, the interview is terminated by the respondent, George, who is replaced by Frank. At this point, B should realise his mistakes, thank the respondents and cease the interview, however he perseveres regardless.

Question 4

By this time, Interviewer A is in her stride and a good rapport has been developed with the respondent. She has control over the interview and the respondent is relaxed in his answers and is happy with the experience of being interviewed. Interviewer B, however, has completely failed – the answers have moved from George to Frank and the muddle anticipated has definitely occurred. In the main, the failure is down to initially misleading the respondent about the length of the interview, not taking control by specifying that a single respondent was required and not following the instructions correctly. Had the interview been completed, the quality of the answers would have been poor.

6.6 Mixed-method approach

It is sometimes useful in research to use a mixed-method approach to develop a deeper understanding of a particular issue. Some examples of this approach, where both quantitative and qualitative methods are used in combination, are shown below:

1. A survey carried out with a staff group in a hotel followed by a series of in-depth interviews to consider the talent management procedures.
2. Questionnaires conducted with tourists followed by focus groups with a small sample of the respondents to discover opinions of a visitor attraction.
3. Participant observation at an event followed by in-depth interviews with attendees to investigate their perceptions of quality.

The example of research in Illustration 6.5 shows how the student used questionnaires in combination with in-depth interviews with experts to investigate the development of agritourism in a region of India.

If you are planning to use a mixed-method approach, you must remember that this will require different skills and will take longer to complete, particularly if you want to analyse the first part of the research before designing the second stage. We will look at the analysis later on in the book in more detail.

Illustration 6.5   A case study approach to research using quantitative and qualitative methods

Methodology

A case study approach was adopted to carry out this research. Semi-structured interviews were employed to gather information from key tourism industry experts. A questionnaire designed for the first part of the research was based on published literature and consisted of 12 multiple-choice questions as well as open-ended questions to solicit personal opinions. The questionnaires were distributed to guests staying at the Casino Group of Hotels, Cochin and Nature Trails, and Yercaud during one week from 8 to 14 February 2010. This hotel chain was chosen because it already had an interest in agritourism and it was anticipated that its guests were likely to be interested in the concept.

The second part of the research, after the analysis of the questionnaires, used a semi-structured interview which was also designed with reference to the published literature. Three interviews were designed as follows: one for the representative of the Agritourism Development Corporation of India, the second for interviews with successful hoteliers in the southern and northern parts of India, and the third for interviews with eminent farmers from different places in the southern and northern parts of India. All of these respondents were personally chosen by the first author of this article because of their perceived interest in the concept of agritourism. One hundred questionnaires were distributed and 75 of them were completed and returned. Some of the respondents even gave some valuable suggestions from an agritour they had taken part in.

The Statistical Package for the Social Sciences (SPSS) version 15.0 and Microsoft Excel version 2007 for Windows Vista were used for analysing the questionnaire and interviews, respectively. An ethical code was developed for the research in order to keep the data collected confidential when required and to handle it correctly.

Source: 'Agritourism in India: the potential for sustainable development and growth' by Avantikka Raghunandan, supervised by Susan Horner, César Ritz Colleges, Switzerland, 2010.

6.7 Ethical issues associated with qualitative research

It is very important for you to develop a strong ethical framework when you are conducting qualitative research. If you conduct in-depth interviews, for example, you may find out very personal things about the person which perhaps they did not mean or wish to tell you. To overcome potential issues, you should develop an informed consent form which details what you are doing in the research, the process the respondent will be asked to participate in and how you will treat the data that you collect. The respondent should sign this before you commence and you should keep these forms for future reference. You will probably refer to the respondents with a pseudonym or call them respondent 1 etc., but it is important to remember that, despite this, readers will be able to recognise them. For example, say you are doing research in a hotel and you talk to the general manager. Even if you hide his or her name, others will be able to spot who he or she is. So care is required, particularly if you are talking about sensitive issues.

You can see in Illustration 6.6 an example of an ethical framework from an undergraduate dissertation. Some of the references in this illustration are particularly interesting for you to have a look at.

Illustration 6.6   An example of an ethical framework from an undergraduate piece of research

'Ethical research involves getting the informed consent of those you are going to interview ... It involves reaching agreements about the uses of this data, and how analysis will be reported and disseminated. And it is about keeping to such agreements when they have been reached' (Blaxter et al., 2006: 158). The study was anonymous, meaning that even the researcher was unable to identify which responses came from which respondents (Finn et al., 2000). The introductory paragraph on the questionnaire reassured this anonymity, outlined the purpose of the study and how the questionnaire should be completed, and which respondents were encouraged to read before being asked to complete the questionnaire (Brunt, 1997; Jennings, 2001; Fleming and Jordan, 2006; Bell, 2010; Bowden et al., 2012). The Plymouth University ethics policy (2015) was also adhered to.

References

Bell, J. (2010). *Doing Your Research Project*. 5th edition. Maidenhead: Open University Press.

Blaxter, L., Hughes, C. and Tight, M. (2006). *How to Research*. Maidenhead: Open University Press.

Bowden, D., Botterill, D. and Platenkamp, V. (2012). *Key Concepts in Tourism Research*. London: Sage.

Brunt, P. (1997). *Market Research in Travel and Tourism*. Oxford: Butterworth-Heinemann.

Finn, M., Elliott-White, M. and Walton, M. (2000). *Tourism and Leisure Research Methods: Data collection, analysis and interpretation*. Harlow: Pearson Education.

Fleming, S. and Jordan, F. (2006). *Ethical Issues in Leisure Research*. Eastbourne: Leisure Studies Association.

Jennings, G. (2001). *Tourism Research*. Chichester: Wiley.

Source: 'Tourist satisfaction: the mythology of King Arthur's Tintagel' by Danielle Chapman, supervised by Natalie Semley, Plymouth University, 2016.

6.8 Summary

We have discussed in this chapter the different ways of conducting qualitative research. Interviewing is a skill which requires training and practice. This is the case whether the survey requires a formal interview with structured questions or an informal interview where there is little standardisation. Where interviewers are recruited, the right sort of individual in terms of administrative skill and personality is needed, as is thorough training. Supervision and ongoing monitoring of interviewers is required to overcome some of the common errors that can occur. Overall, interviewing can be a highly successful and accurate method, which achieves high quality data, providing that interviewers have the necessary skills and sound judgement. The use of focus groups is another interesting approach to research that can yield excellent results. All of the techniques need the development of a clear ethical framework to inform the research.

Exercises

1. What are the main problems that you may encounter when carrying out interviews?
2. Devise a training pack for an inexperienced interviewer to carry out face-to-face interviews at a major event.
3. Devise an interview to find out about guest experience at a hotel front desk. Try this out on a partner and see what issues you encounter.
4. Discuss the issues surrounding participative observation. When would it be useful to use this technique in research?

Further reading

Denzin, N.K. and Lincoln, Y.S. (2003). *The Landscape of Qualitative Research: Theories and issues*. 2nd edition. Thousand Oaks, CA: Sage.
This book provides a comprehensive overview of all the methods of qualitative research that can be used by you as a researcher.

Other useful books on specific topics include:

DeWalt, K.M. and DeWalt, B.R. (2010). *Participant Observation: A guide for fieldworkers*. 2nd edition. Lanham, MD: Altamira Press.
This book outlines the techniques that are required to conduct research as an active participant. It will be useful if you are planning to do research as a participant, either at work or in a leisure situation – say, whilst you are on holiday or attending an event.

Edwards, R. and Holland, J. (2013). *What is Qualitative Interviewing?* London: Bloomsbury open books.
Salmon, J. (2015). *Qualitative Online Interviewing, Strategies Design and Skills*. Thousand Oaks, CA: Sage.
These two books may be of value for you in considering the different approaches to qualitative interviewing including new approaches online.

References

Brunt, P.R. (1990). Tourism trip decision making at the sub-regional level: with special reference to Southern England. Unpublished PhD thesis, University of Bournemouth.

7

ANALYSING THE DATA: A QUANTITATIVE APPROACH

7.1 Overview

In the field of market research in travel and tourism, the analysis of data is clearly a crucial part. Business life generally involves the description, analysis and evaluation of data. This has given rise to a whole series of terms which include statistics, quantitative analysis, models, trends and forecasts. Some of these expressions are specific whilst others attempt to cover a wider range of applications. Take, for example, the term statistics. It could easily be argued that to the general public any numbers, facts and figures, graphs and tables are all statistics. However, statistics is also a subject or body of knowledge which statisticians use. Furthermore, statistics relate to specific calculations of quantities derived from sample data. In the context here, the purpose is not to get too bogged down by terminology but to introduce enough to develop an understanding of a specific range of analytical techniques which the readership of this book can master and use to analyse quantitative data.

There are many sophisticated software packages for analysing quantitative data, including IBM SPSS, Minitab, Stata and Statistica. This chapter will draw on examples from IBM SPSS version 22.0 to illustrate the use of statistics software. Using software to analyse data is clearly sensible and pragmatic, particularly when there is a large amount of data to analyse. Use of software is, however, only effective if the user has a thorough understanding of the basic analytical principles and techniques. Without this, the individual researcher may well be able to get a software package to carry out a series of statistical tests but would be unable to properly interpret the results. This emphasises the point that the analysing of data is much more than a single stage or event in a project. Knowing why particular analytical techniques are appropriate, interpreting the results fully and suggesting or recommending a suitable course of action are equal to, if not more important than, performing a specific statistical test. This chapter will consider a range of tests and discuss the instances in which they are most suitable.

Chapter 3 indicated the need for consideration of the proposed analysis in the early planning stages of a project. It is easy to forget the importance of this aspect in the midst of a project when time pressures are forcing the researcher to get on with designing questionnaires and starting the data collection. Soon the data are collected, coded and put into a spreadsheet or a statistics software package. Suddenly, the question arises 'what do I do now?' The answer is 'well, analyse it'. However, in answer to 'what are you trying to achieve?' there is often an embarrassing silence. In the planning stages of a project, where the aims and objectives are negotiated and agreed, thought must be given to how the analysis will satisfy the objectives. Then, after the pilot stage, when some preliminary results are available, the question of whether the data can be analysed in the way proposed to satisfy the project objectives should be posed. In short, you should always try to anticipate how the analysis will be performed and ensure that the data collected is concordant with the proposed analysis and meets the requirements of the project objectives.

To address these issues, this chapter is now divided into four parts:

- Identifying how to input and code data into statistics software (section 7.2)
- Describing and illustrating data (7.3)
- Describing quantitative data (7.4)
- Analysing quantitative data (7.5).

7.2 Inputting and coding quantitative data

Before data analysis can begin, the researcher must ensure that the information is available in a workable format. Most often, this will involve the use of either a spreadsheet or statistics software to collate all of the results in one database. How the research has been administered will determine how the data is input and how time-intensive the process is likely to be. If paper-based questionnaires have been used, for example, the researcher will need to input the results into the database by hand. Online surveys may be downloaded in compatible formats.

Before creating a data file, you should think carefully to ensure that the structure of your file allows for all the analysis you need. This requires careful consideration well before the data entry stage as a lack of planning can make it difficult to make important comparisons or to find significant relationships. Examples of common errors include: failure to include key variables (such as age or gender) when such variables are central to the study; requesting yes–no answers to complex questions; including many variables without a clear dependent variable to identify the objective of the research; and having a clear dependent variable but no independent variables that are designed to influence it. If the original research has been carefully constructed, then creating a good data file is much easier.

If the data are being input by hand, the researcher is able to code as they go; comparatively, if an online survey has been used, the information that is in the database will need coding. For this, a coding scheme must be developed.

Illustration 7.1   Getting started with SPSS

Start by opening SPSS, once the programme has opened you will arrive at the SPSS data editor window.

Two windows will be shown. The first window asks you which data set you would like to open, and the second window, underneath, is a blank data editor window. Click on 'New Dataset' and OK.

The default screen is the data editor which will appear in variable view. Two tabs are located at the bottom left of the screen which can be used to switch between variable view and data view. Variable view is used to set up and code the database while data view is used to input and view the data.

This data editor window is the central part of SPSS, it's organised like any other spreadsheet, where the rows refer to an individual case and the columns are variables.

(Continued)

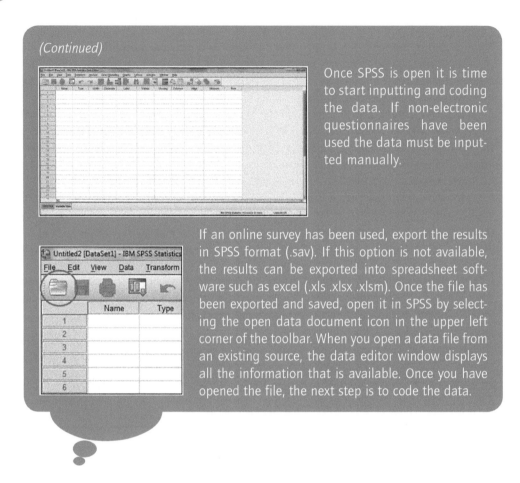

(Continued)

Once SPSS is open it is time to start inputting and coding the data. If non-electronic questionnaires have been used the data must be inputted manually.

If an online survey has been used, export the results in SPSS format (.sav). If this option is not available, the results can be exported into spreadsheet software such as excel (.xls .xlsx .xlsm). Once the file has been exported and saved, open it in SPSS by selecting the open data document icon in the upper left corner of the toolbar. When you open a data file from an existing source, the data editor window displays all the information that is available. Once you have opened the file, the next step is to code the data.

7.2.1 Creating a coding scheme

Responses recorded from a completed questionnaire survey need to be given a code (often numerical) in order to be analysed using SPSS. At the questionnaire design stage, codes can be allocated within the questionnaire. This is called pre-coding. It is important to think through how you are going to analyse your data at this stage of a survey in order to make sure the data are in a format that will allow you to perform the tests you require. Thinking this through may influence the format of your questions. Post-coding is used where questions have open responses. Coding here has to take place after the survey has been undertaken. You will need to read through completed questionnaires to work out what categories will be needed.

A coding scheme is created in order to ensure that all of the data are assigned the correct value. When coding, whether pre-coding or post-coding, it is important to consider the nature of the data. For instance, if you are using ordinal data, which is ranked in a specific order, it is important that your coding reflects this. Illustration 7.2 provides some basic examples of coding data.

Illustration 7.2   Example of a coding scheme

Variable Name	Variable Label	Value Label
Sport	Sport type	1 Value Label
		2 Skiing
		3 Snowboarding
		4 Both
Skilllevel	Skill level	1 Beginner
		2 Intermediate
		3 Advanced
Holidayspend	Holiday spend per person	1 Under £500
		2 £500-£1000
		3 £1000-£1500
		4 £1500-£2000
		5 £2000-£2500
		6 Over £2500
offpiste	Off piste skiing	1 Yes
		2 No
Developnewskills	Importance of developing new skills	1 Always Important
		2 Sometimes Important
		3 Never Important

Illustration 7.3   Setting up the variables and assigning data labels

Once the coding scheme has been designed it is necessary to set up the variables in variable view. SPSS requires that both data and information about the

(Continued)

(Continued)

variables be entered. Each column or variable in the data view window must have a unique 'name' that identifies each variable separately. You'll need to think of a sensible name for each variable.

Sometimes with larger questionnaires it is easy to forget what a variable name means. So that this doesn't happen it is necessary to give a 'label' or description to each variable name.

It is important that the values for each variable are input in variable view. Inputting the values for each variable allows identifi-

cation of the data and enables the software to assign labels to the data when descriptive tests or analysis is run later on which aids the analysis process. In order to accurately input the values, the coding scheme will be needed. When coding the questionnaires each potential answer was given a numerical code. These numerical codes will not only be used to assign a value but will also be entered into the data view.

Illustration 7.4

To assign the values for a variable, click the value cell for the first variable. A second click in the blue shaded area to the right will bring up a value labels dialogue box.

Here you can assign the value labels for this variable. The following window shows part way through the process of doing this for the 'Skill Level' variable.

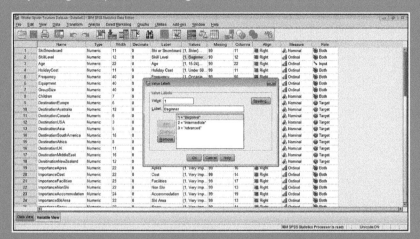

It is important that all missing and not applicable responses are recorded using SPSS as the numbers of non-responses and not applicable questions are an important part of data analysis. Where a respondent fails to answer a question the data is said to be missing. However if the questionnaire contains a series of filter questions then it is possible that some of the questions are not applicable to the respondent and are therefore not applicable.

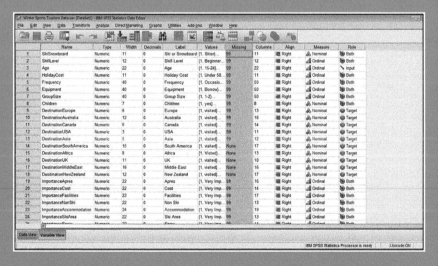

(Continued)

(Continued)

SPSS will treat a 'blank' space in a cell within the data editor window as a missing value (e.g. where values are given within the same column for other cases). However, rather than leave it blank, a code can be entered and assigned formerly as indicating a missing value.

It is common for this code to be 9 or 99 provided that these are not used to signify other value labels. Where a 'not applicable' answer is identified within the question on the questionnaire – this is different than respondents just failing to answer a question, or there being no 'not applicable' box to tick. In this instance you may need to differentiate between this and a true missing value. So you don't get muddled up, always assign 9 or 99 to mean missing values and use another value to mean 'not applicable', establishing a convention within your coding.

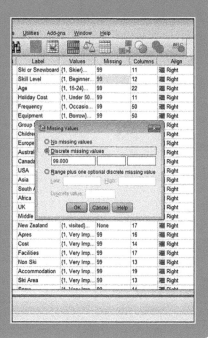

Illustration 7.5   Tidying up variable view

To this point the variables have been defined but there are a few other jobs to do to tidy things up and help make further analysis easier to read. A quick overview of the other columns in the variable view will be given, and suggestions on how to organise these made.

The type column: All the data in this example is in 'numeric' format – i.e.

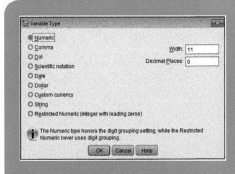

numbers for each value. SPSS can take data in formats other than numeric (although this is the default and expected variable type).

Other options for variable type include:

Date: A numeric variable whose values are displayed in one of several calendar-date or clock-time formats.

Custom currency: A numeric variable whose values are displayed in one of the custom currency formats that has been defined.

String: Values of a string variable are not numeric, and hence not used in calculations. They can contain any characters up to the defined length. Upper and lower case letters are considered distinct. Also known as alphanumeric variable. You might, for example, enter the respondent's name or company and while this isn't used in statistical calculations, it may be useful in charts or tables.

Decimals Column: As none of the data used any decimal places, each variable should be set at 0 decimals.

Align Column: This aligns the values within each cell of the data view either to right, left or centre, depending on your preference.

Columns Column: This sets the width of the column in the data view window, you can play around with the size.

Measure Column: The level of measurement can be selected as scale (numeric data on an interval or ratio scale), ordinal, or nominal. Nominal and ordinal data can be either string (alphanumeric) or numeric. Measurement specification is relevant for Chart procedures that identify variables as scale or categorical. Nominal and ordinal are both treated as categorical.

Select one of three measurement levels:

- *Scale*: Data values are numeric values on an interval or ratio scale (e.g., age, income). Scale variables must be numeric.

(Continued)

(Continued)

Ordinal: Data values represent categories with some intrinsic order (e.g., low, medium, high; strongly agree, agree, disagree, strongly disagree).

Nominal: Data values represent categories with no intrinsic order (e.g., accommodation type). Nominal variables can be either string (alphanumeric) or numeric values that represent distinct categories (e.g., 1 = Male, 2 = Female).

Role Column: Specify the role that will be used to pre-select variables for analysis. By default, all variables are assigned the input role. Changing the variable role alters the way in which the Chart Editor calculates statistics.

Select one of six role subcommands:

- Input: The variable will be used as an input (e.g., predictor, independent variable).
- Target: The variable will be used as an output or target (e.g., dependent variable).
- Both: The variable will be used as both input and output.
- None: The variable has no role assignment.
- Partition: The variable will be used to partition the data into separate samples for training, testing, and validation.
- Split: Included for round-trip compatibility with PASW Modeller. Variables with this role are not used as split-file variables in PASW Statistics.

Illustration 7.6   Inputting data

When it comes to inputting the data, click back to data view and using the coding scheme, carefully input the data from the questionnaires. If you click on a particular cell within the data editor window a 'cell editor', below the menu tools bar, displays the value of the selected cell. At this stage, if data is to be input by hand, the database should be empty.

Using your coding scheme input the data from the questionnaires. To start with bring the cursor to the top left-hand cell (row 1, column 1) and click once. This makes this cell 'active'. Now enter the first number from the coding sheet and press the right cursor key. This makes row 1 column 2 active. Alternatively if you pressed the return key this would take you to row 2 column 1. It is up to you how you wish to input the data. Moving across a row (i.e. by questionnaire or case at a time) is easier. Sometimes you will be able to code directly from a questionnaire, without need of a coding scheme, and it would therefore make more sense to do a row at a time.

Remember each row represents a case (in this case an individual respondent's questionnaire) and each column is a variable (a question). If you make a mistake when entering data, just click onto the appropriate cell to make it active and make your correction. You can also insert new cases and columns via the data menu. Remember to save the data file regularly during the coding process.

If the data has been imported from an online questionnaire the data view should be full of numeric data. It may already be coded, however the values will need to be determined in variable view. Missing data will also need to be assigned a value.

You will have noticed that the data editor window (data view tab) contains columns of numeric data. This data can be viewed either numerically, or with value labels. If you select the view menu, you'll notice that the 'value labels' option is not ticked. If you click and tick this, then the numeric-based columns will transform into columns of data, some which are numeric (e.g. age), and some with text (referred to as non-numeric)

(Continued)

(Continued)

(e.g. skill level). The text in these columns are 'value labels' where, for example a code of 1 means the respondent was a skier and 2 means snowboarder. On the data editor you can view this either in numeric form (1's and 2's) or as the labels where these are assigned (skier and snowboarder). A shortcut to this function can be found on the toolbar as shown above and an example text view is displayed below.

Once complete the data view should look similar to the example below, with all of the cells and missing data coded.

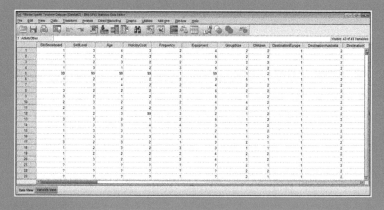

7.3 Describing and illustrating data

The initial stage of data analysis is often the basic description of the data. This will help the researcher to determine the characteristics of their sample and give them an overview of responses. At this stage, the researcher may also wish to visualise this data through the use of charts or graphs. In order to describe and illustrate the data, it is important that the researcher has an understanding of the type of data they are using, is aware of the correct terminology and is familiar with visual methods of data presentation.

7.3.1 Types of data

Quantitative data originate from a variety of different sources. These include surveys, measurements, government statistics and other secondary sources. Quantitative data can be one of three basic types: categorical, ordinal and cardinal.

Categorical data

Categorical data come from, for example, questionnaires where the responses to questions are put into classes, groups or categories. As such, the data do not have a numerical value; rather a label or value is assigned to each category and hence this type of data is often referred to as nominal. Some examples of questions resulting in categorical data are shown in Table 7.1.

Table 7.1   Questions resulting in categorical data

What type of accommodation are you using on this ski trip?	Tick one box
1 Hotel	
2 Aparthotel	
3 Catered chalet	
4 Self-catering chalet	
5 Hostel	
6 Friends and relatives	
7 Other	

Which winter sport(s) do you participate in?   (Circle as appropriate)

1 Skiing

2 Snowboarding

3 Both

As can be seen from the examples, the respondent indicates which category is relevant to them. In the case of gender or other questions where there are only two alternatives (yes or no questions, for example), the data can be referred to as dichotomous.

Ordinal data

Ordinal data are arranged in a specific order. The data are still arranged in categories but must ascend or descend, for example go from best to worst or worst to best. Typically, questions which use ranking scales produce ordinal data. In a similar way to categorical data, it is not possible to measure precisely how much better one category

Table 7.2   Types of question which result in ordinal data 1

Which of the statements best describes the importance of snow conditions when choosing a ski resort?	Tick one box
i Very important	
ii Important	
iii Neither important nor not important	
iv Not important	

Table 7.3   Types of question which result in ordinal data 2

How would you rate the snow conditions in the resort? (Use the following card and indicate a score where 1 means that you thought the snow conditions were excellent down to 5 which means you thought the conditions were poor)	Score
1 Excellent	
2	
3	
4	
5 Poor	

Table 7.4   Types of question which result in ordinal data 3

Indicate your level of agreement of the statements by ticking the appropriate box of whether you:

A   Agree strongly
B   Agree
C   Are undecided
D   Disagree
E   Disagree strongly

	A	B	C	D	E
I was satisfied with the conditions on piste					
I was satisfied with the variety of terrain					
I was satisfied with the provision of services in the resort					
I was satisfied with the management of gondolas and chair lifts					

is than another, other than that one category is higher in the order. Tables 7.2, 7.3 and 7.4 illustrate the types of question which result in ordinal data.

Cardinal data

Cardinal data can be measured against a scale which has a specific numerical value. Thus, often the data can be reported in terms of measurable units, or else are an actual number. Hence, age in years, height in metres, cost in pounds and number of holidays taken are all examples of cardinal data. In the last example, where the amount would refer to a whole number or integer value, the data can also be referred to as discrete cardinal data. In the other examples such as height, age or cost, where the answer could be any value, it is referred to as *continuous* cardinal data.

To summarise, quantitative data can be as shown in Table 7.5.

Table 7.5 Summary of quantitative data

Categorical	Categories, classes or groups
Ordinal	Categories put into some kind of rank order
Cardinal	Measurable against a scale and subdivided into discrete or continuous

Labelling data in SPSS

Illustration 7.5, entitled 'Tidying up variable view', identifies how data can be labelled in SPSS. If statistics software is being used, you are often required to categorise the data into one of these three types. If you have data that is not coded into a numerical form, from free elicitation questions, for example, in SPSS this would be labelled as string data, in the 'type' column.

7.3.2 Variables, values and cases

Often in surveys, the term *variable* is used to define an aspect or question which is measured. You may have asked respondents to state their age, number of children, number of holidays taken, and views of particular aspects of their last holiday. The questions posed can be referred to as a *variable* and the answers given, a *value*. In addition, each person (or sampling unit) can be defined as a *case*. Hence, there will be one value for each variable for each case.

Variables may be sub-divided into *independent* and *dependent*. This relates to the influence which a variable may have within the analysis. It is common to predict that variables such as age, presence of children, income, educational background, social class or gender may influence (or explain) the responses to other variables such as preferred holiday type, satisfaction with accommodation, type of transport used, purchasing behaviour or likelihood to repeat visit. In this sense, it could be said that the latter variables mentioned depend on the former ones. Hence:

- *Independent variables* are likely to be influential in predicting or explaining things. They act independently in the sense that the respondent has little control over the answer. For instance, a respondent is female, with two children, aged 35 and has a particular income.
- *Dependent variables* refer to questions or variables where the respondent is more likely to indicate their feelings or opinions. Dependent variables are usually influenced by one or more variables which may control or relate to them.

Table 7.6 Examples of variables from the Winter Sport Tourism Project

Independent variables	Dependent variables	Both
• Age	• Choice of destination	• Sport
• Gender	• Satisfaction with the destination	• Skill level
	• Frequency of trips	• Motivation for travel
	• Holiday spend	• Behaviour at the destination
		• Importance of destination attributes

It is very often the purpose of market research to find out 'why' certain types of customer are more or less likely to demonstrate particular types of purchasing behaviour. That is, 'who is most likely to want this type of tourism product?' Finding this out to inform a marketing strategy is the obvious and immediate function of market research. Thus, being able to distinguish which independent variables are significant in predicting favourable purchasing characteristics (dependent variables), is a priority.

Labelling independent and dependent variables in SPSS

Illustration 7.5 identifies how independent and dependent variables can be identified in SPSS. Changing the role of the variable alters the way in which the software calculates statistics so it is important that this is correct.

7.3.3 Reporting data

When reporting the results of data collected, it is important that the most effective way of conveying numerical information is considered. Often, it is easier to explain such information in a diagram where the reader can visualise the result. Moreover, diagrams are more likely to both grasp attention and allow better interpretation than a page of numbers or solid text. Hence, the market researcher needs to be sensitive to the readership and report and represent the data in an attractive (and truthful) fashion. Whilst diagrams are useful, simple facts and figures often need to be reported and a decision has to be made whether to simply state the frequency, a proportion, percentage or ratio.

Stating a *frequency* may have little value other than, for instance, '4000 respondents satisfactorily completed the questionnaire'. To a knowledgeable audience, this may have some meaning but out of context it is worthless. Thus, often a *proportion* is used. Hence, '4000 respondents satisfactorily completed the questionnaire from the 5000 that were distributed'. A proportion is therefore a section of the whole (or, more accurately, a section divided by the whole).

Percentages relate to a proportion multiplied by 100%. Thus, rather than saying 4000 out of 5000 completed their questionnaire, you could also state that 80% did so. This is calculated by 4000 divided by 5000 and then multiplied by 100. Another way of expressing numerical information is as a *ratio*. This differs from proportions in that rather than being a section of the whole, it is a section of another section. Using the same example, you could state that the ratio of those completing their questionnaires to those who did not was 80 to 20 or 80/20.

The decision of whether to express results in terms of a frequency, proportion, percentage or ratio is largely up to the preference of the researcher, but it is important to be consistent. Consider the following statement:

Of the 1,000 people interviewed at each of the four sites:

- 200 people at Val d'Isere were from social class B.
- 20% of people at Les Arcs were from social class B.
- 2 out of every 10 visitors to Bansko were from social class B.
- The ratio of those in social classes other than social class B was 10/2 at Vail resort.

The statement is certainly confusing but it is actually an indication that exactly the same number of respondents at each of the four sites were found to be from social class B (200). This stresses the need to be consistent in discussing figures so that the reader can easily follow what is being explained. There is no right or wrong approach (although in the example the ratio expression is unnecessarily complicated). However, in the authors' opinion, expressing small proportions in terms of percentages sometimes appears to be a means of concealing a small sample size. For instance, say 10 skiers are interviewed about what determines their choice of resort. It is found that 7 of the 10 felt that guaranteed snow was important in their choice. Although factually correct, it would be unwise to state that 30% of skiers did not consider good snow conditions to be important in choosing a resort. Percentages should be used to simplify the readers' understanding – in this example it could be argued that using percentages confuses it.

To illustrate data in ways other than within text, tables and diagrams can be used. Examples of a number of useful tables and diagrams will be given and described, and instruction, as to how this can be achieved using SPSS software, will follow.

Table 7.7   **Skill level of respondents**

		Frequency	Cumulative percentage
Valid	Beginner	24	2.9
	Intermediate	398	50.8
	Advanced	408	100.0
	Total	830	

Perhaps the simplest method to illustrate data is a *frequency table*, as illustrated in Table 7.7.

Table 7.7 indicates how 'frequently' each of the responses occurs and the reader can see the results at a glance. By providing a percentage column, the reader can also go further in judging the relative importance of each skill level.

In this example, the percentage given is the percentage of the total, but sometimes where filter questions are used this may include people who are not relevant. Also, this table does not include any missing data, where respondents have dropped out of the questionnaire or failed to complete the question. In this case, it may be necessary to include columns in the table which demonstrate valid and cumulative percentages. Many computer packages perform this function by default. Table 7.8 gives an example.

Table 7.8   **Skill level of respondents including missing data**

		Frequency	Percentage	Valid percentage	Cumulative percentage
Valid	Beginner	24	2.6	2.9	2.9
	Intermediate	398	43.2	48.0	50.8
	Advanced	408	44.3	49.2	100.0
	Total	830	90.1	100.0	
Missing	99	91	9.9		
Total		921	100.0		

In the example in Table 7.8, only 830 out of the 921 answered the question and identified their skill level. These are noted below the table as the valid cases. The 91 missing cases coded as value 99 in the table were respondents who did not finish the online questionnaire. In these circumstances, referring to a percentage of the whole sample (921) is misleading because of the 91 included who did not answer the question. Thus, the *valid percentage* column is based on the percentage of those who actually answered the question (830). In this way it can be seen that 25 respondents were advanced, which represents 44.3% of all respondents but 49.2% of those who answered the question. The final column, *cumulative percentage*, relates to the sum of the valid percentage for a response, plus all the other responses that precede it in the table. Hence, 97.1% of valid cases were either intermediate or advanced.

Illustration 7.7 Creating a Frequency Table Using SPSS

One of the most commonly used statistical functions is the Frequencies command. To open the Frequencies dialogue box, click the word Analyze on the SPSS menu bar, and then select Descriptive Statistics and then Frequencies as shown below.

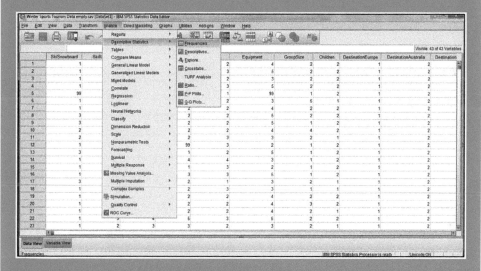

Following this procedure will bring up a new dialogue box that shows each of the variables. From the left hand box select the required variables. More than one variable can be selected.

When there are more variables than can be seen within one or other of these windows a scroll bar appears.

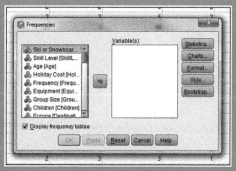

(Continued)

(Continued)

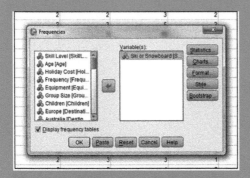

Once the relevant variables have been selected click ok. At this point SPSS performs the commands you have specified – it doesn't take long and quickly you will see a new 'Output' window appear.

This output window is divided into two parts. SPSS refer to the left-hand side as the outline 'pane' and the rest as the display pane. You can obviously change the sizes of these panes by pointing the cursor at the dividing line between them, click and hold, and drag to whatever size you want. In most instances ignore the outline pane and just concentrate on what's happened in the display pane – this is where the actual output is. However, the outline side does contain some handy tricks.

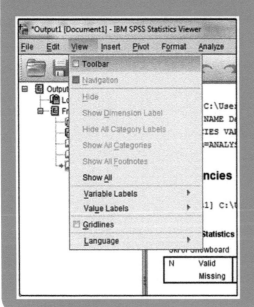

Double click when the cursor is pointing at one of the tables. This function allows you to edit the table in its current location. For example, you can highlight different sections and change the font, size or add additional text. Rows and columns can also be transposed by selecting the relevant item.

Occasionally you will have a lot of output and you can click to different parts of the output.

Alternatively you can simply scroll up and down to find the table/chart you want. The icons on the left-hand side can be moved around or opened and closed, with the little + or – boxes etc.

In the display pane there is as much of the output as can be shown on the screen. Here you will find the frequency tables (actually called pivot tables), charts and titles. Typically you will often want to copy this output and

paste it into word documents (e.g. your report), but might want to change its appearance first so that it better fits into your report.

If the additional tool bar does not pop up automatically, go to the view menu and select it.

What has been described here is a very basic table; SPSS can allow you to construct much more sophisticated tables.

7.3.4 Illustrating data

Whilst the tables in the examples given are straightforward, sometimes frequency tables can be difficult to interpret. In this instance, the researcher must consider how best to illustrate the data in the form of a diagram. The main methods include using *line graphs*, *bar charts*, *histograms* and *pie charts*. These will be discussed briefly followed by some examples.

Line graphs are useful for showing trends over time; data on the horizontal axis can be in numbers or categories, however data on the vertical axis must be

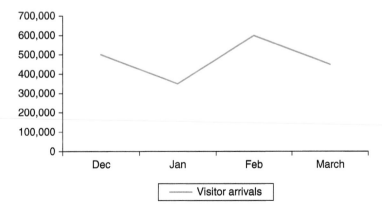

Figure 7.1   Visitor arrivals by month

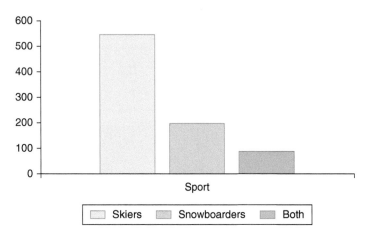

Figure 7.2   Respondents' participation in winter sports

represented by numbers. Because many points can be placed on a line graph, they are most valuable where a bar chart would appear too cluttered. Figure 7.1 illustrates the use of a line graph.

Bar charts are mainly used for categorical data and also allow for comparisons between values. The length of a column in a bar chart is related to the number or frequency it represents. Hence, one of the columns must indicate a frequency, numerical value or percentage, whilst the other axis displays the categories. There is no particular convention as to whether the columns should be presented horizontally or vertically. However, if several bar charts are to be used in a report, a consistent approach is advisable. Figure 7.2 shows an example of a bar chart.

Histograms are similar to bar charts, however histograms are more often used to illustrate cardinal (numerical) data such as age, sales or income. Here, to construct a histogram it must be reasonable to combine adjacent values into columns to form the graph. Combining categorical data may not be possible as the categories may be mutually exclusive. For instance, in Figure 7.2 it would not be possible to combine any of the columns. Hence, where a variable has many different numerical values and it is sensible to group adjacent values together, a histogram is a worthwhile method of illustrating the data.

A pie chart is a circle with segments highlighted to indicate proportionate sections of a total figure. For example, total company sales could be broken down into constituent parts. Sometimes you may wish to emphasise a particular segment by removing it a little way from the others. Pie charts are valuable for illustrating data where there are relatively few categories. Too many segments, especially where several represent a small proportion, can be confusing to the eye. Figure 7.3 shows the equipment rental and ownership of skiers.

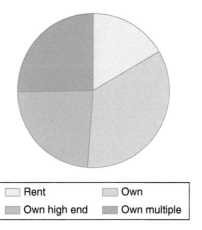

Figure 7.3   Equipment-buying behaviour of skiers

Illustration 7.8   Creating a Chart in SPSS

A chart can be produced (which can be copied and pasted into other documents), through the Frequencies command. When performing the frequencies command, the frequencies dialogue box appears. If after selecting the variable you click the charts button, the following dialogue box appears.

Select the type of chart you need and click 'continue' and then 'ok' on the window underneath.

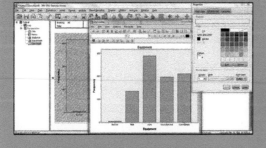

The chart will appear in the output window. Within the output window if you double click on the chart itself, an option to edit the chart is possible.

This is one way of creating charts using SPSS, there is also the graphs

(Continued)

(Continued)

menu which allows you to create a variety of charts and graphs. The chart menu is more extensive, and it is not the intention here to explain all the possible functions. The graphs menu allows you to create bar, line, area and other types and formats of graphs. The software allows you to edit and print the graphs created from data analysis. It is also straightforward to copy graphs and paste them into word documents.

To build a chart, open the tool using the graphs menu and the graph builder. Now drag into the chart preview the required type of chart from the menu in the bottom half of the window.

From the list of variables on the left of the window, drag across the required variable into the 'set colour box'. Edit and click ok.

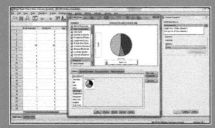

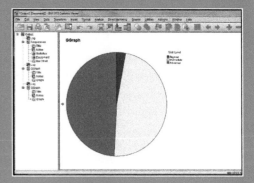

The chart will appear in the output window.

1. Now construct a table

Distance category	Number of respondents
Under 10 miles	5
10 but under 20 miles	24
20 but under 30 miles	35
30 but under 40 miles	31
40 but under 50 miles	23
50 but under 70 miles	8
70 but under 100 miles	5
100 but under 150 miles	3
150 miles or more	1

7.4 Describing quantitative data

Illustrating the data by means of diagrams is not always sufficient to satisfy the aims and objectives of a quantitative survey. The numerical results of survey questions or variables are spread from the lowest value to the highest. This spread of data is referred to as a frequency distribution. For example, in a survey of tourists to a particular destination, 400 respondents were asked, amongst other things, to state their age. It would be unwise to construct a frequency table of the results in a report as it would probably be very large and confusing. The information could be illustrated in a histogram, which would give some indication of the distribution of ages within the sample. However, it may be interesting to report what is the age of the youngest and oldest respondents and what is the average age within the sample. When further information of this kind is required, a variety of descriptive statistical techniques can be used. These techniques can be sub-divided into two broad types:

1. *Measures of central tendency* (also referred to as measures of location)
2. *Measures of dispersion* (also referred to as measures of variation)

Measures of central tendency refer to values within a sample which are typical of all the values. One way of picturing this is to think of measures of central tendency which give the location of a value in the 'centre' of the sample data. The mean, median and mode (in decreasing order of importance) are three measures of central tendency which will be investigated in this chapter.

The second aspect – measures of dispersion – refers to how values are scattered, dispersed or spread within a sample. For example, what is the difference between the highest and lowest values, or how many values lie close to the mean? The range, interquartile range and standard deviation are three measures of dispersion which will be examined later in this chapter.

7.4.1 Measures of central tendency

Mean

The most commonly used measure of central tendency is the mean. The definition of the mean is:

$$\text{Sample mean} = \frac{\text{Sum of observations}}{\text{Number of observations}}$$

As a formula, the mean is represented as x (called x bar). The sum of observations is Σx, where Σ means the sum of and is represented by the Greek capital letter sigma and x is an observation or value in the sample. The number of observations in the sample is denoted as n. Thus, the formula for the mean is:

$$x = \frac{\Sigma x}{n}$$

For an example, consider the information in Table 7.9.

Table 7.9   Data for the mean

Destination	Number of ski resorts
Austria	432
Bulgaria	20
France	254
Germany	288
Italy	288
Norway	109
Switzerland	337

By applying the formula for the mean to these data, we find that:

$$n = 7$$

$$\Sigma x = 1728$$

and therefore:

$$x = \frac{1728}{7}$$

$$= 247 \text{ resorts (rounded up)}$$

This tells us that the mean number of ski resorts per country is 247. Whilst the mean is an accurate and useful measure of central tendency, you should remember that it can be affected by extreme values in a data set. In this example, it can be seen that the values for France, Germany and Italy are close to the mean, yet Bulgaria and Austria are far from it. The effect of extreme values on the mean is particularly pronounced where the data set contains very few values.

Median

The median of a sample of observations is the value of the middle item when the sample is arranged in rank order. Thus, for the same example, if the number of hotels in each country is placed in rank order, we find:

20, 109, 254, 288, 288, 337, 432

The midpoint of the 7 values is the fourth, making the median value 288. If there were an even number of observations in the data set, the median would be the midpoint between the two middle values. The main disadvantage of the median is that equal weight is given to each observation in the data set, regardless of its value.

Mode

The mode of a sample of observations is the value which occurs most often. It should be remembered that a data set may have more than one mode. When a data set has one mode, the distribution of values can be referred to as *unimodal*, whereas if two modes are present the distribution is said to be *bimodal*. In the case of this data set, there is no mode as each value is different. The mode in this case also happens to be the same as the mean, as there are two countries with 288 ski resorts.

7.4.2 Normal distribution

If the mean, median and mode are calculated for a data set and found to be exactly the same value, then the distribution is said to be *normal*. If the values for the data set are plotted on a graph, then the results will be a smooth, symmetrical bell-shaped curve.

If, however, where the mode was a value which was less than the median and mean, then the frequency curve plotted on a graph would have a *negative skew*. Similarly, if the mode was a greater value than the median, which in turn was greater than the mean, then the distribution would have a *positive skew*.

7.4.3 Measures of dispersion

The range

The range of a data set is the difference between the highest and lowest values. For example, in a survey the age of each respondent is recorded in years, as follows:

34, 24, 27, 30, 40, 20, 41, 44, 45, 21, 36, 39

It can be seen that the oldest person is aged 45 and the youngest is 20. Hence, the range is 25 years. Whilst the range is a straightforward way of describing the scatter of values in a data set, it uses the extreme values and therefore the rest of the values are ignored.

The interquartile range

As the name suggests, the interquartile range involves dividing a data set into quarters. After organising the data set into rank order, the first quarter or quartile would come 25% from the beginning. This is called the *lower quartile*. The second quartile would come half way along the data set at the midpoint or median. The next quartile would come at the 75% mark and this is known as the *upper quartile*. The interquartile range is the difference between the upper quartile and the lower quartile, and is therefore concerned with the middle 50% of values within a data set. Hence, for the same data set as used before, to find out the interquartile range we must first arrange the data set in rank order:

20, 21, 24, 27, 30, 34, 36, 39, 40, 41, 44, 45

From the previous section, we can find the median, or middle number. As there are 12 values, the middle value falls between the 6th and 7th, i.e. between 34 and 36, thus the median is 35. To work out the interquartile range, we know that there will be three values in each quartile. The lower quartile will fall between the 3rd and 4th value, i.e. between 24 and 27, and the midpoint between these two values is 25.5. Similarly, the upper quartile, between the 9th and 10th values, 40 and 41, is 40.5.

Thus, in the example the interquartile range is:

$$40.5 - 25.5 = 15$$

The value of the interquartile range is based on the fact that it avoids the influence of any extreme values in a data set, which could be confusing when the range is reported.

Standard deviation

This measure investigates the spread of data in relation to the mean of the data set. Thus, the standard deviation is calculated on determining the average distance of values from the mean.

$$sd = \sqrt{\sum \frac{\left(x - \bar{x}\right)^2}{n}}$$

Where: x = data

$\bar{x}$ = mean

n = number of values in the data set

If the standard deviation is large, then this indicates that there is a greater variability in the data set. The formula for simple, numerical data is as follows:

Example

A sample of ten tourists was asked to indicate how much they had spent on their lunch during a day trip. The amounts were rounded to the nearest pound, as follows:

$$4, 6, 7, 7, 5, 8, 12, 15, 14, 12$$

To calculate the standard deviation (or sigma), you take the following steps.

1. First, calculate the mean:

$$\frac{\sum x}{n} = \frac{90}{10} = £9$$

2. Now construct a table (see Table 7.10).

Table 7.10   Calculating standard deviation

x	$(x-\bar{x})$	$(x-\bar{x})^2$
4	−5	25
6	−3	9
7	−2	4
7	−2	4
5	−4	16
8	−1	1
12	3	9
15	6	36
14	5	25
12	3	9
	$\Sigma(x-\bar{x})^2 \sqrt{}$	138

$$sd = \sqrt{\frac{\Sigma f.x^2}{\Sigma f} - \left(\frac{\Sigma fx}{\Sigma f}\right)^2}$$

Where:

f = the frequency or number of items in a category

x = the midpoint of a category

3. From the table, find the deviations from the mean for each value of x.
4. Square the deviation from the mean for each value of x.
5. Total the squared deviations, i.e. $\Sigma(x-\bar{x})^2$.
6. Now apply the formula:

$$= \sqrt{\frac{138}{10}}$$

$$= \sqrt{13.8}$$

$$= \pounds 3.71$$

When dealing with categorical data which is presented grouped, the formula for standard deviation is:

$$sd = \sqrt{\frac{\Sigma f.x^2}{\Sigma f} - \left(\frac{\Sigma fx}{\Sigma f}\right)^2}$$

Where:

f = the frequency or number of items in a category

x = the midpoint of a category

For example, a survey is carried out to find out how far tourists travelled to an historic building from their accommodation. The result for this question is as seen in Table 7.11.

Table 7.11 **Results of survey to find out how far tourists travelled to an historic building from their accommodation**

Distance category	Number of respondents
Under 10 miles	5
10 but under 20 miles	24
20 but under 30 miles	35
30 but under 40 miles	31
40 but under 50 miles	23
50 but under 70 miles	8
70 but under 100 miles	5
100 but under 150 miles	3
150 miles or more	1

Notice the categories are not all equal in size. Now construct a table (see Table 7.12) and then apply the formula:

Table 7.12 **Calculating standard deviation for categorical data**

Category	x	f	fx	f.x²
Under 10 miles	5	5	25	125
10 but under 20 miles	15	24	360	5400
20 but under 30 miles	25	35	875	21875
30 but under 40 miles	35	31	1085	37975
40 but under 50 miles	45	23	1035	46575
50 but under 70 miles	60	8	480	28800
70 but under 100 miles	85	5	425	36125
100 but under 150 miles	125	3	375	46875
150 miles or more*	175	1	175	30625
*upper limit assumed to be 200	Σ	135	4835	254375

$$Sd = \sqrt{\frac{254375}{135} - \left(\frac{4835}{135}\right)^2}$$

$$= \sqrt{1884.3 - (35.8)^2}$$

$$= \sqrt{1884.3 - 1281.6}$$

$$= \sqrt{602.7}$$

$$= 24.6 \, miles$$

Illustration 7.9   Descriptive tests in SPSS

Although it is necessary to understand how the described tests work and have the ability to perform these by hand, it is often helpful to use statistics software to perform such tests, particularly with a large data set.

Descriptive tests can be found through the analyse menu, following descriptive

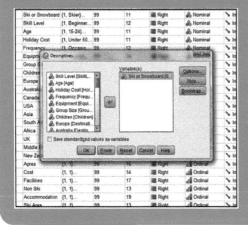

statistics and finally selecting descriptives.

The descriptives window will appear. Select the relevant variables from the list on the left and then select the options button on the right.

The descriptives procedure displays univariate summary statistics for several variables in a single table. Variables can be ordered by the size of their means (in ascending or descending order), alphabetically, or by the order in which you select the variables (the default).

The statistics available are: sample size, mean, minimum, maximum, standard deviation, variance, range, sum, standard error of the mean, and kurtosis and skewness with their standard errors. You will need to think of the type of data you have for a variable as to whether this procedure is appropriate or not.

Illustration 7.10   Cross-tabulation in SPSS

In many instances, when you are analysing data, you will want to study the relationship between two or more variables. In most cases this scenario is likely to be where the data is 'categorical' and has a small number of values. In this situation, you can use a 'crosstabulation' – a table that contains counts of the number of times various combinations of values of two variables occur. In some of the literature you may come across crosstabulation tables may also be referred to as contingency tables. Sometimes crosstabulations or crosstabs are a useful command to perform when checking your data to ensure consistency in the data.

(Continued)

(Continued)

Crosstabs are reasonably straightforward to carry out. From the menu bar select analyze, then select descriptive statistics, finally select crosstabs. This will bring up the crosstabs dialogue box.

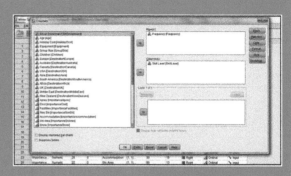

Select the first variable that you want to compare, then using the arrow, move it into the row(s) box. Now select the second variable from the list and click across to the column(s) box, then click ok. SPSS will now compute the analysis and show the crosstabs table in the output window.

Analyse the table to identify any trends within the data.

Frequency * Skill Level Crosstabulation

Count

		Skill Level			Total
		Beginner	Intermediate	Advanced	
Frequency	Occasional	8	29	7	44
	Annual	8	175	84	267
	Multiple	6	186	262	454
	Lifestyle	2	6	55	63
Total		24	396	408	828

7.5 Analysing quantitative data

7.5.1 Overview

In the previous section, we referred to the expression 'normal distribution' where the mean, median and mode of a data set occupied the same value. If the distribution for a data set is normal, then the laws of probability are such that:

- about 68% of all observations will fall between the mean and 1 standard deviation
- about 95% of all observations will fall between the mean and 2 standard deviations
- about 99% of all observations will fall between the mean and 3 standard deviations.

You may be wondering what in real life is a normal distribution and how you would know if your data set was one. When very large surveys are undertaken of the general public, variables such as age, height and weight are considered to be normally distributed, thus over 99% of all answers or observations will fall within 3 standard deviations of the mean. If you can assume that your data set is normally distributed (for example, instructing the computer to graphically represent the distribution and noting that it is a smooth, symmetrical bell shape), then this has an implication for the nature of analytical statistical techniques you can perform on the data. When it comes to analytical techniques, there is a broad twofold distinction:

Parametric statistics: This assumes that the sample data set has a normal distribution. Often, these tests will use the mean and standard deviation and involve cardinal (numerical) data.

Non-parametric statistics: These tests do not assume that the data set approximates a normal distribution and are therefore more common in the analysis of market research information. Often, the data can be in the form of categories or ranks.

7.5.2 Hypothesis testing

In the statistical analysis of market research information, we are often concerned with comparing whether a particular variable, such as income, for example, has any influence on another variable, such as type of holiday purchased. When results of a statistical test to determine the influence of a variable in this way are produced, we are often required to indicate whether the differences found are sufficiently large to state that, say, income level has a significant bearing on holiday type. Before learning how to undertake such a statistical test, it is important to express the question which lies behind the analysis in the correct way.

Statisticians do this by stating what is called a *hypothesis*. It is convention to be cautious when writing statements and therefore it is normal at the beginning of any statistical test to state what is termed the *null hypothesis*. This assumes that there is no difference, association or relationship between the two variables or samples in the analysis. Thus, before investigating the effect of income on holiday type we would start by expressing a null hypothesis, namely:

There is no significant relationship/difference/association between a respondent's income and the type of holiday which is chosen.

This gives the researcher a context with which to apply the test, after which the null hypothesis can be accepted or rejected.

7.5.3 Levels of significance

If we are in a position to reject a null hypothesis, we are indicating that there are significant differences between the two variables or samples we are testing. The immediate question which follows this is 'how big does the difference have to be before it becomes significant?' In a sense, deciding on a 'cut-off' point may seem rather arbitrary, like asking 'how far does a tourist have to travel to say they have been "far away"?' In statistical analysis, there are, conventionally, two cut-off points. These are the 5% level and the 1% level (often referred to as the 0.05 level and the 0.01 level).

What this means is that at the 0.05 level we are indicating that we are 95% confident that there is a significant difference and there is a 5% probability that the result has occurred by random chance. Consequently, the 0.01 level is more stringent. Here we are 99% confident of a significant difference and there is a 1% probability that the result has occurred by chance.

When carrying out statistical tests to measure the difference between two variables or samples, it is important to decide at what level to accept or reject a null hypothesis. Sometimes a difference that is significant at the 0.05 level is said to be 'significant', whilst at the 0.01 level 'highly significant'. Such words may add very little to the actual figures but may make the researcher feel more confident in reporting the results.

In carrying out analytical statistics, it should be remembered that:

- the tests should have been previously specified and must relate to the objectives of the research
- a null hypothesis is written prior to each test
- an appropriate level of significance is determined prior to each test.

It is now possible to review some of the commonly used statistical methods in the analysis of survey data.

7.5.4 Useful quantitative tests

When planning a research project, it is necessary to have a clear idea of the type of statistical test that will be used to analyse the data. Some tests require that data are collected in a specific format or that a certain type of data is collected. This section will introduce a number of useful statistical tests and identify when they might be used, before demonstrating how to perform two of those listed, step by step (Table 7.13).

Table 7.13   Useful tests

Statistical test	When the test is useful
Spearman's Rank Correlation Coefficient	Spearman's rank measures the strength and direction of an association between two ranked variables. In order to use this test, ordinal data is needed and use of a larger sample will increase reliability. Again, Spearman's rank is commonly used in hypothesis testing.
Chi-square test	Chi-square tests are used to identify significant relationships between categories of data. A null hypothesis is formed as to the existence of a relationship between two variables and Chi-square can be used to prove or disprove this null hypothesis. The test examines the extent to which correlation in the data has occurred by chance. In order to use Chi-squared effectively, a larger sample size is required.
Pearson's Correlation Coefficient	Often used after the Chi-square test to establish the strength of the relationship identified by the Chi-square test. In addition to the strength of the relationship, it can be used to identify the direction of the relationship, that is, if it is positively or negatively correlated.
Multiple regression analysis	Multiple regression analysis allows the effects of multiple independent variables on a dependent variable to be examined. It is often used in forecasting. Multiple regression analysis not only identifies the correlation between the independent variables and the dependent variable, but also identifies the correlations between the independent variables. Again, the direction of the correlation can be identified. The dependent variable needs to be measured on a continuous scale so cardinal data must be used; the independent variables can be ordinal, nominal or cardinal.
t-tests	t-tests are used to identify when two groups differ from one another with regards to an ordinal variable. They can be useful in comparing perception of different groups. The t-test examines the difference in the mean of the two categories to ascertain if it is significantly different. T-test can be used to prove or disprove hypotheses/assumptions made about two groups. In order for this test to be successful, data for the dependent variable must be cardinal, while the independent variable uses categorical or ordinal data.
Mann-Whitney U test	The Mann-Whitney U test is a non-parametric test that is often used instead of a t-test. A non-parametric test can still be used to test hypotheses yet it does not require the distribution of results to be normal, unlike the t-test, so it is useful when data do not show normal distribution. The Mann-Whitney U test is used to compare the distribution of two samples, yet, rather than testing the mean, it tests the median of the two groups. Like the t-test, in order for this test to be successful data for the dependent variable must be cardinal, while the independent variable uses categorical or ordinal data.
ANOVA	Analysis of variance (ANOVA) tests are similar to t-tests in the sense that they identify variance between the mean of different groups. While t-tests identify variance between two groups, ANOVA is used when there are more than two groups. Again, categorical and ordinal data are tested, however ANOVA tests require a larger sample, as more groups are being tested, in order to be reliable.

Two tests have been selected for illustrative purposes here. These are:

- Spearman's Rank Correlation Coefficient
- the Chi-square test.

These tests are both non-parametric, thus assumptions about the data set relating to a normal distribution are not necessary. These tests are also very relevant to the analysis of questions from survey data. Whilst statistical computer software packages can easily perform these tests, undertaking them with a calculator is feasible and should not be ruled out for small samples.

Spearman's Rank Correlation Coefficient

This test is used to describe the relationship in ordinal (ranked) characteristics. This can be useful where it is difficult to measure a particular characteristic and ranking the data can overcome the problem. For example, a tour operator sells eight different holiday programmes (family holidays, young adult, retired, winter sports, etc.). These holidays are sold in the UK and Germany, as shown in Table 7.14.

Table 7.14   Sales of different holidays in the UK and Germany

Holiday type	UK (£) (000)	Germany (€) (000)
1	15,004	38,424
2	22,483	25,500
3	7,896	12,986
4	14,283	44,824
5	78,975	93,611
6	3,242	3,100
7	28,227	13,819
8	4,591	2,986

Because of exchange rates changing over a season, together with the different size of each market, it is difficult to compare the relative value of the information. However, in comparing the popularity of each holiday type in the two countries, one way of simplifying the information would be to rank it, as shown in Table 7.15.

Table 7.15   **Rankings of holidays sold in the UK and Germany by holiday type**

Holiday type	Rank in the UK	Rank in Germany
1	4	3
2	3	4
3	6	6
4	5	2
5	1	1
6	8	7
7	2	5
8	7	8

Here the holiday types have been ranked by the value in each country. To test whether there is a statistical association between the sets of rankings, we can apply the Spearman's Rank Correlation Coefficient, explained in the following stages:

Stage 1: Determining a null hypothesis and the significance level

Null hypothesis – there is no association between the rankings of the holidays sold in the UK and Germany. This is to be tested at the 0.05 level.

Stage 2: Calculating the differences between the ranks, squaring them and summing the total

Table 7.16   **Calculating differences in the rankings**

Holiday type	Rank in the UK	Rank in Germany	Difference (d)	d²
1	4	3	1	1
2	3	4	−1	1
3	6	6	0	0

(Continued)

Table 7.16   (Continued)

Holiday type	Rank in the UK	Rank in Germany	Difference (d)	d²
4	5	2	3	9
5	1	1	0	0
6	8	7	1	1
7	2	5	−3	9
8	7	8	−1	1
				$\Sigma = 22$

Stage 3: Applying the formula

The formula for Spearman's Rank Correlation Coefficient (r_s) is:

$$r_s = 1 - \left[6\Sigma d^2 / n(n^2 - 1) \right]$$

Where: n = number of ranks

In our example, this gives:

$$r_s = 1 - 6 \times 22 / 8 \left(8\sqrt[2]{-1} \right)$$
$$= 1 - 132 / 8 \times 63$$
$$= 1 - 132 / 504$$
$$= 1 - 0.26$$
$$r_s = 0.74$$

The formula will always produce a figure for r_s which lies between +1 and −1. If the value of r_s is very close to +1 then the two countries will have similar ranks (be positively correlated), and if the value of r_s is −1 they will have opposite ranks (negative correlation). A value of 0 represents no statistical correlation. However, as in this case, achieving extreme values is quite rare. As a general rule, if the value of r_s lies between −0.5 and +0.5 you can accept the null hypothesis and indicate that there is no statistical association (unless you have in excess of 15 ranks). Values greater or less than this may indicate some degree of statistical significance and tables are again needed to determine the acceptance or rejection of the null hypothesis.

Stage 4: The test statistic is compared against probability tables for Spearman's Rank Correlation Coefficient

Appropriate tables are shown in Table 7.17.

Table 7.17   Spearman's Rank Correlation Coefficient probability tables

| n | Probability level | |
Where n = number of ranks	0.05	0.01
4	1.000	–
5	0.999	1.000
6	0.829	0.943
7	0.714	0.893
8	0.643	0.833
9	0.600	0.783
10	0.564	0.746
12	0.504	0.701
14	0.456	0.645
16	0.425	0.601
18	0.399	0.564
20	0.377	0.534
22	0.359	0.508
24	0.343	0.485
26	0.329	0.465
28	0.317	0.448
30	0.306	0.432

Hence, we see that at the 0.05 level with 8 ranks, a test statistic of 0.74 exceeds the table value of 0.643.

Stage 5: The null hypothesis is accepted or rejected and an inference is made from the result

At the 0.05 level, we can reject the null hypothesis and indicate that the rankings for the UK and Germany are associated. The inference from this would be that the popular holiday products sold in the UK are similarly popular in Germany. Note, however, that had a higher significance level been set, this would not be the case, as the data show that there are some differences.

The Chi-square test

Suppose that in a survey we found the results seen in Tables 7.18 and 7.19.

Table 7.18   Skill level of skiers and snowboarders

Skill level	Number of respondents
Beginner	24
Intermediate	398
Advanced	408
Sub-total	*830*
Missing	99
Total	921

Table 7.19   Frequency of trips to participate in winter sports

Frequency of trips	Number of respondents
Occasional	52
Annual	296
Multiple	500
Lifestyle	70
Sub-total	*918*
Missing	3
Total	921

Next, it is common to *cross-tabulate* the answers to the two questions. What this involves is showing how frequently beginner, intermediate or advanced skiers or snowboarders participate in winter sports trips. The result of this is shown in Table 7.20.

Table 7.20   Cross-tabulating how frequently beginner, intermediate or advanced skiers or snowboarders participate in winter sports trips

Count		Beginner	Intermediate	Advanced	Total
		Skill Level			
Frequency	Occasional	8	29	7	44
	Annual	8	175	84	267
	Multiple	6	186	262	454
	Lifestyle	2	6	55	63
Total		24	396	408	828

Table 7.20 shows that of the 63 people that made winter sports a lifestyle, 55 of them were advanced skiers or snowboarders. Of the 44 who participated occasionally, only 7 were advanced skiers or snowboarders. The cross-tabulation table itself gives some indication of a relationship in that it appears that the higher the skill level, the more frequent the participation. However, there are more intermediate and advanced respondents than beginners, so is there a significant relationship? This is where the Chi-square test is valuable, and it is carried out in several stages.

Stage 1: An assertion is made

By examining the frequency tables of 'observed' values in the survey, an assertion can be made. For example, from the observed values we can see that there is a divide between advanced and beginner skiers and snowboarders. Similarly, we can ascertain that the frequency of trips ranges from occasional to those that have made skiing a lifestyle. Therefore, we may assert that the skill level of the respondent (independent variable) may have an effect on the rating of the frequency of trips (dependent variable).

Stage 2: The assertion is converted into the form of a null hypothesis and the required level of significance determined

The assertion is converted into the form of a null hypothesis; the null hypothesis for this example would be:

There is no association between the skill level respondent and the frequency they participate in winter sports.

When carrying out statistical tests to measure the difference between two variables or samples, it is important to decide at what level to accept or reject a null hypothesis. The 0.01 level is determined as suitable for this test, being sufficiently stringent to be confident.

Stage 3: The information is arranged in the form of a cross-tabulation table and the column and row totals noted

Doing this by hand takes a long time! Basically, it would involve making two piles of questionnaires – one for males and one for females. Each of these is sub-divided by the scores for the rating question. Producing a crosstab using statistics software is much more efficient (see Table 7.20).

Stage 4: The frequencies expected by chance are calculated for each cell of the table

This assumes what the frequency for each cell would be if there were no association between the two questions, i.e. that they were independent of each other. To calculate the expected values for each specific cell, you must multiply that cell's row total by its column total and divide by the grand total (that is, the total number of people interviewed or sample size). Thus:

$$\text{Expected value} = \frac{\text{Row total} \times \text{Column total}}{\text{Grand total}}$$

Table 7.21 shows the result of this exercise. Note that there is slightly different terminology used in different texts (probably deliberate on the part of statisticians to confuse others). Some refer to the frequency you found in your survey as the 'count' or 'observed value' and the frequency you might expect to find as the 'expected value' or 'expected count'. To get your head round the logic of this, consider the crosstab in Table 7.21.

Table 7.21   **Stage 4 exercise result 1**

	Female	Male	
Yes	5	45	50
No	45	5	50
Total	50	50	100

In this survey of 100, there were 50 males and 50 females, where 5 females said yes and 45 said no, 45 males said yes and 5 said no. If there were no differences between males and females, we would expect to find 25 responses in each category, as shown in brackets below. If you multiply the row total by the column total ($50 \times 50 = 2500$) and divide by the number in the survey (100), then the answer is 25.

Table 7.22   **Stage 4 exercise result 2**

	Female	Male	
Yes	5 (25)	45 (25)	50
No	45 (25)	5 (25)	50
Total	50	50	100

Coming back to our worked example, using the formula, Tables 7.23 and 7.24 are produced.

Table 7.23   **Cross-tabulation of skill level and frequency of trips**

	Skill level			
Frequency of trips	Beginner	Intermediate	Advanced	Total
Occasional	8	29	7	44
Annual	8	175	84	267
Multiple	6	186	262	454
Lifestyle	2	6	55	63
Total	24	396	408	828

Table 7.24   Cross-tabulation of skill level and frequency of trips 2

| | | | Skill level | | | |
			Beginner	Intermediate	Advanced	Total
Frequency	Occasional	Count	8	29	7	44
		Expected count	1.3	21.0	21.7	44.0
	Annual	Count	8	175	84	267
		Expected count	7.7	127.7	131.6	267.0
	Multiple	Count	6	186	262	454
		Expected count	13.2	217.1	223.7	454.0
	Lifestyle	Count	2	6	55	63
		Expected count	1.8	30.1	31.0	63.0
Total		Count	24	396	408	828
		Expected count	24.0	396.0	408.0	828.0

Stage 5: Applying the Chi-square test using the formula

The formula for Chi-square is as follows:

$$\chi^2 = \Sigma \frac{(O-E)^2}{E}$$

Where

O = the observed value

E = the expected value

Breaking down the formula, we can use a table (Table 7.25) to work out the different stages of Chi-square.

Table 7.25   Calculating Chi-square

O	E	O – E	$(O - E)^2$	$(O - E)^2 \div E$
8	1.3	6.7	44.90	34.54
8	7.7	0.3	0.09	0.01
6	13.2	−7.2	51.84	3.93

O	E	O – E	(O – E)²	(O – E)² ÷ E
2	1.8	0.2	0.04	0.02
29	21.0	8	64	3.05
175	127.7	47.3	2237.29	17.52
186	217.1	–31.1	967.21	4.46
6	30.1	–24.1	580.81	19.30
7	21.7	–14.7	216.09	9.96
84	131.6	–47.6	2265.76	17.23
262	223.7	38.3	1466.89	6.56
55	31.0	24	576	18.58
			Σ	135.16

Thus, the Chi-square statistic is 135.16.

Stage 6: Calculating the degrees of freedom

The degrees of freedom give some meaning to the test statistic. In this case, it relates to the number of items in the sample upon which the test was based; in this example, there were four rows and three columns. The degrees of freedom are given by:

$$df = (r - 1) \times (c - 1)$$

Where: r = the number of rows

                                    c = the number of columns

In this example: $df = (4 - 1) \times (3 - 1)$

                                    $= 3 \times 2$

                                    $= 6$

When doing the Chi-square test by hand, the test statistic must be applied to a set of appropriate Chi-square probability tables for the given degrees of freedom. Table 7.26 can be found in many statistical texts.

   In this example, the table value for 6 degrees of freedom is 12.6 at the 0.05 level, and 16.8 at the 0.01 level. Taking a significance level of 0.01, the value of 16.8 is taken.

Table 7.26   Percentage points of the Chi-square distribution

Degrees of freedom	Probability level	
	0.05	0.01
1	3.84	6.63
2	5.99	9.21
3	7.81	11.3
4	9.49	13.3
5	11.1	15.1
6	12.6	16.8
7	14.1	18.5
8	15.5	20.3
9	16.9	21.7
10	18.3	23.2
12	21.0	26.2
14	23.7	29.1
16	26.3	32.0
18	28.9	34.8
20	31.4	37.6

Stage 7: The null hypothesis is either accepted or rejected depending on the required level of significance

In this example, the Chi-square statistic of 135.16 is more than the value in the table (13.3); therefore, we can reject the null hypothesis and conclude that the differences between the scores of males and females are statistically significant. Thus, we are 99.9% confident that there is some association between the skill level of the respondent and the frequency they participate in winter sports, and acknowledge that there is a 0.1% probability that this result has occurred by chance. If the Chi-square value had been less than the value in the table for the given significance level and degrees of freedom, we would have accepted the null hypothesis.

Stage 8: Explaining the findings

Having rejected the null hypothesis, we are now indicating that there is an association between the skill level of the respondent and the frequency they participate in winter sports, but the Chi-square test does not tell us what the association is. This we must infer. The easiest way to do this is to return to the table where the observed values in the survey were set against the expected values if no association was apparent (Table 7.26) and note where there are large differences in the cells.

Here we see that more than expected advanced-level skiers and snowboarders took multiple holidays or made winter sports their lifestyle, whilst fewer than expected participated occasionally or just once a year. More than expected beginners and intermediate-level skiers and snowboarders, however, participated occasionally and annually. Thus, we can infer that the higher the skill level, the more frequently respondents are likely to participate in winter sports.

Whilst Chi-square is a valuable and useful analytical technique in market research, there are some conditions which affect its validity. The principal problem with Chi-square is where the cross-tabulation has a large number of rows and columns but the sample size is small. When this happens, there may be many cells which are empty or have very low observed values and expected frequencies. This can severely weaken the test. As a general rule, you should not use the Chi-square test if more than 20% of the cells have expected frequencies of less than 5 and if any of the cells have an expected frequency of less than 1. If this is the case, you should consider combining categories together to reduce the size of the cross-tabulation table, but only if there is a rationale for doing so. For example, excellent and good could be combined as could poor and very poor, reducing the rows from 5 to 3. However, putting together males and females into one category would defeat the object of the test and be without logic.

On this latter point, it can be seen that sample size influences whether a test such as Chi-square is suitable or not. Where you anticipate using Chi-square, the requirements of the test may help you to judge the overall sample size of a survey in the planning stages (see Chapter 4).

Illustration 7.11   Chi-square test using SPSS

While I hope you can follow the logic of doing this by hand, it is a long-winded affair, and SPSS does it for you in a fraction of a second. Begin by opening the crosstabs menu as previously illustrated.

Select the dependent variable and move it into the rows dialogue box, select the

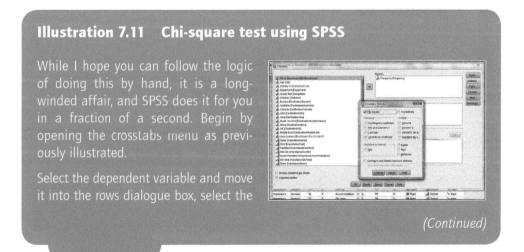

(Continued)

(Continued)

independent variable and move it into the columns dialogue box. Select statistics, select Chi-square.

Back in the crosstabs dialogue box select the cells button, check both observed and expected, click continue. Click ok and the crosstab will appear in outputs window with a chi-square output.

The chi-square output table shows the chi-squared score to be 135.87, degrees of freedom as 6 and significance as 0.000

Chi-Square Tests

	Value	df	Asymp. Sig. (2-sided)
Pearson Chi-Square	135.877[a]	6	.000
Likelihood Ratio	127.311	6	.000
Linear-by-Linear Association	105.802	1	.000
N of Valid Cases	828		

a. 2 cells (16.7%) have expected count less than 5. The minimum expected count is 1.28.

In this example, if we were to use the table values (see above) for 6 degrees of freedom, you will recall that the value is 12.6 at the 0.05 level, and 16.8 at the 0.01 level. Our Chi-square statistic of 135.87 is greater than both; hence we can reject the null hypothesis (there is no association between skill level and frequency). This meant that we could be 99% sure that there was an association between skill level and frequency of participation (acknowledging that there was a 1% probability that this result has occurred by chance).

However, when working with SPSS, there is no need to use probability tables as the SPSS output provides the significance level for us. The top right-hand box indicates this. If this value is less than 0.05, we can reject the null hypothesis at the 95% level and if it is less than 0.01, we can reject the null hypothesis at the 99% level. Here, with a significance value of 0.000, we can be 99.999% certain that there is an association between the variables.

Even when using SPSS, this value does not tell you what the association between the variables is, so having rejected the null hypothesis you must then consider what the association is and make a statement. As previously mentioned, where you have large differences between the count and the expected count in your crosstabs table you are more likely to find an association. This final statement is absolutely vital; otherwise there seems little point in doing the statistics. The Chi-square test doesn't tell you what the association is, rather that there is a probability that there is an association. The final inference or explanation you must work out for yourself.

7.6 Summary

This chapter has attempted to convey some principal issues which the researcher faces when dealing with quantitative data. This chapter has also introduced a basic guide to using IBM SPSS 22.0 to analyse quantitative data. Some of the statistical vocabulary has been presented and the need for careful prior planning has been stressed. It was not intended that this chapter should be a shortened statistical text or guide to statistics software, as that is better dealt with elsewhere and requires formal training. However, the information provided should enable you to be more informed and more critical of the data presented to you.

Exercises

1. Outline the differences between categorical, ordinal and cardinal data. Give examples of each form.
2. Explain what is meant by the terms variable, value, case, independent and dependent variable.
3. When using a frequency table, assess when it would be more appropriate to use the valid percentage or cumulative percentage to explain a result.
4. Determine when it is more appropriate to use a histogram rather than a bar chart.
5. Define the terms mean, median and mode.
6. Discuss the principal difference in the assumptions of parametric statistics and non-parametric statistics.
7. Explain when it would be appropriate to use Chi-square tests.

Further reading

Pallant, J. (2016). *SPSS Survival Manual.* 6th edition. Maidenhead: McGraw-Hill Education.
The sixth edition of this book provides an easy-to-follow guide to using SPSS for both basic and advanced statistical techniques.

8

ANALYSING THE DATA: A QUALITATIVE APPROACH

LEARNING OBJECTIVES

From reading this chapter, you should be able to:

- recognise the different approaches to reading and interpreting qualitative data
- understand some basic principles and techniques of qualitative data analysis
- apply the process of thematic analysis to qualitative data sources.

8.1 Overview

Unlike quantitative analysis, where there are tried-and-tested techniques of data analysis, qualitative methods of analysis are not so clear cut. It is not possible to state that under certain circumstances the 'such and such' test should be used. There are no clearly agreed qualitative rules or procedures to follow. This may well leave you unsure of whether your attempt to categorise the transcript from an interview, for example, is appropriate. What is called for here, instead of one specific test, is creativity on behalf of the researcher, with the ability to systematically search for answers. Or, as Ritchie and colleagues (2014: 270) put it, the researcher requires a 'blend of inspiration and diligent detection' when dealing with qualitative data.

The original purpose of the qualitative research, stated by the researcher when planning a project, is instrumental in determining how the data itself should be analysed. Qualitative research, as mentioned in Chapter 2, is sometimes used to explore a particular topic and inform the design of a quantitative inquiry (i.e. triangulation). In these circumstances, detailed notes which the researcher makes from the experience of conducting lengthy interviews and focus groups (Chapter 6) may be sufficient to help in the construction of a structured questionnaire (Chapter 5) for pilot testing. However, to consider qualitative research as being solely for this exploratory function is to miss the point and value of the approach. Qualitative research has a deeper and more profound place in contemporary research. It can offer insight into and interpretation of a social phenomenon, and it can act as a tool to 'tell a story' (Fox et al., 2014: 169). Qualitative data enables exploration within the social sciences; it allows a researcher to uncover insights and information about people. After all, research within the THE industry is about people, as a component of the social phenomenon and the world as it exists. But this should not be the first time you have considered the role of qualitative research. Your decision about qualitative research did not start here. It started back in Chapter 2 and will continue throughout your knowledge generation until you complete the final write-up in Chapter 9.

Analysis is inherent in the start to the end of a qualitative enquiry (Ritchie et al., 2014). After all, you have already decided to conduct qualitative research (Chapter 2). You have identified your ontological and epistemological position and you have outlined a clear rationale for your investigation (Chapter 2). You have identified your data sources and the methods for generating data from them. You have planned your project (Chapter 3), identified a suitable sample and sampling strategy (Chapter 4) and decided on the most suitable technique for undertaking and recording data (Chapter 6). All you need to know now is *how* to make sense of and analyse the data. It is only now that you need to know how to process the information, the data and your newfound understanding; and this is what the chapter is designed to help you with. However, this does not mean that you should wait until you have collected data to read this chapter! This chapter should be read prior to undertaking data collection, because you need to determine if there are any specific requirements of the selected analysis tool that has a bearing on your actual data collection process (Chapter 3 on planning a project – ring any bells?). Otherwise, you may find that your data cannot be analysed in what you deem to be a suitable manner.

Planning is crucial to any project and, therefore, throughout this chapter, it is important to remember that you should still be designing your project – not just looking for a quick fix analysis method. This is because there is no such thing as a quick fix in qualitative analysis. It is at this stage that the hard work begins. You may find the transcription process time and resource intensive, and the analysis stage confusing and overly subjective. Therefore, it is important that you remember the purpose of the underpinning project and that you allow the analysis process to be directed by the aim and objectives of the research itself. Whilst this may seem an obvious and unnecessary statement to make, a particular feature of qualitative data is the huge amounts of paper, words, recordings and time that it takes to get to the analysis stage; and that enables the researcher to become easily side-tracked!

To keep you on track, there is a series of questions that need to be asked and decisions which need to be made, prior to data collection, based on your stated research POEM. As stated by Fox et al. (2014), you need to decide on:

- *The degree of subjectivity* you are consciously basing your interpretation on (Chapter 2). In Chapter 2, we discussed the need to strike a balance between subjectivity and objectivity (your personal opinions and your detachment from the subject matter). The degree of subjectivity is important to establish because even though it is assumed by this stage that you followed the principles of the interpretivism paradigm that led you to qualitative methods, there are different levels of subjectivity to consider (see section 2.2.2). You need to be clear about the role that you, as a researcher, play as a source of data, and, inevitably, about the advantages and limitations (e.g. bias) of this.
- *The level, degree and nature of transcription* you are applying to the data itself (Chapter 6). There are many ways in which data from an interview or a focus group, for example, can be transcribed. It can be transcribed verbatim (word for word) with the inclusion or exclusion of verbal tics and social talk (Savin-Baden and Howell Major, 2013). Some transcripts will therefore only contain the words spoken, whilst others will include additional aspects that correspond to tone, pitch and non-verbal cues, which the researcher determines as being an element of importance when it comes to data interpretation (section 8.2.3).
- *The form of coding* that you will employ within the analysis stage also needs to be identified. There is not one single agreed process as to how data can be 'coded'. Neither is there agreement about the use of and implications for the terminology that can be utilised to describe the process of categorisation. Whether it is labels, codes, categorisations or theming, you utilise a process that is systematic and reflective of the data that is presented (see section 8.2.1).

To help you with the decision making at this stage, the chapter is designed to remind you about key terminology and open up the possibilities for managing and exploring data. Consequently, the chapter is split into two distinct sections:

1. *Recognising data and making decisions about how data are read*: this section (8.2) will give you an overview as to how data can be recognised and read. The purpose here is to illustrate the various ways data can be acknowledged, and how you can describe and then interpret data to create your coding scheme, which will then be put into practice in the second section.
2. *Analysing qualitative data*: this section (8.3) is designed to showcase two tools that you can use for qualitative data analysis to complete a thematic analysis of the written word. The section will also review additional processes of analysis, which do not necessarily conform to the process of thematic analysis, just to give you an alternative approach if you are not considering undertaking a substantive interpretation of the data.

8.2 Recognising and reading qualitative data

The process of recognising data should have been happening since the research POEM was established in Chapter 2. This is the process by which you identify your data sources, the phenomena from or through which you believe data can be generated (Mason, 2002). A list of potential data sources, the most commonly used data sources in qualitative research (Mason, 2002), is reviewed in Table 8.1.

Table 8.1   Identifying potential data sources

Data sources

- People (as individuals, groups or collectives)
- Organisations, institutions and entities
- Texts (published and unpublished sources including virtual ones)
- Settings and environments (material, visual/sensory and virtual)
- Objects, artefacts, media products (material, visual/sensory and virtual)
- Events and happenings (material, visual/sensory and virtual)

Source: adapted from Mason (2002)

Once the data source has been identified, you need to determine how data can be generated from these sources and what the main methods are for conducting a qualitative enquiry (Chapters 2 and 6, respectively). Whether you are choosing in-depth interviews or focus groups as a method of generating data, you are, in essence, creating audio files which require transcription and transformation into the written word. Or, if you are keeping observational logs, you are also working with the written word and so you need to start to consider how the text can be analysed effectively. Working with visual material is slightly different, because you are not analysing the written word in the first instance. Nevertheless, there are many similar questions to ask and lessons to be learnt.

8.2.1 Organising data

The key questions with regards to the written word and visual material are how you may impose order and start to make some interpretive sense (Mason, 2002) of the data; to build an argument or an explanation about the phenomena under investigation. To *impose order*, you are considering how you can organise the material to make the breadth and depth of information more manageable. There are two main ways in which you may decide to impose order upon your data sources:

1. Putting the data in a *chronological order*, meaning you are considering the order in which the data was produced/recorded/transcribed/published. You may identify the oldest transcript and work through to the newest. Alternatively, you may identify a specific sequence which is a more appropriate order for the data that has been collected.
2. Putting the data in a *thematic order*, meaning you are identifying a topic and applying that topic to the data, rather than paying attention to the order in which the data was produced/recorded/transcribed/published. For example, if you are working on a case study approach and you have two specific destinations in mind, you may theme the data according to each destination.

The key is that, whatever decision you make, you are consistent across the whole data set. It is about you deciding, as the researcher, what constitutes data in the context of your research, and working with that rationale. Once the data are ordered, you can start to make some interpretive sense of the data, and build explanations and arguments, in line with the research aim and objectives. However, before you do make interpretive sense of the data, you should stop and think in a little more detail about how you are going to read your data.

8.2.2 Reading data

According to Mason (2002), there are three ways in which data can be read: literally, interpretively and reflexively. Each one is discussed in more detail below and has an implication for what you treat as data. To aid your understanding and to illustrate the different ways in which data can be read, Image 8.1 has been read for you by the author, and cues to how you can achieve the different statements are also given in Illustrations 8.1, 8.2 and 8.3. The same practices and principles can be applied to written sources.

Image 8.1   A street in Benidorm, Spain

Source: Semley (2014)

1. *Literal readings* are about articulating factual information about what is seen in the data. It is about articulating the actual content, the precise information and the actual occurrences within the data. The content, the structure, the style and the layout are of importance here; and the way you read the data will depend on the source you are reading. For a photograph like Image 8.1, you will focus on what is there (Mason, 2002), whereas for a transcript you will focus on the language used and the sequence of interactions that take place between the researcher and the respondent. However, as a qualitative researcher, why would you wish to stop there? After all, a literal reading does not conform to the desire of subjectivity and interpretation outlined in Chapter 2. Therefore, you may start here and progress to the other readings because 'what we see is shaped by how we see it' (Mason, 2002: 149).

Illustration 8.1   The literal reading of Image 8.1

The square photo contains a street found in Benidorm. Along both sides of the street there are a number of businesses operating. These businesses include retail outlets (clothing and souvenirs) and eateries (tapas bars). The street is adorned with neon signage and it appears that all the businesses are open for trading. The one-way street is for both traffic and pedestrians. Although there are no cars in the picture, there are two people dressed in cut-off trousers/shorts and t-shirts walking up the street together, away from the photographer, whilst a third person dressed in trousers and a shirt is looking down at an artefact located within the retail shop. The photo is taken during the day and showcases artefacts relating to Spanish culture (local cuisine).

2. *Interpretive readings* are based on assumption. It is about the reader documenting a version of what they think the data means or represents. You read through and beyond the data in one way or another, and articulate the data source to illuminate meaning. For an image like Image 8.1, you may decode the content of the picture to have meaning beyond the literal reading provided above. For written material, the reader may articulate what they can infer from the dialogue, as to what someone's attitude to a particular topic is.

Illustration 8.2   An interpretive reading of Image 8.1

The photo represents a street scene often found in Benidorm, Spain. The photo encapsulates the interaction between the local population and the tourism industry in a destination which is popular with British tourists. The high-rise building acts as evidence of the fashionable period of Mediterranean holidays and of the demand for properties by the sea. It appears that the photo is taken in the shoulder season, whereby shops are open and trading but tourists are few and far between. The narrow streets depict the old streets of Benidorm and fail to showcase the new developments that have taken place since the destination's fall from fashion in the 1980s. However, it is still evident that the destination caters for the British market due to the English signs and the lack of authentic Spanish artefacts.

3. *Reflexive readings* are a reflection of the researcher's reactions to the data that is presented. This means that the reader can, once again, interpret what they think the data means and represents. This type of reading also means that the researcher can locate themselves as part of the data they have generated. The reading can therefore capture the relationship between the researcher and the data source and express those connections to the intended audience. The researcher therefore becomes part of the data and explores their role and perspective.

> ### Illustration 8.3   A reflexive reading of Image 8.1
>
> Having taken the photo on 27 February 2014, the image depicts the desolate streets of the older town in Benidorm, Spain. The location was sparsely populated, with the exception of one (English) couple. Having been approached by a retailer, the couple quickly departed the shop and it appeared that they could not get away from the establishment quick enough. The temperature that day was relatively warm for the time of year, and that feeling was echoed by the busy British bar around the corner from this street. In the newer parts of town near the railway station, Brits were sat drinking outside and soaking up the sun. This street had character and a distinctive sense of place. The narrow streets made for an intimate atmosphere, but at the same time the proliferation of neon signs meant that the local culture had been lost and was not considered as an appealing location to explore for very long.

As stated, the different ways in which data can be read can be applied to other forms of data, not just imagery. For the written word, the process of reading data is similar. However, the focus is placed on what is said and how it has been said, via the transcripts. Obviously then, the level of subjectivity embedded within the transcripts were predetermined as well as the style, level, degree and nature of the transcription. However, for a brief insight, the following verbatim transcript, taken from a focus group with local residents in Glastonbury by Semley and Busby (2014), can be used to consider the different ways of reading written data, as outlined in Table 8.2:

00:10:55	R1	There's a, there's a point that linked to the Rosslyn Chapel because, er, they started renovation work on it. I don't know whether that coincided with the impact of the… (Overlapping Conversation)
00:11:05	R2	Well the renovation could have been going on for about 10 years or more…
00:11:09	R1	…but did they receive increased donations to support that?
00:11:10	R2	That I don't know. (Overlapping Conversation)
00:11:11	R3	I think they did.
00:11:15	R2	It certainly would have helped. It would have been massively important to the economy.
00:11:19	R3	One of the curators for Rosslyn was down at the weekend and I had lunch with her, she, she's a friend. I didn't realise she was involved with Rosslyn, but I can ask her … erm … because she is involved with Lady Rosslyn and the restoration project … erm … so I can just drop her a line when I get back and see you know…Well I think it did make a difference… (Overlapping Conversation)
00:11:37	R2	The restoration has finished now but er … I think they're a bit more geared up. It is beautiful land (Overlapping Conversation) … its coped very well, but it is only a tiny little village … and (Overlapping Conversation) er, but the spiritual impact as well, but I think it did invite a lot of erm … tourists that were just tourists, they didn't come from the spiritual aspect… (Overlapping Conversation)
00:11:56	R3	We went to a very small village in France, in er, in Brittany a couple of years ago which er, er, has strongly associated with the Arthurian legends and the Holy Grail from the Bratton site, and er … it's a lovely little village, but it's much, much more smaller than Glastonbury and a, an awful lot of land around it is car parking. There are massive, massive coach parks, because it is completely inaccessible by any other means. You can't get there by train erm … coach and car is the only way to get to it (Overlapping Conversation) and that's kinda of a wow, how big are your car parks?

Table 8.2   Considerations for reading the written word

Type of reading	Focus and consideration could be placed upon:
Literal	The words and language used
	The sequence of interactions: R1, R2, R1, R2, and so on
	The form and structure of the dialogue
Interpretive/reflexive	The perceptions of Glastonbury residents towards the other named locations and people
	The level of agreement and disagreement between the residents themselves
	The overlapping conversation: Does it mean anything to you as a researcher?

8.2.3 Reading secondary sources

Another key item to address here is the nature of the data sources themselves. For example, to this point it is assumed that you have been out and collected primary qualitative data. However, there is no reason why you cannot read data in a qualitative manner that has been prepared by others, meaning you can utilise secondary data as a qualitative data source. If you are planning to use images produced by an event attendee and displayed on a social media site, or a range of tourist brochures to determine the influence of image formation upon destination choice, then you are likely to be using secondary sources. If you are intending to use secondary sources, then you need to ask a number of questions of the sources, such as:

- Why were these sources prepared?
- Who prepared these sources?
- Under what conditions were these sources prepared?
- According to what/whose rules?
- What have these sources been primarily used for?

You may also wonder if they are authentic. Once you have answered these questions and ensured that they represent appropriate data sources (in relation to your research POEM), you want to start thinking about how you are going to read the data and apply the logic/process outlined in section 8.2.2.

You can also read film. Once again, you need to decide on how you are going to read the film, but once that is established you can go through a process of reading data in a systematic manner, as outlined in Table 8.3. Once you have composed your notes, you can type up your notes as transcripts and identify themes for analysis. Once the notes are analysed, you can then make interpretations and statements about the data (in relation to the project aim and objectives, of course).

Secondary resources such as published documents can also be read. An example is given in Illustration 8.4 from a tourism and event context, whereby three academics (Semley et al., 2017) wished to review the value of planned events in the destination

Table 8.3   Stages involved in reading film

Viewing	Actions
1st	• Watch film in un-deconstructed way
	• Write down impressions at the end
2nd	• Watch the film again
	• Make notes as the film is being watched
	• Start to identify themes
3rd	• Watch the film again
	• Pause the film as themes associated with particular scenes are identified
	• Make more detailed notes

Source: adapted from Goldberg (2000)

management plans (DMP) of destination management organisations (DMO) in England. For this study, a literal interpretation of the DMP was made, and the results showcased how planned events were of some value to the DMO, but not of key importance. This was despite the recorded value of events to the UK economy (DCMS, 2016) and the belief that events can act as a catalyst and an animator for a destination area (Getz, 1997, 2007).

Illustration 8.4   DMO, DMP and event tourism – are planned events valued?

As part of a broader project, the researchers aspired to determine the policy importance of a planned event for DMOs in England. To do this, the authors identified a number of objectives, including a need to identify the number and nature of DMOs that exist in England, whilst also identifying the portfolio of events that contribute to achieving the DMP. Consequently, the value of these events was not determined by the number of events being held, but by broader characteristics and properties that were outlined by their DMP. A strategy outlines the aspirations of an organisation and allows for interpretation to be made about the prominence and portfolio of events which were included, and within what context. Consequently, an extensive search for DMOs was undertaken, and as information was gathered about the English-based DMOs the strategy for each was also obtained and stored in a thematic manner (by the regional location of the actual DMO). Once all the DMO DMP had been gathered, the data was read literally and given appropriate labels and codes. It was then, from this perspective, that the value of planned events could be established.

Source: Semley et al. (2017)

8.2.4 Applying labels, codes, categories and themes

To this point, the chapter has simply discussed the many ways in which qualitative data can be recognised and read. Now we have such an understanding, it is important to discuss what is next: reflect on what has been said and consider what it is we do intuitively as we read data; we identify themes and codes.

In the previous section, the idea of themes and coding has been touched on, but I have purposefully not said why or how themes and coding can be developed, or even if the word *coding* is the most suitable terminology for the process of sifting, sorting (Brunt, 1997), characterising, cutting, coding, categorising, converting and creating (Savin-Baden and Howell Major, 2013) qualitative data. After all, the word coding does pertain to the numerical applications found in quantitative research (Ritchie et al., 2014). This section is, therefore, designed to clearly articulate the meaning of the various terminology and to draw conclusions over what it is exactly the qualitative researcher is expected to do. The definition of each term is given in Table 8.4.

Table 8.4   Defining the terminology

	Definition
Labelling	Attach a label to something
	Tag something
	Put a mark on something
	Create a ribbon
Coding	Assign a code to something
	Create a systematic collection
Categorisation	Place something in a particular group
	Place something in a particular order
	Create groupings
Theming	Present participle
	Assign a character to an activity

Source: Oxford Dictionaries (2016)

From reviewing the terminology and considering the definitions of these words, it is clear there are similarities in meaning, and therefore we could say that the panacea would be to pick a term you prefer and apply it to your procedure! For example, Miles and Huberman (1994: 56) note that 'codes are tags or labels for assigning units of meaning to the descriptive … information compiled during a study'. Therefore, coding captures the way data are labelled and re-labelled within the data analysis process. Consequently, for the purposes of this book the term coding has been selected, because it is well documented within the research methods literature and in THE-specific research publications. However, you personally may have an alternative perspective!

Coding can happen in different ways and for different purposes. Coding can happen in cycles (first and second cycle), and, in essence, what the researcher is attempting to do is 'fix meaning' (Ritchie et al., 2014: 278) to the data. Coding can be executed in three specific ways, as first noted by Glaser and Strauss (1967) and utilised by Savin-Baden and Howell Major (2013):

1. *Open (or initial) coding*: this is an example of first-cycle coding, when the researcher working with qualitative data makes initial codes. This can happen in the margins of field notes or transcripts and involves conceptualisation of the data.

2. *Axial coding*: this is an example of second-cycle coding and is representative of a process which has much more structure than initial coding. The researcher here follows a set of procedures to review the data and put it together in different ways. The focus therefore is placed on identifying causal relationships in the open coding and then framing generic relationships together.

3. *Selective coding*: this is another example of a second-cycle stage, if not third, whereby the researcher determines a core variable in the data that is common/identifiable across all the data and then applies that code to the transcripts. This involves reading through the data again, looking for cases of illustration and explanation.

However, these are not the only ways data can be coded. Saldana (2012), for example, identifies 32 different ways to code! Coding could therefore be descriptive, interpretive or pattern coding; topic or analytical; emotional, values-driven or verses coding (Fox et al., 2014). The list is comprehensive, but for the level of analysis that is applicable to research at this stage in your career, it is only the basics that we are interested in. Therefore, we shall just focus on the cycles of coding that may intuitively occur, and then reflect on how coding, itself, makes *things* part of a classification system and makes things similar; which, in essence, makes the data more manageable and easier to interpret. This is how you start to tell your story, the story of your data.

Sourcing codes

By this stage, it may seem obvious as to where codes can be sourced. If you have been paying attention to the content of the literature when planning your project, then the codes themselves may come from those themes. Or you may be developing a new theory and have a stronger focus on the inductive design of the research. Therefore, you allow the coding to emerge from the data. It doesn't really matter. If you have immersed yourself in the data, then the coding may be personal to you as an individual. However, you need to be cautious. Coding should be replicable to some extent, meaning that another researcher should be able to decipher the meaning of the coding to the material that they have consumed. They may attach subjectivity to different elements of the transcript, for example, but they can see where and why your code has been applied.

As described by Fox et al. (2014: 170), from an events management perspective you can create or identify codes when you are:

- writing a literature review
- writing up your field notes
- transcribing your data
- doing the analysis.

Therefore, when writing your methodology, you may already have pre-specified themes, or not. It will all depend on the nature of your research POEM and on your epistemological assumption (Ritchie et al., 2014). It is, after all, down to your level of intuition and creativity as a researcher to determine the best practice for your research project.

Applying codes

In terms of actually applying the codes, there are many ways in which this can be done. There are different tools which can be utilised to apply codes. It can be done by hand or by computer, and if you select a computer you can utilise a word-processing application or a specific piece of software that is designed to analyse qualitative data. Some of these tools are briefly explored by Fox et al. (2014) and include colour highlighting in Word (p. 172), coloured highlighter pens and paper (p. 173), cutting paper into sections (p. 174), cutting and pasting sections using Word (p. 174) and utilising CAQDAS (Computer Assisted Qualitative Data Analysis Software) (p. 175). Alternatively, you can source specific books which focus on a particular CAQDAS, such as Bazeley and Jackson (2013), who perform qualitative data analysis with the NVivo software.

The important thing to remember here is being consistent and concise when coding. Yes, more than one code can be given to a specific piece of data (an excerpt of a transcript of an image), but the rationale for coding should be consistent and transparent in order to allow others to interpret the process effectively and connect the process of thinking behind the coding process. An example of initial coding and giving 'others' a transparent insight into the coding scheme is shown in Illustration 8.5.

Illustration 8.5   Coding guide for a PhD researcher

When conducting qualitative analysis of 28 in-depth interviews, Table 8.5 was used as an initial coding scheme for the data to ensure consistency and transparency across the data set. The PhD focused on establishing the nature of community responses to tourism-related crime.

(Continued)

(Continued)

Table 8.5   Initial coding scheme

Initial code	Explanation
Active behaviour	When respondents recall active behaviour in a positive or negative manner
Birthplace	Was the respondent born locally?
Changes in behaviour	Respondents note that tourism changes their behaviour
Community distribution	Are the respondent groups developed through spatial distribution or through mutual interests?
Community feelings	Feelings towards being a part of the local community
Community groups	Types of community groups respondent believes they belong to
Community issues	Changes and thoughts about the community as a whole and in passing
Community problems	Highlights the problems respondents may have with the community
Coping strategies	Respondent's statements towards 'coping' with tourists and tourism
Crime experience	Respondent's examples of how they have been a victim of crime
Crime levels	How the respondent perceives the level of crime in the community to be
Crime reduction	Actively involved in community efforts to help reduce crime
Daily involvement	Involvement level with tourists on a regular basis
Definition of community	How the respondent defines a community
Development	Thoughts about development within the town
Discourage crime	Does the respondent act to discourage crime? Act as a guardian?
Employment	Type of employment the respondent is in
Express views officially	Does the respondent have sufficient opportunity to express views?
Fear of crime	Does the respondent fear becoming a victim of crime?
Impacts of tourism	Positive and negative impacts of tourism
Importance of tourism	How important tourism is to daily life
Length of involvement	Time respondent has been involved with tourists and tourism
Length of residency	How long has the respondent lived in the community?
Level of influence	Does the respondent have a good enough level of influence, should they want it, within their community?
Neighbourhood Watch	Opinions about the scheme
Offenders	Who the respondent thinks causes crime in the community
Passive behaviour	Where respondent acts passively in a positive or negative manner
Place distinctions	Talk about features and facilities of the community and destination
Proximity to CBD	How far the respondent lives from the town centre
Resident groups	Is the respondent a member of any resident groups?

Initial code	Explanation
Seasonal distinctions	Comments about seasonal distinctions noted within the community
Social bond	Strength of social bond with the community
Tourism impacts the community	Feelings towards the implications of tourism having an impact on their community
Tourist behaviour	Respondent's opinions about how tourists behave
Weight of impacts	Whether or not respondent feels as though the positives outweigh the negatives

As you can see, this is quite a comprehensive list to digest. Many studies do not operate with such an extensive list; instead, they work on a number of basic coding criteria. The key here is to ensure you are able to answer the research question effectively and that the design of this stage is reflective of the project aim and objectives. The amount of codes is not the important part.

Source: Semley (2012)

8.2.5 The role of numbers

The role and purpose of quantifying qualitative data have been a personal topic of contention for me. As a qualitative researcher, I have been asked to assign numbers to each category to showcase how frequently a code has been presented in the data. However, I do not personally see the value of the number; I think it removes the creativity, intuition and interpretation placed on the data set and creates a factual formative statement from which the analysis stage will be judged. As Krane and colleagues (1997: 214) state: 'placing a frequency count after a category of experiences is tantamount to saying how important it is; thus value is derived by number. In many cases, rare experiences are no less meaningful, useful, or important than common ones. In some cases, the rare experience may be the most enlightening one.' Therefore, I am confident in my belief that at no stage should a number be assigned to the data set, the coding scheme of the output from data analysis. However, this is a contentious issue, and if you are conducting consultancy research for a client who wants quantification of the data, then you are going to have to just do it! Likewise, there are some CAQDAS which automatically generate numbers, statistics and figures for you, so it doesn't cause a time delay or an inconvenience. I personally though believe that the number value added to a code detracts attention from the rare, unique, yet clearly important statements that may be made in the data. Therefore, from this point forward you will not find many examples (if any!) of the quantification of the coding scheme and/or data analysis process.

8.3 Analysing qualitative data

Analysing qualitative data requires a belief in your personal intuition as a researcher, and a certain level of creativity. To analyse data, you need to examine the data, study it, scrutinise it, question it and evaluate it to draw out knowledge from it. Therefore, it is a time-consuming and immersive experience for the researcher. It is not a job which can be done with a few clicks of a button (as I sometimes view SPSS analysis to be!). You need to prepare the data and engage with it to enable effective dissection and quality exploration. Therefore, from this point forward, careful consideration is required as to why you are analysing data in the way you have chosen. The main items to focus on here are the tools which can be used to aid analysis and, of course, being able to support and explain the value of conducting the type of data analysis that you chose. Judgement is something which is often placed on qualitative data, not only in the sense of the level of subjectivity (section 8.1) but also in terms of justification and broader application of the newfound knowledge (section 8.3.1). However, it is no longer about proving its value, but, instead, about just clearly articulating the validity and reliability of the data to others.

The value of qualitative enquiries has altered. Since Walle (1997) examined the importance of qualitative enquiry to the tourism industry and Crang (2003) reviewed the nature of the enquiry, perceptions have changed. This change was evident after it was felt that qualitative techniques had gone through a period of 'mature reflection and evaluation' (Crang, 2003: 494). It is, therefore, no longer a paradigm of versus (qualitative versus quantitative) or a question of science versus art (Walle, 1997); instead, it is a case of showcasing the value added through this constructive approach to knowledge generation. It is about articulating the value of a single exploration of a case study area to the broader THE industry, and illustrating how knowledge can be transferred and not just generalised upon (we will return to this issue in section 8.3.1). Such information about qualitative data and its analysis can influence the verdict placed upon the suitability of the data, create judgements about its application and influence the perceived importance of the data itself.

8.3.1 Judging qualitative research

As qualitative research is open to the judgement of the researcher, it is often difficult to critically evaluate its worth. Moreover, in many instances considerable attention is given to the interpretation of the results rather than the methods devised by the researcher to achieve this analysis. Strauss and Corbin (1990) suggest that when evaluating qualitative research sufficient attention should be given to the 'validity, reliability and credibility of the data … the adequacy of the research process … [and the] judgements made about the empirical grounding of the research findings'. Of particular importance then, in the judgement of qualitative research, is the reporting of the whole research process; to demonstrate rigour and logic in the methods adopted. This is something which needs to be considered in detail, because there is some criticism of this arts-based focus (Walle, 1997) from scientific researchers who may only be focusing on Chapter 7 of this book. The central concepts to consider here are noted by Ritchie et al. (2014) and are, in essence, scientific terms applied to qualitative approaches:

1. *Reliability*: one belief in the realm of research methods that allows outsiders to judge the quality of the data is reliability. Reliability is depicted within the scientific, quantitative enquiry as being how replicable the study's findings are. This implies that a second researcher should be able to gain similar results if the same processes were undertaken and analysis was applied. However, this is not always possible with qualitative techniques because of the level of subjectivity that may be introduced to the data. However, instead of utilising different terminology, which may be deemed by some as being more appropriate to the qualitative techniques, it is instead important to articulate good practice and transparency within the research agenda. Good practice and transparency are required to showcase exactly which processes were followed and how conclusions were drawn. This leads to a rigorous and consistent interpretation of data which are logical, consistent and dependable. Therefore, application of the science to the arts is about operationalisation of the terminology, and not replacing these central concepts with an alternative. If this is then achieved by the researcher in their description of the methods, there is no reason why the process cannot be replicated.

2. *Validity*: a second central concept to consider is the extent to which the findings are well-founded and reflect the phenomenon being studied. Validity is a question of the data accuracy, credibility and broader application of the knowledge gained. Similarly, it is a question of operationalisation and ensuring that the data are validated through a clear interpretation of just how well the data have been captured and interpreted, rather than comparing qualitative to quantitative interpretation. After all, the focus here is on giving the methods adopted credibility and allowing qualitative techniques to stand alone as a tool for developing new knowledge. There are authors however, like Guba and Lincoln (1994), who prefer the judgement of authenticity over validity, but why should qualitative techniques not be treated in the same manner as quantitative techniques?

3. *Generalisation*: the third concept to consider is better known as transference within the qualitative research world. Even though the above operationalisation of scientific-based terminology is outlined, it is here where I personally stop. I do not believe that qualitative data should be generalised upon. Data are not universal here and should therefore not be simplified when you are supposedly exploring the depth and uniqueness of social phenomena. Although the initial two concepts clearly relate to generalisation, here I operationalise the third concept differently. There are still clear links to (measurement, internal and external) validity and the methods can be utilised as a part of (methods, sources, analysis or theory) triangulation, however the difference here is not about making sweeping statements from the data/giving an overview of how things work. Instead, it is important to consider how data can be transferred to a different situation, how conveyance can provide a different interpretation of the data to reflect the new application of the knowledge. However, given my explanation of the initial two concepts, you may wish to choose to continue to use the terminology associated with the sciences, to give your work additional credibility. If you decide to do this, you may come up against some criticism, but if you have a clear, justified and well-substantiated rationale for doing this, then you should. It is your causal puzzle and it is you that needs to believe in the strength of your data collection process.

Once these three central concepts have been explored and digested, the researcher is in a good place to understand the extent to which qualitative data (and therefore its analysis) can be judged by others. It also allows the researcher to make well-informed decisions about the specific tool which will be utilised for analysis itself, as the question of judgement does not stop here. Judgement will be made based on the entire research process and on the quality of the final publication (Chapter 9).

8.3.2 Tools to analyse qualitative data

For the purposes of this book, there are two analysis tools which are being considered: analysis by hand or by computer. There is little, in my mind, which separates them, and therefore they will be briefly outlined here, before being treated in a similar fashion for the rest of the chapter, because, regardless of tool, it is the process which needs to be given the additional focus. Nevertheless, there is a difference in opinion about this; some academics believe a computer can interfere with the analysis process, whereas others believe it enhances it (Bazeley, 2007; Bazeley and Jackson, 2013).

Depending on the time and resources you have available to you, you may find that it is not a decision that has to be made, because you are left with no choice. Nevertheless, it is worth considering the options here, because you may change your mind once it has been reviewed. Now, the tools (hand or computer) have already been noted in this chapter (Fox et al., 2014: 172–6) and go from utilising paper and pen through to CAQDAS, with a reflection on basic computer programs which can assist your analysis. Each of these options reflects the personal preferences of the researcher alongside the resources available to that researcher. This means that the time and money the researcher has for the data analysis process may result in the selection of the analysis tool.

When reflecting back on some of the content in Chapter 2, it was clear to depict that transcription was a lengthy process, and therefore resource (time) intensive. Here, the immersion and the application of coding can also become resource-intensive; furthermore, the purchase of a CAQDAS can be expensive. The expense can be for the actual purchase and also the necessary training which is required to utilise the CAQDAS. This means that the money and time invested in data collection is considerable for the researcher or the organisation. Therefore, instead of using the computer, it may be concluded that it is more effective to do the data analysis by hand. However, by hand you have to allow for human error and you have to acknowledge that there is no instant overview (that is provided by some CAQDAS) that can inspire and motivate the researcher to code their data after a long period of transcription.

The advantages and limitations of each tool are summarised in Table 8.6. This is important to note because CAQDAS can raise methodological concerns.

Based on a sound understanding of the tools, there is then just the question of building a methodological rationale for using the preferred tool, and ensuring that you can articulate and justify your choice of tool. For example, shortly thematic analysis (Savin-Baden and Howell Major, 2013) will be explored via the 'framework method' (Ritchie and Spencer, 1994; Brunt, 1997) and for this type of thematic analysis, either tool can be utilised. It is therefore up to the researcher to determine the rationale for selecting the most appropriate tool and conveying

Table 8.6 Advantages and limitations of qualitative data analysis tools

	By hand	**By computer**
Advantages	• The researcher remains in control of the data analysis process • Cost-effective, in terms of not having to purchase any (or many) tools to begin with	• A quick overview of the data can be obtained once imported into the software and before any real analysis has been undertaken • Analysis can be at the cutting edge of technological advancement
Limitations	• Human error can become an issue within the coding and interpretation process • The interpretation of data is somewhat limited by the researcher's creativity • Expensive in terms of time and resource intensity	• Purchasing CAQDAS and becoming proficient in using the software can be expensive • Programmes can create issues relating to the contextualisation of the research and closeness of the researcher to the investigation

Table 8.7   Issues and advantages of using NVivo in qualitative research analysis

Issues identified with using NVivo	Advantages of using NVivo
• Inability to see the whole document once the transcript has been uploaded and coded	• The software still provides the researcher with the ability to view retrieved segments of text in their original context
• The process of using software supports a code-and-retrieve activity, rather than immersing the researcher in the actual data	• The researcher can recontextualise the data through the coded category rather than just the original transcript
• There is fear that the analysis is mechanised rather than being emergent	• Metacognitive awareness ensures the researcher remains in control of the process they are engaging with
• The loss of context is possible as the codes are applied and removed from the original transcription	• The researcher can integrate their perspective and conceptual framework into their coding choices
• The process distances the researcher from their data because the interface is not 'natural' like the phenomenon under investigation	• With the IT proficiency of many researchers these days, using a computer is a natural reflection of the social world which may be under investigation
• There is a misconception that computers support only grounded theory	• The software allows the researcher to code the data more efficiently and build theory effectively

Source: Bazeley (2007)

this to the reader. Throughout section 8.3.3, the analysis outlined in the six illustrations was conducted by hand, with the help of a word processor. Therefore, Table 8.7 is an example of justification that was used by Semley (2012) when NVivo was utilised in conjunction with the framework method. The table outlines the issues and advantages of using NVivo (a specific CAQDAS), which I used within the methodological chapter of my own PhD.

From reviewing Table 8.7, a justification could be made for using or not using NVivo within a study. There really is nothing that distinguishes the two options other than the researcher's preference and possibly their research POEM. For my own study, the main rationale for why the software was utilised was that it was a larger set of in-depth interviews than I was used to dealing with, and the software enabled me to view the whole sample whilst comparing and isolating the data in the same instance. Therefore, it was beneficial to me as a researcher, but I had to clearly articulate this to the audience, to ensure they could understand the process and rationale of my work. After all, I wanted them to place a fair judgement on my work!

8.3.3 Focus on: thematic analysis

Thematic analysis is one of many ways in which data can be analysed. Thematic analysis, as defined by Savin-Baden and Howell Major (2013), is a method of identifying, analysing and reporting patterns in the data set. The analysis process is one of characterising, cutting, coding, categorising, converting and creating knowledge (Savin-Baden and Howell Major, 2013). Therefore, in essence, it is about identifying the themes and applying these to the data itself. Now, there is no one set way to conduct thematic analysis; it is more a case of identifying with the work of a seminal author and effectively following their guidelines. Therefore, if conducting thematic analysis, it is important to identify with a specific technique which supports your research POEM and aligns with your capabilities as a researcher. In general, thematic analysis involves a series of stages, and, through each stage, you become more immersed in your data and you start to code the data to manage it more effectively, before you conclude with a clear and well-informed understanding of the data set. My personal preference for thematic analysis comes through my personal understanding of Ritchie and Spencer's (1994) framework method. The focus here, therefore, is placed on the framework method because it is flexible and versatile in application. It provides a logical sequence to approaching the mass of qualitative material, and it helps to keep the analyst on a pathway which will keep the original purpose of the research in mind.

The framework method

The framework method is a specific method associated with systematic and disciplined research, and involves the 'systematic process of sifting, charting and sorting material according to key issues and themes' (Ritchie and Spencer, 1994: 177). As a form of thematic analysis, it provides a good way to analyse qualitative data (Brunt, 1997) and requires immersion, conceptualisation and judgement to be made, before data can be 'lifted' from its initial context and interpreted and defined. Furthermore, the methods validity relies heavily on the creative and conceptual ability of the analyst to 'determine meaning, salience and connections' (Ritchie and Spencer, 1994: 177) from within and about the data.

The method was initially developed by Social and Community Planning Research (SCPR), as reported by Ritchie and Spencer (1994), and is a generic method providing a versatile means for qualitative analysis, rather than being a highly specific technique. It provides a procedural structure which you, the researcher, can apply to your own data. As such, it can be applied to a wide variety of qualitative methods of data collection with differing aims and objectives.

It should be remembered that, often, qualitative studies are concerned with exploring and investigating deeply a particular phenomenon. Thus, when analysing qualitative data, the approach taken should be complementary to this. The data from qualitative studies is often in the form of transcripts of recorded interviews with individuals or groups and observational logs. Typically, it may take several hours before the researcher has transcribed a single recording, whilst he/she feels fully aware of the content of a short interview with a single respondent.

Therefore, when working with larger samples, a considerable amount of time may pass before the researcher gains certain 'hunches' about the data and how aspects of the data relate to the research questions posed. The benefit of a method such as the framework method is that it allows the mass of data and hunches from the transcription stage to be organised in a structured way, and to contribute to a holistic analysis process.

Essentially, the framework method involves five key stages:

1. Familiarisation
2. Identifying a thematic framework
3. Indexing
4. Charting
5. Mapping and interpretation.

Each stage will now be explored in more detail. Furthermore, to demonstrate the process, an illustration will be provided throughout the section, taken from the work of Brunt and Hooton (2010), who explored community responses to tourism and crime in the Cornish seaside resort of Newquay.

Illustration 8.6   Analysis in practice 1 – the Brunt and Hooton (2010) POEM

The logic and rationale behind Brunt and Hooton's (2010) article was the aim to identify trends in a host's behaviour in relation to crime and their fear of crime within both the home and the work environment. The academics believed that the host and their perceptions of tourism-related crime were meaningful constituents of the social world in themselves (Mason, 2002), as they (the authors) had a specific interest in determining how the host's perceptions affected resident behaviour on a daily basis. The researchers also believed that these perceptions could be recollected and articulated by the respondent to the researcher, acting as evidence of their perceptions (i.e. the individuals were the data source, whilst the perception was the method of generating data). However, the researchers needed to gain insight into the destination and ensure they were asking the right people the right questions, because it was not clear how and why issues of tourism-related crime were of a particular concern within the resort. Based on the research aim and objectives, and the POE(M) to that point, the authors decided to undertake three stages of data collection:

1   A series of *observational logs* was designed to provide knowledge about the destination and provide insights into the behaviour pattern of people, in general, within the resort. This resulted in field notes and observational logs being recorded and analysed via the framework method, which then informed the second stage of data collection.

2   *Postal questionnaires* for hosts provided the authors with an account of local residents' experience and interpretations of their level of fear of crime in the resort. This resulted in quantitative data that was analysed separately in SPSS.

3   A series of *in-depth interviews* with key stakeholders and residents resulted in conversations being recorded and analysed via the framework method.

This mixed-method approach allowed the phenomena to be viewed from more than one source (Decrop, 1999; Davies, 2003), known as triangulation. Furthermore, it ensured that the phenomenon under investigation could be uncovered more effectively, given the fact that deviance is not something people are willing to discuss if they fear being incarcerated or that it would have a detrimental impact on their livelihood (i.e. an impact on the tourism industry).

In summary, the POEM for this investigation was one of: (P) Interpretivism, (O) Relativism, (E) Subjectivism and (M) Induction; with both qualitative and quantitative data collection stages.

Framework stage 1: Familiarisation

The first stage of the framework method, as outlined by Ritchie and Spencer (1994), involves the researcher, the person who is to perform the analysis, becoming familiar with the scope, nature and richness of the data that has been collected. This is particularly important where staff other than the analyst have undertaken the interviews, led focus groups or transcribed the recordings. Thus, the analyst must gain an overview of the data to conceptualise the material and put their hunches into context.

In essence, the analyst reads the transcripts/logs and starts to make notes about the themes which they believe are coming from the data. These themes relate to the aims and objectives of the research and are, at this stage, just hunches about the data and have not been applied to the entire data set. Put simply, the data are read and brief notes are made on the data – this may be on the transcripts themselves or within a separate log book/journal.

Illustration 8.7   Analysis in practice 2 – familiarisation in action (Brunt and Hooton, 2010)

Based on the stage of observation, a series of logs was recorded. These logs took place on different days at different times and in different locations within the resort. The locations were informed by secondary data that was collected prior to visiting the destination, which revealed distinct areas in the resort and crime hot spots areas which should be visited. The date and timing of the observational logs were informed by the nature of the tourism industry perceived in the resort (i.e. seasonality, the night-time economy), which were once again informed by secondary data sources. The researcher depicted that the best way to observe the environment, and the interaction of people within the setting, were through covert participant observation. Following the period of observation, field notes were transcribed, which constructed the researcher version of what they thought the data meant. Consequently, the researcher was part of the data (i.e. an interpretive and reflexive reading of the situation) and read through and beyond the data itself in conjunction with the secondary data that was previously collected.

Below is an excerpt from an observational log that was recorded by the researchers (log number 3 of 12). You should now read the excerpt and become familiar with the nature of the data that was collected and with the destination it was collected in:

> I am starting to think that it is my own behaviour patterns that I should be recording. I have to be telling myself something. I am sat outside another pub! Are these the only places where you can come and people watch without feeling unwelcome? Is this why people spend all their time in the pub rather than the café across the road? Who knows, but I am very conscious about the location, I hope no one recognises me from the previous location, they will think I am out on the tiles as well as me perceiving other people's actions as being as such!

> Regardless of the way I am feeling this location is pretty similar to that at the central. There is a main road which passes outside the establishment. In fact, 3 roads meet outside of here. It seems very busy as far as the traffic

is concerned. There are a lot fewer people within the establishment though. The few that are in here are either watching the sports inside with a beer or two or soaking up the sun outside. In fact, there is quite a distinction between the people sat inside and those lazing outside. Inside the establishment it is dark and cold and the people in there are much older looking. If we were to criticise them and place them into a box I would say they all look like they are addicted to beer, betting and the pub on the weekend. They all actually feel like locals to the area. There is no sign inside of anyone who is unfamiliar with their surroundings, and there is no sign of a woman anywhere, just men. In fact, I am sure that if the majority of these men stood up their name would be carved into the seat where they are sat. I am sure of it. Outside though, it is a whole new kettle of fish. The few people who are sat here seem like they are soaking up the leisure time that they have found to have a beer within, with no big groups hanging about the place. They seem more like non-native cavemen that hang out in the deepest darkest corners of this seedy bar. Instead, they most likely made it all the way from the hotel next door and had been partying in the underground club all night. My I must learn not to judge people!

Two doors up are the bookies and today is the Grand National! So maybe that is why all the men inside the pub are looking the way they are. Who knows? With this in mind though and the amount of alcohol people seem to be consuming, you can't help but think that there could be trouble later.

Once the race starts, if it hasn't already, in fact there are signs stating that there is live coverage of the race here, place your bets here!! I think there could be a few happy and depressed all within this bar at once!

Outside other than the traffic which has been congested since I have sat here, there is also a fair ground ride type ball thing. This seems to be stopping a few people as they pass just enough space through on the street side to not cause a problem. Why don't people just stand on the grass the other side through?!? The place where this attraction is located is on the forecourt of a large hotel, and there is a large grass area where people could stand and watch. Not these people, instead they are congregated on the pavement causing an obstruction to others. Maybe it is the close vicinity to the pub that puts them off?

(Continued)

(Continued)

> I really am starting to feel a little conscious of my location. I feel much less comfortable outside of here as opposed to the other. I am not sure why either. Maybe it is due to the nature and the lay out of the area. There are fewer people about but the traffic is causing a problem and I do feel as though I am sat amongst it all here. Whilst standing out like a sore thumb. I think I have seen enough for now and I think it is time to wait to see what the night brings. Hopefully a win on the Old Grand National, come on the Cornish one!

Although this is only one excerpt, you should be feeling relatively aware of what the researcher was seeing, and have a hunch over the content of other logs that were recorded. In practice, you would record some of these hunches as you read all the other 11 observational logs. It is only then you would move on to the next stage of identifying the thematic framework.

Note, if you do not have any hunches about the data at this stage, then perhaps it would be worth exploring the literature which pertains to the relationship between tourism and crime to understand the context of the investigation a little further. In particular, review Brunt and Hambly's (1999) article, 'Tourism and Crime: A research agenda'.

Framework stage 2: Identifying a thematic framework

This stage requires the further development of the notes from the familiarisation stage, with hunches becoming organised into recurring themes. Again, reference to the original aims and objectives is crucial. Eventually, the data are sorted into a framework of themes which relate to the research questions of the study. This stage remains fairly descriptive in character in the sense that it represents a stage beyond initial sifting but only as far as the identification of general themes goes. However, within this stage the thematic framework which is developed can be tested for its suitability against several transcripts. Often, there will be discrepancies or anomalies where the themes identified do not hold up against the actual data. It is likely that several attempts at 'to-ing and fro-ing' between a framework of themes and its applicability to the data will take place. Once a suitable thematic framework has been developed, the next stage flows naturally.

Illustration 8.8   Analysis in practice 3 – thematic framework in action (Brunt and Hooton, 2010)

The original aim of the project was to identify responses in hosts' behaviour as a consequence of tourism-related crime and their fear of such crime. To achieve this, an objective was set to develop observational studies to provide knowledge of the destination area and insights into behaviour patterns within the resort. Based on this information, the data (meaning all the logs that were read and utilised) was sorted into a framework of themes which related to these.

For example, from reading the excerpt in Illustration 8.7, the general themes appear to be: the gender divide; the nature of the location itself; the type of people present; and the traffic congestion in the area. These were recorded on a piece of paper, and, as the other 11 logs were read, additional hunches were drawn. Some of these hunches were the same as the ones noted here, whilst others were recorded which later were determined to be anomalies, meaning that not all the hunches were felt to be applicable to all the logs.

This stage can be confusing and time-consuming as you start to sift through the data and try to make sense of your data. However, with a little perseverance and recollection of the aim and objectives of the research programme, it is rewarding when you start to narrow down the themes and decide to index the data with your final chosen themes.

Framework stage 3: Indexing

This stage relates to the thematic framework being applied to the whole data in a systematic way. Thus, specific comments and phrases made by the respondents can be 'indexed' within the thematic framework. Depending on the nature of the data collection and the form of the data, the indexes may be numbers, symbols or annotations on the margins of the transcripts. Index cards which are colour-coded may also be useful. Inevitably, as this stage is applied to the whole data, there will be instances where the researcher must apply a certain degree of judgement over how particular statements are coded within the indexing system. To improve accuracy, Ritchie and Spencer (1994) recommend that the researcher tries out their indexing system on a friend or a colleague to allow judgements and assumptions to be evaluated. Perhaps, if you are undertaking a project at university, you could discuss the judgements and assumptions you are making with your supervisor!

Illustration 8.9   Analysis in practice 4 – indexing in action (Brunt and Hooton, 2010)

From reviewing all the observational logs, the researchers were able to identify a range of emergent themes. The themes included:

- general atmosphere
- location
- type of people
- group sizes
- distinction between the sexes
- age
- traffic congestion
- signs of antisocial behaviour
- additional comments.

These themes were applied to the logs via a colour-coded system in a computer software package.

Framework stage 4: Charting

Following the indexing of statements and phrases, it is now possible to develop a more complete assessment of the data. To represent the extent of the material, charting can be undertaken. This involves the removal of the key phrases which were indexed in the transcripts and placing them in a table, matrix or chart in relation to a particular theme. The precise nature of the chart will relate to the nature of the data, the research questions posed and the thematic framework defined by the analyst. Typically, a chart will have a research question as a column heading and each case (or respondent) as the rows of a table. Within each cell, the themes identified can be located together with the phrase or statement which was indexed from the transcript. It is recommended that when reporting data in this way the same chart layout is used for each research question to ease comparisons between the charts.

Illustration 8.10   Analysis in practice 5 – charting in action (Brunt and Hooton, 2010)

Once coded, the observational logs were charted. The indexing highlighted in the previous illustration was separated from the original transcript and combined into a single, simple-to-read table (Table 8.8).

Table 8.8   Charting in action

Theme: General atmosphere	
Day	'Feel as though I am sat amongst it all'
Night	'It has changed considerably'
	'There is something about this location that I am not at ease with'
	'You can sense the potential of this place and the problems which could be caused'
	'It has progressively got busier'
	'I don't really feel welcomed at all within the bar'

Theme: Location	
Day	'People ... are congregated on the pavement causing an obstruction to others'
	'Seems to be the meeting place for everyone'
Night	'The terrace outside has enough people on it to suggest a maximum capacity'
	'You could describe this place as the bottleneck of the area'

Theme: Type of people	
Day	'There is ... a distinction between the people sat inside and those lazing outside'
	'There are a variety of groups about ... hens and stags to youthful groups'
	'Boy racers'
	'There are also families evident'
Night	'There are still a lot of groups about, a lot of stag and hens'
	'Definitely not family orientated'

Table 8.8 was then refined further and used for interpretation within the final publication of Brunt and Hooton (2010). This was, of course, positioned alongside the other research findings that were associated with each stage of data collection!

Framework stage 5: Mapping and interpretation

The charting process of the previous stage is a means to facilitate the mapping and interpretation of the data as a whole. The final stage of the framework method represents the most difficult and the most creative. It involves the evaluation and discussion of the data in relation to the original aim(s) and objectives of the study. Ritchie and Spencer (1994) suggest that six features of qualitative research are often what the analyst returns to at this stage, namely:

1. defining concepts
2. mapping the range and nature of phenomena
3. creating typologies
4. finding associations
5. providing explanations
6. developing strategies.

The emphasis on each of these is guided by the study aims. What is involved is comparing charts, looking for patterns and connections, seeking instances where respondents complement or contradict each other and searching for explanations to the research questions. To be useful, the researcher must evaluate the data and draw out conclusions rather than simply reporting how many cases supported a particular theme. This stage requires reflection, intuition and imagination on the part of the analyst. If the framework process has worked, then it should be possible for the analyst to visualise the results, judge their importance and provide an appropriate interpretation.

Illustration 8.11   Analysis in practice 6 – mapping in action (Brunt and Hooton, 2010)

The final mapping and interpretation of the data was included within the publication itself and covered the main findings of the project to an academic audience. The main results which were articulated and explored, not just noted, were that of seasonal trends in activities and the variation of activities and types of people within distinct districts of the destination. For additional insight, it is recommended that you access the published journal article:

Brunt, P. and Hooton, N. (2010). Community Responses to Tourism and Crime. *Crime Prevention and Community Safety: An International Journal.* 12 (1): 42–57.

These five stages of the framework method are extremely transparent, intuitive and informative for the researcher. There are some areas where the stages become merged together – for example, the familiarisation and the start of the indexing stage. Nevertheless, it is important that the researcher acknowledges and evidences each stage within the methods section of their study. This level of articulation will ensure that the process can be judged as being reliable by others and that replication is possible, allowing for the technique to be praised as a standalone investigation.

For a second example of thematic analysis via the framework method, Mansfield's (2016) work about Nantes can be reviewed. This research is outlined in Illustration 8.12 and provides an overview of the same process, but with the tool of a qualitative analysis software programme, rather than using the tool of the hand as noted above.

Illustration 8.12   Place branding in Nantes by Mansfield (2016)

Mansfield (2016) provides free access to his *toureme* website, where insight into his postdoctoral work is apparent. The website itself presents lecturers and content in the area of tourism knowledge and heritage management, and is hosted by Google Sites to ensure access is open to all. Within the content, Mansfield (2016) provides a 'walk through' of his own coding process, via the utilisation of the framework method and NVivo. The focus of this work is discovering how Nantes has been framed by the media, and determining then if the media can be utilised to brand a specific place. This is an interesting and insightful study, therefore engaging with the site and its content is important for two reasons. First, the site acts as a working example of how the framework method can be applied to the role of the media in place branding, in the city of Nantes. Second, it will introduce you further to NVivo, which is also discussed in section 8.3.5 below.

8.3.4 Focus on: content analysis

There is no one, simple right way to *do* content analysis (Weber, 1985), but it is a widely used research technique (Hsieh and Shannon, 2005) and is perceived as being systematic, rule-guided analysis. The *ways to do* content analysis vary according to 'coding schemes, origins of codes, and threats to trustworthiness' (Hsieh and Shannon, 2005: 1277), whereas the similarities come in the form of the way data are handled and the way in which the analysis method is perceived as a classical procedure for 'analysing textual material' (Flick, 2002: 190).

As described in Chapter 6, this is a well-defined technique for making inferences by systematically and objectively identifying specified characteristics of a method (Frankfort-Nachmias and Nachmias, 1992; Hoyle et al., 2002). This means that this is an analysis method which can draw inference from the communication itself and ensure data are classified via the identification of words, phrases or other units of text; and those which are 'classified in the same category are presumed to have similar meaning' (Weber, 1985: 12). Now this does not mean that it is an easy option or tool to adopt, because, as with other methodological decisions, the decision to undertake content analysis should be linked to the research questions that have been developed prior to analysis (Chapter 3). Therefore, it is a question of suitability – suitability to the research at hand to discover the answers to the questions set and to add value to knowledge, understanding and theory about the social phenomena.

Content analysis can be viewed from both a quantitative and qualitative perspective, and this in itself is an area of confusion and concern for many researchers. There are some authors who assume 'repetition is the most valuable indicator of significance' (Ericson et al., 1991: 50) and there are others who prefer to draw inference 'on the basis of appearance or non-appearance of attributes in messages' (Holsti, 1969: 10), without counting. One deals with many texts and much counting (quantitative), whilst the other believes that the qualitative analysis of 'a limited number of crucial communications may often yield better clues to the particular intentions of a particular speaker at one moment in time' (Holsti, 1969). Even so, there is the contention that all content *variables* are quantifiable (otherwise they are not variables – see Chapter 7). But this is something that does not necessarily need to be addressed here; instead, it is important that you are aware that an alternative perspective exists!

To identify *variables* in qualitative content analysis, you begin by searching the text for the appearance of an attribute. These attributes are then highlighted and coded, before being interpreted into meaning and perhaps being detached from the original text. Qualitative content analysis can then be *done* in many different ways. In fact, it is possible to categorise qualitative content analysis into three specific approaches: conventional, directed and summative content analysis, as noted by Hsieh and Shannon (2005) and outlined below:

1. *Conventional* content analysis is generally used when a researcher is aiming to describe some phenomena. When theory is limited and there are no preconceived categories for coding, the researcher allows categories to emerge from the text itself. Consequently, immersion in the data is necessary and the process very much replicates the practices of thematic analysis (and the framework method) noted in section 8.3.3, meaning data are read to derive codes and then codes are sorted into categories, and those categories are used to organise and group meaningful clusters of codes and categories. The reporting of the content

is then expressed through identifying exemplars of each cluster, category or code and this knowledge is then linked to the relevant theory highlighted within the literature (of what may have existed).

2. *Directed* content analysis is used when there is existing theory or prior research about the phenomena under investigation, yet there is a need to further describe the phenomenon. The process here could be described as being more deductive in nature than conventional content analysis, because of the use of theory and how it may be further understood, because the researcher is validating (to some extent) a priori theory. Furthermore, the theory can provide preconceived codes and initial coding schemes, because the researcher is looking out for examples of a certain element or aspect of the theory. This is, therefore, a more structured way to undertake content analysis and the process starts with theory, which leads to a coding scheme, and then to interpretation via the content of the texts (if it exists of course). The results will then represent support for or difference in opinion to that which was originally stated by the theory. However, the goal of content analysis remains the same – to make inferences about the communication itself; and the presentation of the data is similar to conventional content analysis. Exemplars are highlighted, and these data are detached from the original text and presented as a theme. Note that this is not a quantitative analysis technique because we are still considering how things are said, and not how many resources say it – we are interested in the contextualisation of the data!

3. *Summative* content analysis, however, is slightly more quantitatively focused than the two named above. Here, the study starts with identifying and quantifying words in text, but with the purpose still being to understand the context, not the volume of appearances; therefore, it remains qualitative. If the analysis simply stopped after identifying and quantifying the frequency of words, then it would be quantitative. However, summative analysis does not stop there. Summative content analysis goes further and requires the researcher to interpret meaning from the text and to discover the underlying meaning of the content. Data collection therefore starts with a search for occurrences, and then this information is used to identify patterns in the data and to contextualise the codes, allowing for an interpretation of the context associated with the use of the word/phrase.

Moreover, each of these three approaches resembles a similar, analytical, process. Hsieh and Shannon (2005) outline these similarities as seven classic steps for qualitative content analysis:

1. Formulating the research questions (to be answered)
2. Selecting the sample to be analysed
3. Defining the categories to be applied

4. Outlining the coding process and the training required for the coder
5. Implementing the coding process itself upon the text
6. Determining the trustworthiness of the data sources
7. Effectively analysing the results of the coding process.

There are, of course, many advantages and limitations to each of the ways you *do* content analysis (see Hsieh and Shannon, 2005). Therefore, it is up to the researcher to ensure that a competent analysis of the texts/documentation is undertaken. This includes questioning the context and the social situation surrounding the documents in question (step 6 or 7 listed above). It is important as a researcher to grasp the significance of the document itself, to understand the process of production (in relation to the meaning and message of the document) and to then consider these aspects when the topics and themes emerge (Altheide, 1996) because they may be influential.

A key example of this is when newsprint is analysed. Newsprint, depending on the source of publication, can be seen as being sensationalistic, informative, didactic or a feature story (Cousins and Brunt, 2002). The nature of reporting can influence the type of words and stories which are conveyed to the audience and, therefore, the qualitative analysis of these publications may lead to bias, as such. To overcome these types of issues, it is therefore important that the researcher considers the purpose and process of the publication and searches for relevant information in a systematic and consistent manner (to allow for replication if nothing else). An example of the content analysis of newsprint is given in Illustration 8.13.

Illustration 8.13   A conventional form of content analysis (Hooton, 2005)

When researching the media interpretations of a tourist destination, Hooton (2005) outlined the need to explore the nature and extent of media representation of a Cornish seaside resort. To successfully address this need, the researcher decided to identify the nature of media representation of the resort through a qualitative analysis of newspaper print. Consequently, a structured process was followed to identify (and then evaluate) newsprint that had depicted the town over the past four years. With the use of LexisNexis Professional, a pioneering, electronic and accessible repository of documents, the researcher was able to systematically search for newsprint, as shown in Table 8.9, via a four-stage elimination process.

Table 8.9   Four-stage elimination process

Stage	Process	Outcome
One	One key word: 'Newquay' To view the quantity of articles related to this investigation and the destination	Over 1,000 articles which the program was unable to display
Two	Key word search for 'Newquay' and 'tourism' within the same article To ensure the documents' relevance to the investigation	936 articles Some showed no relevance Newquay only mentioned in passing
Three	Key word search for the appearance of 'Newquay' three times or more, and in addition still displayed the word 'tourism'	248 articles 48 appeared in national newspapers and 200 were articles sourced from local print
Four	Familiarisation of text and discovery of relevance	24 of the national prints were deemed irrelevant 41 of the local articles were also considered irrelevant
	Result	24 national articles and 159 local articles

Once the articles were accessed, and the trustworthiness and suitability of the sources were reviewed, analysis was then undertaken. The sample was structured in terms of the national and local audiences that they were targeted at, and resulted in nine national newspapers (e.g. *Daily Mail*, *The Guardian* and the *Observer*) and three local papers (e.g. the *Cornish Guardian* and the *Western Morning News*) being assessed.

The researcher at this stage immersed themselves into the data and allowed for the codes and categories to emerge. Therefore, the categorisation process was achieved through the familiarisation of content and noting themes along with brief descriptions. The results were as follows.

National newsprint

Hedonism

'Drug dealers ply their evil trade on the beach as under-age girls swig booze and shamelessly hunt for sex in Newquay'

'Sleazy older men target vulnerable young girls for sex'

(Continued)

(Continued)

'Hard drugs are freely available, whilst cannabis and ecstasy are sold openly on the beach'

Development

'Rick Stein venture could revive the fortunes of the Cornish resort of Newquay'

'Rick Stein is extending his empire'

'Many Newquay hoteliers are poshing their places up'

'Reverse decades of decline'

Infrastructure

'Ryanair burst on to the scene'

'Ryanair's arrival is the most significant economic regeneration factor'

Activities/Attractions

'Newquay has become the centre for British surfing'

'Tourist officials talk about the nearby Eden Project as if it is the Hoover Dam'

'Surfing has gone up market'

'Surfing capital of the country'

Visitor profile

'The playground for wild child Britain'

'All display the most predictable and disgusting characteristics of British Youth'

'High spending bachelor parties have become big business'

Beach emphasis

'International Surf Centre will open on Fistral Beach'

'Fistral Beach is gorgeous'

Organisations

'Newquay Town Council demanding a bylaw to end all night revels'

Negative implications

'Family bookings are very down this year after all the bad press'

'Property prices have more than doubled in two years'

'Prices are being driven up by a buy-to-let bubble'

External elements

'Worried that images of flood devastation will keep tourists away'

Local newsprint

Hedonism

'A few detained for violence and public order offences'

'Labelled this month as a boozy resort'

'All night drinking is finally getting its way'

Development

'Every big new development creates its own spin-offs'

'Holds the key to the development of the region's tourist industry'

'Surf reef will be a big boost'

Infrastructure

'It has been a fantastic year for Newquay Airport'

'Newquay Airport seems to go from strength to strength'

'Ryanair came to Newquay around two years ago'

Activities/Attractions

'Run to the Sun is a massive asset for Newquay'

'The unique environment of the Eden Project'

'The Eden Factor'

(Continued)

(Continued)

'Surfing capital of the UK'

'Importance of the Eden Project in revitalising tourism'

Visitor profile

'Well-heeled holidaymakers, young and old, are now flocking'

'Young people from around the country head for the town each year'

'A younger crowd has laid claim to Newquay'

Beach emphasis

'Watergate Bay is a growth area'

'Upturn in fortunes for Watergate Bay'

'Fistral more than a match for Bondi'

'Fistral Beach is thriving'

Organisations

'Newquay Town Council has also reinforced its commitment to supporting tourism'

Negative implications

'Family cancelled their reunion party'

'National press has been blamed for holiday cancellations'

'Perceived decline in popularity of coach tours'

'The loss of further bed spaces'

External elements

'Weather forecasters predicted glorious sunshine'

'Continuing problems with foot and mouth are having a significant effect'

From these charts, it was determined that the nature and extent of media representation of the resort differed in terms of how the key themes were expressed.

The charts identified the sensationalistic style of writing within the national press and a more mundane reporting of everyday occurrences within the local press.

Note: to make this analysis process *directed*, the researcher could have utilised a preconceived list of codes from existent theory. Alternatively, to provide a *summative* analysis, the researcher could have counted how often key terms were expressed and then utilised Spearman's Rank Correlation Coefficient to determine the significance level of association between the themes and key words from both the national and local press.

8.3.5 Focus on NVivo

As highlighted in section 8.3.2, there are two ways of doing qualitative data analysis – by hand and by computer. One specific CAQDAS that can be used for qualitative data analysis by computer is NVivo. NVivo is software produced by QSR International (2016) and software that intuitively helps a researcher to characterise, cut, code, categorise, convert and create knowledge about a phenomenon that Savin-Baden and Howell Major (2013) describe as thematic analysis. There are many textbooks which highlight the use of NVivo (e.g. Savin-Baden and Howell Major, 2013) and others whose central focus is to inform the reader of how to make full use of the NVivo software (e.g. Bazeley, 2007; Bazeley and Jackson, 2013). Therefore, the purpose of this section is not to replicate the contents of either type of entry, but simply to raise key areas of interest, to share insight into its application via a live case study and to offer some personal evaluations of how the computer *tool* can make the process of thematic analysis more effective and efficient than conducting it by hand.

First and foremost, it is important to know exactly what NVivo is. NVivo is a piece of software that supports qualitative data analysis (QSR International, 2016) and it is designed to help a researcher to record, sort, match and link data without losing access to the original data (or contexts from which the data have come) (Bazeley, 2007). The software is, therefore, an appropriate tool for analysis that supports thematic analysis (section 8.3.3) and the framework method (section 8.3.3), as described earlier in this chapter. However, instead of conducting thematic analysis by hand, the software increases the effectiveness and efficiency of the analysis process. At the same time, it provides the researcher with 'a more complete set of data for interpretation than might occur when working manually' (Bazeley, 2007: 3).

NVivo is an intuitive programme that allows the researcher to organise their data in a naturalistic manner, and provides the researcher with both quick interpretations of data sets and functions that allow for more detailed interpretation of the data set. With regards to the analysis process, NVivo can be used in isolation of any other analysis processes already named in this chapter (e.g. by conducting key word searches) in conjunction with thematic analysis and the framework method, which involves five key steps. These steps were discussed in section 8.3.3 and include the process of familiarisation, coding and charting. The process is extremely similar if utilising the NVivo software and is outlined in Table 8.10. Although the terminology alters, the process is comparable. For example, the data sources are identified (e.g. interviews are transcribed) and the researcher becomes familiar with the process before developing free nodes (open codes) and tree nodes (axial codes) to index the data. Once the sources are then coded and clustered (in nodes) patterns can be detected.

Table 8.10   Utilising NVivo as a tool for thematic analysis via the Framework Method

Step	Framework stages	NVivo processes
1	Familiarisation	Transcribe and import data
2	Identifying a thematic framework	Reconsider free nodes; transform free nodes into tree nodes and allow relationships to emerge
3	Indexing	Use tree nodes to index the research and present themes and relationships within the data
4	Charting	Export data from the original context to form charts and tables to support the emergent themes
5	Mapping and interpretation	Use charts to illustrate and define concepts, map the range and nature of the phenomena, find associations and provide explanations through the development of strategies

The process of thematic analysis has been used by numerous academics (Mansfield, 2016; Semley et al., 2017) within the THE industry to quickly explore the data that has been collected, and then to appropriately code and sort the data once an initial understanding has been obtained. This is conducted through the content analysis of published material (e.g. newsprint and destination management plans, respectively). Therefore, NVivo can be used to analyse all types of data sources and at many different levels: from conventional content analysis to summative and anywhere in between.

From a tourism and events perspective, NVivo has been used as a tool to quickly identify the key themes of a destination's management plan to determine if planned events are of value to the destination's strategic goals. As noted in Illustration 8.4, Semley et al. (2017) aspired to determine the policy importance of planned events for DMOs in England, and the authors painstakingly collated the DMPs for DMOs based in England. Once these were obtained, the authors imported the files in bulk (see steps 1–7 in Illustration 8.14) and quickly interpreted the data via a series of word clouds; these were simply produced to get an initial feel for the content. By no means was this where the analysis ended. After the result of the initial *word cloud*, as illustrated in step 6, the sources were grouped and codes were formed to help the academics to tell a more effective, insightful and considered story about the data and the research question posed.

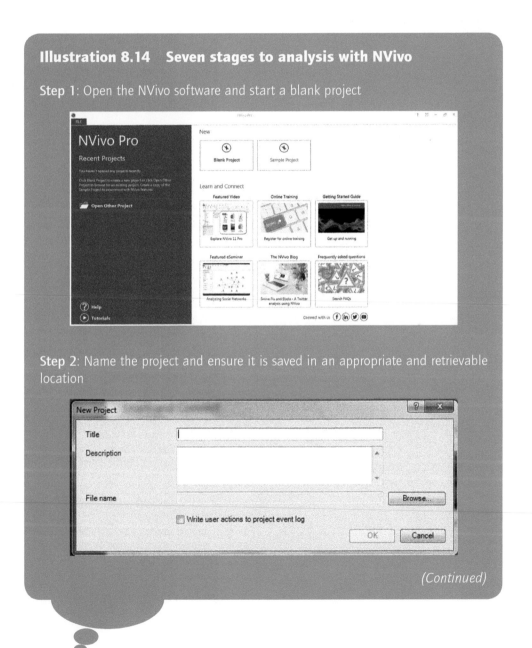

Illustration 8.14   Seven stages to analysis with NVivo

Step 1: Open the NVivo software and start a blank project

Step 2: Name the project and ensure it is saved in an appropriate and retrievable location

(Continued)

(Continued)

Step 3: Create and classify sources via the 'data' tab

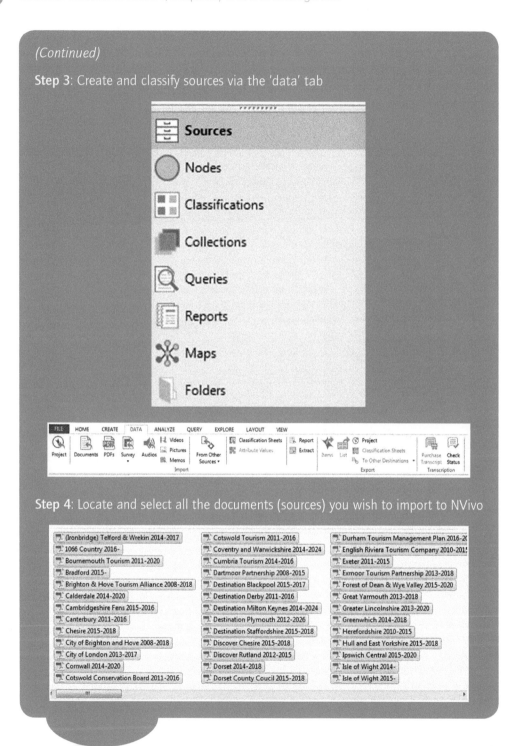

Step 4: Locate and select all the documents (sources) you wish to import to NVivo

Step 5: Run a query to generate a word frequency

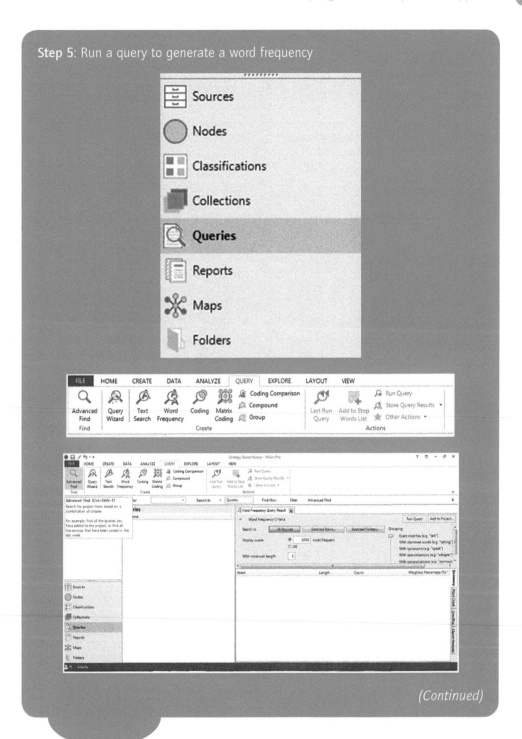

(Continued)

(Continued)

Step 6: View the word cloud for a visual interpretation of the data

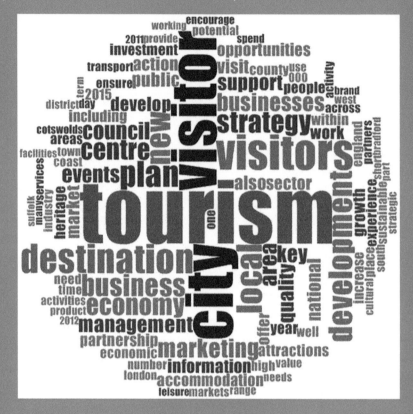

Step 7: Interpret the word cloud in conjunction with the research enquiry and, if of value, ensure you 'add to project' before moving on to undertake a more detailed assessment of the data sources

At this stage, evidently, there are *results* (as such) for the researcher to consider. You can view the word cloud and you can interpret the content. However, the real question about this quick and dirty insight into the data set is: what does this actually tell us about the DMPs of DMOs?

Well, not a lot really. Yes, it does provide you with a starting point and a hunch as such to the presence of key terminology within the DMPs themselves. The word event is there, but can you see it? Furthermore, the size of the word 'events' depicts the frequency of its use, and if I wanted to quantify the usage of the word itself 'events', then I could tell you that it appears 1,723 times within the 74 DMPs covering 0.33% of the overall content:

Word	Length	Count	Weighted Percentage (%) ▽
economy	7	2158	0.41
centre	6	2152	0.41
marketing	9	1954	0.37
businesses	10	1852	0.36
area	4	1833	0.35
council	7	1790	0.34
key	3	1753	0.34
events	6	1723	0.33
management	10	1708	0.33
support	7	1634	0.31
quality	7	1616	0.31
also	4	1456	0.28
develop	7	1455	0.28

Summary | Word Cloud | Tree Map | Cluster Analysis

However, as I stated in section 8.2.4, numbers are of little value to the qualitative interpretation of data. Instead, what is needed is a contextual understanding of the way in which the word (events) is used in the text. Therefore, instead of leaving the analysis (if we could call it that!) here, you would need to go back to the data set and begin to familiarise yourself with the content before coding and categorising the data for later interpretation, as did Semley et al. (2017).

A similar process can also be applied to online information, for example data drawn from social media. Illustration 8.15 outlines a quick exercise that can be undertaken to determine the themes tweeted by an organisation of your choice. Obviously, this illustration only outlines the process to undertake; it does not give you the answers to the data analysis. It is at this stage that you still need to be creative and develop the ability to systematically search for answers. This is, as described in Table 8.5, where the hard work begins!

Illustration 8.15   Using NVivo to analyse social media content on Twitter; by Jennifer Phillips (2016)

Getting started:

- Step 1: Open NVivo and select 'New Project'
- Step 2: Name your project and add a description, click OK
- Step 3: Select 'Sources' in the menu on the left and then open 'Internals'
- Step 4: Select the 'create' tab on the toolbar and click on document as shown
- Step 5: Name your new document and provide a description, click OK; the new source will now show in Internals
- Step 6: Double-click on your new source; this will open a blank document. Copy and paste five tweets from a business or organisation of your choice.

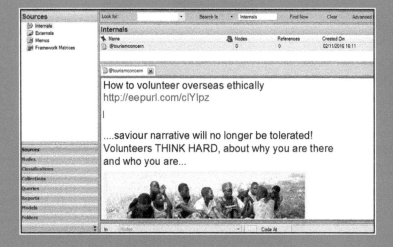

Repeat steps 4-6 for a second business or organisation. Choose an example that is of a similar nature to the first source. This example uses two tourism charities

- Step 7: Click on the classifications tab in the left-hand panel. Right click in the source classifications box in the centre of the screen and select 'New Classification' from the drop-down menu
- Step 8: Name and describe the classification for the new sources
- Step 9: Click on the Sources tab in the left-hand panel. Right click on each of the sources and select 'Classification' from the drop-down menu and click on the new classification.

Creating and classifying nodes:

Nodes can be created in three ways dependent on what you already know about your data:

- Add nodes before you start coding:
    1. From the navigation panel on the left select 'Nodes'.
    2. Click on the create tab and select 'Node'.
    3. When the new dialogue box opens, enter a name and description for the Node.
- Create nodes as you code:
    1. Open a source in detail view.
    2. Select the content that you want to code.
    3. On the Analyse tab under 'Code Selection at' click 'New Node'.
- Name a node from a selected word:
    1. Open a source in detail view.
    2. Select the content that you want to code.
    3. On the Analyse tab click 'Code In Vivo'.

In addition to sources, nodes can also be classified:

- Click on the 'Classifications' tab in the navigation panel and select 'Node Classifications'.
- Right click in the node classifications box and select 'New Classification' from the drop-down menu.
- Name and describe your new classification.

There are three different types of coding to consider:

1. Topic coding – what topic is being discussed?
2. Analytical coding – what is the content really about? Why is it of interest?
3. Descriptive coding – what is the material for? Who is speaking? Etc.

Once you start coding, you will also need to code at existing Nodes:

1. Select the material you wish to code.
2. On the Analyse tab, click Existing nodes and select the appropriate Node.

(Continued)

(Continued)

3. This can also be achieved through the drop-down menu if you right-click select 'Code Selection' and 'Code Selection At Existing Node', or by using the Quick Coding Bar at the bottom of the detail view.
4. To see what you have coded, use the 'Highlight' function or 'Coding stripes', both located under the View tab.

Visualising the data:

- Create a model to visualise connections. This function can be used to visualise, explore and present connections in the data:

  1. Click on the Explore tab and select Create a new Model.
  2. Name and provide a description for your model.
  3. To get started, click 'Add Project Items'.

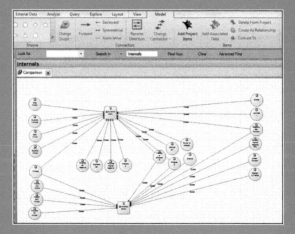

- Display data in a chart. This function can be used to visualise the different nodes that code a source:

    1. Click on the Explore tab and select chart.
    2. Follow the chart wizard to create your chart.

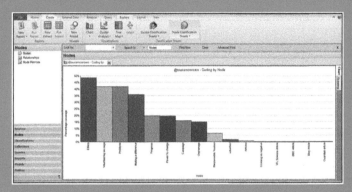

Queries for text analysis:

- Explore the text using:

    1. Text search query: search for a word or phrase. View all instances that occur or create a word tree.

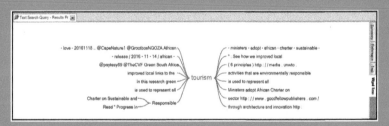

    2. Word frequency query: list the most frequent words and visualise the results as a tree map, word cloud or cluster analysis.

As you can see from the examples included in this section, NVivo can be a welcome support for the thematic analysis of qualitative data. The software is versatile and offers numerous additional functions which are not noted here. To gain a more detailed insight, and a more thorough 'how to' guide, it is recommended that you access the QSR International website (www.qsrinternational.com) which contains video tutorials and helpful resources. The possibilities are endless; again, they will only be limited by the researcher's level of creativity and understanding of their research POEM and the coding, themes and interpretation process.

8.4 Summary

This chapter has acknowledged a range of different ways in which an individual can 'do' research and tell the data story. The chapter has outlined how qualitative data analysis, in all of its guises, needs to be led by creativity, inspiration and the meticulous uncovering of meaning. This deeper and more profound way of developing our understanding offers both insight into and interpretation of a social phenomenon that is under investigation. There is no quick fix to qualitative analysis; instead, there are a range of different approaches to reading and interpreting qualitative data that need to be considered. Furthermore, the researcher needs to understand a range of techniques that can sometimes result in confusion and the generation of overly subjective findings. Nevertheless, if you allow for the project to be underpinned by the original aim and purpose, you can overcome these issues and produce an effective and efficient analysis of various data sources.

Whether conducting the process by hand or by computer, there are different ways in which qualitative analysis may be tackled, even if there is no one set technique, test or procedure to follow. There are universal processes which can be followed, to some extent, that allow for successful thematic analysis, regardless of tool. However, this should not override the creativity and detailed interpretation that have been demonstrated throughout the chapter. Just remember, to succeed you need to believe in your personal intuition as a qualitative researcher!

Exercises

1. Identify five reasons why a researcher within the THE industry may decide to organise

    a. written material; and
    b. visual material
       in a chronological order.

2. Read one of the following three images (8.2, 8.3 and 8.4). Start with a literal interpretation. Then progress to an interpretive reading of the image. What are the key distinctions you have drawn from these readings? Which 'reading' do you perceive as being most suitable when discussing the topic of each photo?

Image 8.2   **A Foo Fighters concert at The National Bowl, Milton Keynes**

Image 8.3   **Boardmasters Festival, Newquay**

Image 8.4   **Field Good Music Festival, Trevarrian, Cornwall**

3. Explain the five stages of the framework method of qualitative data analysis.
4. Take to social media and undertake the activity outlined in Illustration 8.15. How intuitive did you find NVivo? What did the word cloud reveal to you?

Further reading

Bazeley, P. and Jackson, K. (2013). *Qualitative Data Analysis with NVivo*. 2nd edition. London: Sage. This book provides you with an in-depth introduction to NVivo and a comprehensive 'how to' guide to get you started with the qualitative data analysis software.

Brunt, P. and Hooton, N. (2010). Community Responses to Tourism and Crime. *Crime Prevention and Community Safety: An International Journal*. 12 (1): 42–57. This article offers you a working example of how observational logs and in-depth interviews can be obtained, analysed and presented via the framework method discussed in section 8.3.3.

Mason, J. (2002). *Qualitative Researching*. 2nd edition. London: Sage.
This book is my go-to text for a clear understanding of the research POEM. Jennifer Mason's style of questioning encourages the researcher to search for in-depth and detailed answers to understand their causal puzzle.

Ritchie, J. and Spencer, L. (1994). Qualitative Analysis for Applied Policy Research. In A. Bryman and R.G. Burgess (eds). *Analyzing Qualitative Data*. London: Routledge.
This chapter of the book gives you a detailed insight into the framework method as a form of thematic analysis. This is the first publication to name and outline the process itself, which was later adopted and adapted by other academics.

Semley, N. and Busby, G. (2014). Film Tourism: The pre-production perspective – A case study of Visit Somerset and the Hollywood story of Glastonbury. *Journal of Tourism Consumption and Practice*. 6 (2): 23–53.
This article offers you a working example of how elite interviews and focus groups can be analysed using the framework method.

Semley, N., Huang, R. and Dalton, J. (2016). Feedback for Learning Development: Tourism students' perspective. *Journal of Hospitality, Leisure, Sport & Tourism Education*. 17 (2): 41–53.
This article offers you a working example of how in-depth interviews can be analysed utilising thematic analysis.

References

Altheide, D.L. (1996). *Qualitative Media Analysis*. Qualitative Research Method series 38. London: Sage.
Bazeley, P. (2007). *Qualitative Data Analysis with NVivo*. London: Sage.
Bazeley, P. and Jackson, K. (2013). *Qualitative Data Analysis with NVivo*. 2nd edition. London: Sage.
Brunt, P. (1997). *Market Research in Travel and Tourism*. Oxford: Butterworth-Heinemann.
Brunt, P. and Hambly, Z. (1999). Tourism and Crime: A research agenda. *Crime Prevention and Community Safety: An International Journal*. 1 (2): 25–36.
Brunt, P. and Hooton, N. (2010). Community Responses to Tourism and Crime. *Crime Prevention and Community Safety: An International Journal*. 12 (1): 42–57.
Cousins, K. and Brunt, P. (2002). Terrorism, Tourism and the Media. *Security Journal*. 15 (1): 19–32.
Crang, M. (2003). Qualitative Methods: Touchy, feely, look-see? *Progress in Human Geography*. 27 (4): 494–504.
Davies, B. (2003). The Role of Quantitative and Qualitative Research in Industrial Studies of Tourism. *International Journal of Tourism Research*. 5 (1): 97–111.
Decrop, A. (1999). Triangulation in Qualitative Tourism Research. *Tourism Management*. 20 (1): 157–61.
Department of Culture, Media and Sport (DCMS). (2016). Home page. Available at: www.gov.uk/government/organisations/department-for-culture-media-sport (accessed 16 December 2016).
Ericson, R.V., Baranek, P.M. and Chan, J.B.L. (1991). *Representing Order: Crime, law, and justice in the news media*. Milton Keynes: Open University Press.

Flick, U. (2002). *An Introduction to Qualitative Research*. 2nd edition. London: Sage.

Fox, D., Gouthro, M.B., Morakabati, Y. and Brackstone, J. (2014). *Doing Events Research: From theory to practice*. London: Routledge.

Frankfort-Nachmias, C. and Nachmias, D. (1992). *Research Methods in the Social Sciences*. 4th edition. London: Edward Arnold.

Getz, D. (1997). *Event Management and Event Tourism*. New York: Cognizant Communications Corp.

Getz, D. (2007). *Event Studies: Theory, research and policy for planned events*. Oxford: Elsevier.

Glaser, B.G. and Strauss, A.L. (1967). *The Discovery of Grounded Theory: Strategies for qualitative research*. Chicago: Aldine.

Goldberg, M. (2000). *Some suggestions on 'how to read' a film*. Available at: https://faculty.washington.edu/mlg/students/readafilm.htm (accessed 16 December 2016).

Guba, E.G. and Lincoln, Y.S. (1994). Competing Paradigms in Qualitative Research. In N.K. Denzin and Y.S. Lincoln (eds). *Handbook of Qualitative Research*. Thousand Oaks, CA: Sage, pp. 105–17.

Holsti, O.R. (1969). *Content Analysis for the Social Sciences and Humanities*. London: Addison-Wesley.

Hooton, N. (2005). Community responses to tourism and crime. Unpublished MSc thesis, University of Plymouth.

Hoyle, R.H., Harris, M.J. and Judd, C.M. (2002). *Research Methods in Social Relations*. 7th edition. Wadsworth: Thomson Learning.

Hsieh, H.-F. and Shannon, S.E. (2005). Three Approaches to Qualitative Content Analysis. *Qualitative Health Research*. 15 (9): 1277–88.

Krane, V., Anderson, M. and Stean, W. (1997). Issues of Qualitative Research Methods and Presentation. *Journal of Sport and Exercise Psychology*. 19 (2): 213–18.

Mansfield, C. (2016). *NVivo*. Available at: https://sites.google.com/site/touremetkt/home/nvivo (accessed 16 December 2016).

Mason, J. (2002). *Qualitative Researching*. 2nd edition. London: Sage.

Miles, M. and Huberman, A. (1994). *Qualitative Data Analysis*. Thousand Oaks, CA: Sage.

Oxford Dictionaries. (2016). Home page. Available at: www.oxforddictionaries.com (accessed 16 December 2016).

QSR International. (2016). *Discover NVivo*. Available at: www.qsrinternational.com (accessed 16 December 2016).

Ritchie, J. and Spencer, L. (1994). Qualitative Analysis for Applied Policy Research. In A. Bryman and R.G. Burgess (eds). *Analyzing Qualitative Data*. London: Routledge.

Ritchie, J., Lewis, J., Nicholls, C.M. and Ormston, R. (2014). *Qualitative Research Practice: A guide for social science students and researchers*. 2nd edition. London: Sage.

Saldana, J. (2012). *The Coding Manual for Qualitative Researchers*. 2nd edition. Thousand Oaks, CA: Sage.

Savin-Baden, M. and Howell Major, C. (2013). *Qualitative Research: The essential guide to theory and practice*. London: Routledge.

Semley, N. (2012). *An evaluation of tourism communities and community responses to tourism and crime: a case study of two Cornish destinations*. Available at: https://pearl.plymouth.ac.uk/handle/10026.1/1238 (accessed 16 December 2016).

Semley, N. (2014). A Street in Benidom, Spain. Unpublished photo.

Semley, N. and Busby, G. (2014). Film Tourism: The pre-production perspective – A case study of Visit Somerset and the Hollywood story of Glastonbury. *Journal of Tourism Consumption and Practice*. 6 (2): 23–53.

Semley, N., Bellingham, T. and Young, R. (2017). DMO, DMP and Event Tourism: Are planned events valued? (ed.) H. Seraphin, *International Events Management: Bridging the gap between theory and practice*. Forthcoming.

Semley, N., Huang, R. and Dalton, J. (2016). Feedback for Learning Development: Tourism students' perspective. *Journal of Hospitality, Leisure, Sport & Tourism Education*. 17 (2): 41–53.

Strauss, A. and Corbin, J. (1990). *Basics of Qualitative Research: Techniques and procedures for developing grounded theory*. London: Sage.

Walle, A.H. (1997). Quantitative versus Qualitative Tourism Research. *Annals of Tourism Research*. 24 (3): 524–36.

Weber, R.P. (1985). *Basic Content Analysis*. Quantitative Applications in the Social Sciences series. London: Sage.

9

WRITING UP, PRESENTING AND PUBLISHING THE RESULTS

LEARNING OBJECTIVES

From reading this chapter, you should be able to:

- appreciate the different approaches to writing up and presenting findings in relation to the type of research carried out
- understand how to organise the main sections of research reports
- learn how to prepare and arrange presentations
- identify publication opportunities for research.

9.1 Introduction

As mentioned in Chapter 3, the final stage of the research process is the communication of the findings. Normally, this will involve a written report and may also include giving a presentation. The format for the report or presentation will, to a certain extent, be dictated by the type of research you have undertaken.

In academic research, reports of the findings of research projects are often published as articles in journals such as *Tourism Management* or *Annals of Tourism*

Research. Here, the format of the article is often prescribed by the 'house style' of the journal. Aspects such as the illustrations, method of referencing as well as the length of the text must fit with the journal's own criteria. Moreover, before publication may proceed, the article is 'refereed' by other academics who may sit on an editorial board for the journal. Referees may recommend rejecting the publication or suggest amendments before the article is accepted. Academics may, alternatively, report their findings in books either as a whole text or as a chapter in an edited text. Here, again, there may be certain requirements of format made by the publisher or editor. Often, academics will aim to present a paper at a conference where they can speak about their research findings to others interested in the subject. Most conferences issue the 'proceedings' of a conference which represent a written form of the academics' speech.

A form where students report their findings is in support of a particular qualification. These can range from a special study or major project for a Higher National Diploma, through an honours project or dissertation for a first degree, to the thesis for a masters' or doctorate qualification. Here too, the awarding body may require certain features to be included in the format of any written material. Additionally, the qualification may involve an oral presentation or examination.

With applied or action research where, typically, projects are undertaken on behalf of an employer, the results are often communicated in both written and verbal form. Reports of research may be read by senior management, councillors or shareholders depending on the nature of the employer. In this case an executive summary, which is a shortened version of the principal findings, is usually required. This is because busy executives or councillors can get a 'flavour' of the report and decide how much of the rest of the report they need to (or are willing to) read. In addition, employee researchers will often be asked to give a presentation of their work to a meeting of senior colleagues.

Where the nature of the research has been a consultancy project, a similar pattern is usually found. The format for the results in terms of a written report and any presentation will have been specified in the contract. Additionally, the consultant may be required to submit written interim reports and give presentations at client meetings.

It can be seen that, whatever the type of research, and whilst there may be certain guidelines or constraints in terms of format, the reporting and presentation of the project are crucial to the researcher. For academics, future funding opportunities, reputation and promotion prospects are, in part, determined by the success of the publication of their research. For the HND, BA/BSc, MA/MSc or PhD student, a significant part of passing their examination is down to skill in writing up their findings and defending them orally. For the employee researcher, their opportunities to get future interesting projects, promotion prospects and company performance may, to a certain degree, be directly related to completing and reporting on their research. Finally, for the consultant their chance of future contracts and financial survival are directly related to their performance and ability to communicate effectively. Hence, it would seem that if any researcher is to be truly successful and achieve job satisfaction, writing up and presenting results must be done well!

When embarking on the writing-up process, it is necessary for you to first consider the readership. This can influence the type of language and emphasis given to particular sections. The consultancy report may have a greater focus on the findings and give specific recommendations than would an academic paper. In the latter case, the academic may need to give greater depth to the methods of data collection, sampling techniques and types of analysis than would a consultant's report.

Writing up and giving presentations are not easy but can be very rewarding. Unfortunately, however, they are often left until the very end of a project when time pressures for completion are greatest. Too often, data collection and analysis overrun and eat into the time allowed for writing up. Whilst, for some, the deadline looming helps to focus the mind and motivate the writer, it is probably safer to recognise the difficulty and plan ahead. Some sections of a report could be written as a first draft whilst the data collection is under way. The aims and objectives, introduction, methodology, bibliography and some appendices could be prepared in advance before the researcher becomes too involved in the data analysis. The aim of this chapter is to help in this process. It is divided into three parts to give you some practical guidelines for preparing a report, planning a presentation and publishing your research.

9.2 Writing up a student research project

9.2.1 The sequence of a research report

As previously mentioned, the type of the research approach, readership and place of publication will influence the nature of a report. However, commonly, most student research reports will include a variation of the following:

Title

Preface or Foreword (or both)

Acknowledgements

Summary or Abstract

Contents page

List of tables

List of figures

Introduction

Literature review

Aims and objectives

Methods

Results

Discussion

Recommendations

Conclusion

References or Bibliography (or both)

Appendices

Each of these components will be examined in turn and examples of key aspects of the report will be provided.

Title

On the front cover of a report will be the title of the work, the name of the author and the year in which it was completed. If the research is carried out for an employer (action research) or a client (consultancy), their name will also appear on the front cover. In the case of a student research report, the name of the academic tutor or module code may also be included. It is common in books that the first page will also be a title page that repeats similar information.

The title should reflect the purpose of the study and be as concise as possible. We have seen a lot of examples of titles throughout the book as we have been considering examples.

Preface or Foreword

Inclusion of a preface or foreword is uncommon in student research projects, but it is mentioned here for completeness. A foreword is most commonly found in books and is normally written by a series editor or an eminent individual in the subject area. It is an introduction in support of the book covering its purpose and scope. A preface is usually written by the author and typically outlines the principal themes to be covered, the general approach, intended readership and other similar points.

Acknowledgements

This is an expression of gratitude to those who have helped the author in the research. As such, it is common to student research, books and reports. It is usual in student research to acknowledge the help of academic tutors who have provided advice throughout the duration of the project. It is also common to give thanks to organisations or individuals who have provided access to information. Acknowledgements are often personal, with thanks being given to family and friends. Where permission from another author or organisation was sought to include some of their work in the text (especially when the report is published), this is also acknowledged. Here is an example of acknowledgements from an undergraduate dissertation for you to have a look at:

> I could not have achieved this final report without the assistance, assurance and guidance from numerous people. I would therefore like to take the opportunity to acknowledge a few, predominately Dr Nigel Jackson for his dedicated time, insight and helpful feedback. To the industry professionals who gave their valuable time for me to interview them. But most importantly, I thank my family, for their emotional support and their grammatical assistance. (Lucy Cairns, undergraduate dissertation, Plymouth University, 2016)

Here is another good example of acknowledgements in an undergraduate dissertation that is a bit more personal:

> First and foremost, my eternal gratitude must be expressed to my parents and family who have given me unfailing support throughout the course of my studies. To them I owe my investigative nature and passion for active travel which have been the inspiration for my project. My sincerest thanks must also go to my honours project tutor Derek Shepherd whose expert guidance and timely advice have spurred me on to achieve great successes with my thesis and to Dr Charlie Mansfield whose constant interest and insight have had a great impact on the progression of my academic studies. My gratitude must also be expressed towards all those who willingly took part as respondents to the surveys and interviews, and last but not least to all those friends who have patiently supported and encouraged me through the process of writing up my thesis. (Antonio Calogero Nobile, undergraduate dissertation, Plymouth University, 2016)

Another example of acknowledgements is shown below:

> Foremost I would like to express my deepest gratitude to my supervisor Andreas Walmsley. His patience, encouragement and immense knowledge were the key motivations throughout the process of my dissertation project. His support and dedication have guided me throughout this year to complete my research project. I would also like to thank my family for their support and encouragement, which helped me to stay motivated throughout the process of my dissertation. (Karolina Valichova, undergraduate dissertation, Plymouth University, 2016)

Summary of report or Abstract

A summary is of the whole report, providing the reader with a shortened version of the aims and objectives, methods, results, recommendations and conclusions. Only the most important findings are included, which allow your reader to be aware of any recommendations prior to reading the main text.

For research reports which are published as articles in journals, the summary is often replaced by an abstract and these are also common in student research projects. In student research projects, the abstract is usually included before the contents page and states what has been done, why, what was found and what was concluded. As journal articles do not normally include contents or lists of tables and figures, the abstract will follow the title. Sometimes journals will additionally require key words which are pertinent to the theme of the research. These enable key word searches to be facilitated. Abstracts vary in length but rarely exceed 300 words. An example of a well-written abstract is given below:

The aim of the research was to explore the contemporary talent management process in a 4 star hotel in Plymouth. The research objectives included the examination of the role of different managers in the management of the talents in the hotel, to try to identify the difference between talent management and a traditional human resource approach, to identify the importance of employee engagement and to identify the positives and negatives of the inclusive and exclusive talent management processes. The researcher consulted key areas of the literature including the meaning of talent management, employee engagement, the human resource and organisational perspective of talent management, and the inclusive and exclusive talent management approaches to the talent management process. The research used a qualitative data collection method. The empirical research method included qualitative, semi-structured interviews and the personal observation of the researcher. The data analysis used transcript analysis followed by thematic analysis. In the conclusion of the research, employee engagement seems to be the most critical in the talent management process and the work finishes with recommendations for the sector, including improvement in the efficiency of hiring and the importance of recognising employees in the workplace. The limitations of the research are discussed and recommendations are made for further research including suggestions for research from a larger sample of hotels. (Rohit Reji George, undergraduate student dissertation, supervised by Susan Horner, Plymouth University, 2016)

Contents page

This reports the page numbers of each major section and subsection to guide the reader. Contents pages can be automatically generated in word-processing software such as Microsoft Word by use of the heading styles. Use of these functions allows the table of contents to be updated automatically and will save time when it comes to formatting the final document.

An example of a contents page is shown below:

Table of Contents

Source: Rebecca Makepiece, undergraduate dissertation, supervised by Craig Wight, Plymouth University, 2014

Lists of tables and figures

Where tables or figures have been included in the main body of the report, they are titled and listed following the contents. Sometimes tables and figures are numbered consecutively throughout the text (e.g. from 1 to 40) or by each section (4.1, 7.2, meaning the first table or figure in Chapter 4 and the second in Chapter 7). The page number is supplied by each entry. As with the contents page, a list of tables and figures can also be generated automatically. From the same dissertation as above, see below an example of a list of tables and figures:

Table of Figures

Main text – introduction

This, the first major section of the report, sets the scene and background of the research. Introductory sections identify the need or problem which is to be investigated and comments on how the research relates to other research undertaken in the past. In essence, the introduction builds a picture of what will happen in the rest of the report. It may be useful at the end of the introduction to specify how the remainder of the report is organised. Doing this assists the reader in knowing what to expect and helps them to follow your logic. From this base, the next section naturally flows.

For an example of an introduction to a student dissertation, see Illustration 9.1.

Illustration 9.1   An example of an introduction in an undergraduate student dissertation

This research project seeks to investigate what effect consumer behaviour towards discount promotions has on business strategy for restaurant organisations. *The Guardian* (2010) reports that the use of discount promotions in the restaurant industry has been a major phenomenon. It is said that more than one in five consumers won't go to a restaurant unless it is offering a discount voucher. Diners are said to be typically saving £3 million every day on the cost of eating out and the number of people using discount promotions in restaurants is on the rise (*The Guardian*, 2010). Therefore, it can be said that there is a need to see how this phenomenon, the large savings that consumers are able to obtain, is affecting businesses who engage with these types of promotions. More recently and in contradiction, *The Telegraph*

(Continued)

(Continued)

(2013) reports that the use of discount promotions within the restaurant industry is in decline. These tactics have been used to gain a bigger market share, however using discount promotions as part of business strategy is said to be unsustainable. It is said that restaurants using this type of promotion have become more discriminant, because they were selling many products at a loss. This research seeks to find out how these changes are impacting businesses' use of discount promotions – for example, how consumers are reacting to restaurants being more discriminant; using academic theory such as self-perception theory can explain consumer behaviour and give recommendations on how to overcome future challenges when using discount promotions in the restaurant industry.

Aims and objectives

This research aims to investigate the use of discount promotions within the restaurant industry in Plymouth. It seeks to find out how consumer behaviour towards discount promotions affects restaurant organisations' business strategy. The objectives of the research are as follows:

1   To review literature surrounding the use of discount promotions, linking in relevant theory and researching Plymouth's population.
2   To consider the literature review and investigate concepts including consumer behaviour, repeat patronage and marketing through technology.
3   To conduct research according to methodology. A questionnaire will be issued to the appropriate sample and will be used to collect data from questions surrounding relevant concepts. The data collected will be input into SPSS for use of analysis and validity testing.
4   To draw on findings and the literature review to further analyse any gaps associated with how consumer behaviour towards discount promotions affects restaurant organisations' business strategy. From this, future implications and recommendations can be made.

Source: 'How is consumer behaviour towards discounted promotions affecting restaurant organisations?' by Lauren Read, final-year dissertation, supervised by Christina Kelly, Plymouth University, 2016

An introduction to a student paper is a shortened version of the introduction in a full dissertation. The aim of this is to give the reader a flavour of the research that was undertaken in a short piece of writing. You can see an example of this in Illustration 9.2.

Illustration 9.2   An example of an introduction to a conference paper

Introduction

The purpose of this paper is to discuss the view that an understanding of talent management in hospitality organisations can be advanced through the adoption of a career perspective. The concept of talent management is not new, and it remains a popular and contemporary concept in hospitality and wider research fields due to its importance for both individuals and organisations. According to Brown et al. (2004), there have been numerous debates about the competitive advantage of companies that focus on fitting the right people with knowledge and expertise to the right organisations in order to maintain business success. Despite the wealth of research from the hospitality field on the topic of talent management (Lashley et al., 2007; Baum, 2008; Hatum, 2010; Steward and Harte, 2010; Kalaisevan and Naachimuthu, 2011), there are still many areas for debate, with evidence that theoretical development, transparency and on the whole the goals and conceptual boundaries of the topic are not clearly defined. Moreover, researchers still argue about what actually constitutes talent management. According to Hatum (2010), the talent management literature connected to hospitality incorporates talent management practices and activities. Overall, scholars focus largely on the attraction, selection, development and retention of talented individuals.

This paper argues that the adoption of a career perspective could be beneficial to our understanding of talent management. In pursuit of this aim, the paper is organised in the following way. First, it discusses conventional approaches to talent management, where talent management is observed through a human resource lens (Paditporn and Verma, 2003; Boudreau and Ramstad, 2005; Hugles and Rog, 2008; Hatum, 2010). Second, it discusses the adoption of a career perspective to talent management with its focus on individual career outcomes, and drawing on examples of graduate careers and career perspectives of hotel managers in hospitality (Buckingham and Vosburgh, 2001; Briscoe et al., 2006; McCabe

(Continued)

(Continued)

and Savery, 2007; Vance and Vaiman, 2008; Ladkin and Webber, 2010). This paper draws from a wider research project currently in its initial stages exploring talent management in hospitality small and medium enterprises in the UK.

Source: 'Understanding talent management in hospitality: developing the conceptual framework' by Aliaksei Kichuk, Adele Ladkin and Susan Horner, Bournemouth University, pp. 1–2. Paper presented at EuroCHRIE, Dubai, 6–9 October 2014. Note that references are for illustration purposes only.

Literature review

For student research reports, the literature review is a crucial part of the research. The background reading which was carried out, which influenced the style or context of the project, should be referred to. The literature review is used to highlight key topics relating to the research area, to identify existing understanding of that area and identify gaps in current knowledge. The most successful literature reviews will draw on a wide range of sources and refer to current research which has not been superseded. One aspect where literature can support the design of a research project is in the acknowledgement of any limitations. Where other authors have tried and tested certain aspects pertinent to the project, their work can be cited to justify your approach. You can see an example of a student literature review in Illustration 9.3.

Illustration 9.3   Example of a literature review in a student paper

Literature review

Culinary tourism represents a research area that gained prominence over the last decade as a result of a growing interest devoted to the relationship between food and tourism (Mazza, 2013). Whilst it is accepted that food fulfills biological and functional needs, it is increasingly being used as a stand-alone niche tourism product (Jones and Jenkins, 2002). Several authors have subsequently developed their own terminologies, thus the relationship between food and tourism is also referred to by researchers as cuisine tourism, food tourism, gastronomy tourism and culinary tourism (Okumus et al., 2007). However, Ruben (2008) suggests that 'culinary tourism' is now the most established terminology and concept that is increasingly used to describe travel and tourism activity, of which food is a primary motivation. Long (2003) explains that the term 'foodways' suggests that food is a network of activities and systems – physical, social, economic and aesthetic. Other prominent authors on the subject include Hall et al. (2003), who explain that culinary tourism involves visits to primary and secondary food producers, food festivals, restaurants and specific locations for which food tasting and experiencing the attributes of specialist food production regions are the primary motivating factor for travel. However, Shenoy (2005) argues that this definition narrows the scope of culinary tourism by stating that it can only occur when the food of a destination acts as a primary motivator to travel to the region.

More recently, the International Culinary Tourism Association (2006) defined culinary tourism as dining whilst on vacation and as something every visitor does. Steinmetz (2010) challenges this definition, stating that it is very broad and that little distinction is made between tourists who are specifically motivated to travel to a destination and take part in food tourism activities and others for whom food is not the primary motivation for travel. Subsequently, Mazza (2013) segments these tourists into either 'committed gastronomic tourists' or 'non-gastronomically focused tourists'. An alternative approach has been adopted by Wolf (2002) who states that culinary tourism is a form of travel with the goal to explore and enjoy local delicacies and gain memorable culinary experiences. Similarly, MacDonald and Deneault (2001) add that food tourists fulfill their expectations when they immerse themselves in the culture they are visiting through authentic and engaging experiences with people, cuisine, wine and other cultural activities.

Boniface (2003) is of the opinion that culinary tourism is by no means limited to urban regions and five-star restaurants, and suggests that farm shops, fruit-picking sites, cheese manufacturers, artisan food producers are amongst potential sites in the culinary tourism experience. Likewise, Horng and Tsai (2012) state that the facilities of culinary tourist destinations include all buildings and land use related to food preparation, including food-processing factories and farmers' markets. Daniszewshi (2013) and Quan and Wang (2003) argue that the existing literature fails to mention the role of the accommodation sector when discussing culinary tourism providers. After all, tourism by definition involves tourists travelling to and

(Continued)

(Continued)

staying in places outside their usual environment (World Tourism Organisation, 1995), therefore those who participate in culinary tourism require accommodation during their visit. Consequently, Daniszewski (2013) stresses that accommodation establishments have an important role in the culinary tourism experience.

Whilst each author interprets culinary tourism differently, the various terminologies connote almost the same notion, which is that culinary tourism involves participation in food-related activities, with food being the key focus of travel behaviour, rather than an ancillary motivation (Shenoy, 2005). The definitions presented in this section are very much consumer-focused and lacking in supply-side perspectives. Seasonality is an issue for tourism economies which are known to peak in the summer months and reach a trough during the winter (Beatty et al., 2010). This makes it hard for small businesses to survive during off-peak periods and creates an unstable job market (Devon County Council, n.d. a). However, Sims (2009) explains that local produce adds authenticity to the tourist experience and provides a motivation for visitors to come to a location, thus creating potential revenue streams throughout the year.

According to Quan and Wang (2004), over a third of tourist spending is devoted to food, and therefore the cuisine of the destination is an aspect of utmost importance in the quality of the holiday experience and has a great impact on travellers' decisions when choosing their vacation destination. Furthermore, it has been reported that the cuisine of a country can showcase its cultural or national identity (Du Rand et al., 2003). France has long been famed for its food and drink (Frochot, 2003); in fact, a study determined that gastronomy was the main focus for 60% of both domestic and international tourists to France (Frochot, 2000). Destinations and hospitality and tourism companies are becoming increasingly aware of the importance of gastronomy in order to diversify tourism and stimulate local, regional and national economic growth (Herrera et al., 2003).

Although several nations in mainland Europe have been traditionally well regarded in terms of their gastronomic offering (Blakely and Bradshaw, 2002), in the past two decades there has been a resurgence in demand for quality products made by traditional methods in the UK (BBC, 2005). In 2005, the BBC identified the West Country as one of the UK's most popular culinary destinations (BBC, 2005). More recently, Henley (2013) stated that Cornwall is experiencing a growing number of small, high-quality producers who, despite the extreme seasonality and distance from market, have helped the county establish itself as a county making and consuming some very good food. Comparably, Devon has also developed a growing reputation as a 'foodie paradise' with quality, seasonality and traceability all high on the agenda (ilovesouthdevon.com, 2013).

A visitor survey conducted by the South West Tourism Research Department (SWTRD) (2007) discovered that visitors to Devon and Cornwall typically fell into the middle/older age brackets with 58% of all visitors aged 45+ years. Visitors were also relatively affluent with 53% classified as ABC1's, thus comparable to Wade and Martin's (2005), Murray's (2008) and Daniszewski's (2013) profiles of the culinary tourist. The same study revealed that for the majority of visitors to Cornwall, the main purpose for the visit was for leisure, with over four in five on a leisure trip to the region. The majority of visitors were also happy to try local food and drink if they came across it (42%), but do not go out of their way to find it or visit Cornwall especially for its food and drink. Devon and Cornwall are host to a number of organisations who trade to culinary tourists, including award-winning food and beverage producers, cookery schools, high-end restaurants, food and drink festivals and a range of high-quality accommodation providers. Some of the better-known establishments include the two-Michelin-starred hotel and restaurant Gidleigh Park, Hugh Fearnley Whittingstall's River Cottage HQ and Rick Stein's numerous eateries in Padstow (Lonely Planet, 2010). It is understood that culinary tourists are drawn by the opportunity to participate in educational activities such as cookery schools (Ignatov and Smith, 2006). Such establishments exist in both counties, including 'Cookery School of the Year 2013' winner Ashburton Cookery School, and Rick Stein's Seafood School. In addition, both counties have become renowned for producing a number of regional delicacies such as Plymouth Gin, Sharpham and Camel Valley wines, Salcombe Dairy Ice Cream and St Austell Ales (Lonely Planet, 2010). Consequently, both regions increasingly celebrate their culinary successes through annual regional food and drink festivals such as the 'Cornwall Food and Drink Festival' and Plymouth's 'Flavour Fest'.

Sheaves (2013) indicates that the current success of Devon and Cornwall as culinary tourism destinations is a result of exceptionally high-quality food and drink producers. DMOs such as Visit Devon (2012) also suggest that quality and regional produce, teamed with a fantastic landscape and high-quality facilities, are central to the success of Devon and Cornwall's emerging foodie scenes. Whilst culinary tourism is an emerging market in Devon and Cornwall, the evidence suggested by other international destinations such as France, Spain and Italy indicates that there is potential for further growth.

Source: 'Culinary tourism in Devon and Cornwall: a supply-side perspective' by Rebecca Makepiece, Craig Wight and Susan Horner (2015), CHME annual conference, Manchester, 20–22 May 2015, pp. 2–5.
Note that references are for illustration purposes only.

Aims and objectives

Aims and objectives are commonly used in student research projects to establish the purpose of the research. Whilst some see a statement of aims and objectives as part of the introduction, it is such an important section that it may well be better to highlight it separately. Out of the introduction, background and literature should come your specific research aims (principal questions to be investigated) and objectives (secondary questions posed to assist in the answer of the project aims). The inclusion of the aims and objectives after the introduction or after the literature review may come down to personal preference, however as the literature review informs these aims and objectives it is often more logical for them to appear after this section.

In some reports, a section called *Terms of reference* is included as an alternative to the aims, objectives and, to a certain extent, the introduction. This is more common in consultancy reports where the project aims are specified in the research contract. Thus, it is unnecessary for the consultant to write a lengthy introductory section because the client has already stated why the project is to be undertaken. Terms of reference, therefore, relate to a statement of the subject matter of the report, its purpose and who the report is for (the client). We saw an example of the aims and objectives of an undergraduate dissertation previously in Illustration 9.1.

Methods

All reports include a section on the method(s) used in the research and this follows whatever variation of introductory section(s) is used. In student research or other academic projects, this is often referred to as the methodology. To this point you have set the scene in your introduction, referred to other work, acknowledged limitations, stated your aims and objectives and now are ready to say how the work was done. The method section, therefore, explains how the research aims were approached, why particular techniques were used and how they were put into action. For surveys it is necessary to explain aspects of data collection, sampling, respondent selection, questionnaire design, principal methods of analysis and any other features of methodology that are applicable. It may be useful to refer back to the literature for assistance in the justification of your methodology. A feature here (particularly for academic research) should be that another researcher could read this section and be able to repeat the research. Although precise replication of method is more a feature of natural science research, as a theme to guide the writer in this context it is useful. Examples of methodology sections from both a student dissertation and a paper are shown in Illustrations 9.4 and 9.5 respectively.

Illustration 9.4   An example of a full methodology section from an undergraduate dissertation

Chapter 4: Methodology

4.1 Overview

The purpose of this research was to find solutions to the research question through objective and methodical analysis (Rajasekar et al., 2013). The research methods of this dissertation align with the project's aims and objectives. The methods used for this dissertation are semi-structured focus groups. These will be recorded with digital aids to assist transcription.

4.2 Approach

4.2.1 Qualitative versus quantitative (deductive vs inductive)

Before research can be gathered, the investigator must isolate the correct research method in order to fit the project; this should be either qualitative or quantitative. Both qualitative and quantitative research methods have their inherent strengths and weaknesses. Bogdan and Biklen (2007) define qualitative research as 'an approach to social science research that emphasizes collecting descriptive data in natural settings, uses inductive thinking, and emphasizes understanding the subject's point of view'. Denzin and Lincoln (2005) emphasise that qualitative research turns a series of representations, including interviews, conversations, photographs and recordings, to the self. Creswell (2014) denotes that quantitative research examines the relationship amongst variables. These variables, in turn, can be measured typically on instruments, so that numbered data can be analysed using statistical procedures. Earl (2010) adds that quantitative methods emphasise objective measurements using statistical and mathematical data collection techniques such as questionnaires or surveys. Whilst these are both valuable methods of research, the investigator must consider the paradigm that is qualitative and quantitative research. Walsh (2011) argues that the qualitative versus quantitative debate is a dichotomy, however false. He reasons that the methods assume all research approaches somehow fit in either a qualitative or quantitative technique. However, many qualitative approaches use quantification, and quantitative studies make qualitative judgements.

(Continued)

(Continued)

4.2.2 Ontology versus Epistemology

Before determining an accurate methodological approach, additional research must be done into the research philosophy. This will enable an in-depth understanding of how the project will achieve the objectives set out at the beginning of the study. There are two philosophical approaches that underpin the development of social research. The first is ontology which concerns the nature of reality and what there is to know about the world (Ritchie et al., 2014). The second approach concerns epistemology which involves the way in which individuals know and learn about the world, and focuses on issues such as how we can learn about reality (Ritchie et al., 2014).

This can be further broken down into two additional approaches: induction and deduction. Induction is generally known as a bottom-up approach. Smith (2010) describes induction as a collection of specific events that indicate a common trend on which general conclusions are made. It focuses on knowledge development that can involve observations of key trends (Basford and Slevin, 2003: 174). To a certain extent, the research undertaken in this study was based on the authors' personal experiences. This may suggest therefore that the origins of the research question were of an inductive nature. In contrast, however, there is the deduction view which is seen as a top-down process and represents the commonest view of the nature of the relationship between theory and social research (Bryman, 2004). According to Ary et al. (2014), deductive reasoning can be described as a thinking process in which you proceed from general to specific knowledge through logical argument. Some sources suggest that inductive reasoning tends to be paired with qualitative research (Moody, 1990) and deductive approaches usually involve quantitative methods (Basford and Slevin, 2003). The researcher therefore will adopt an inductive approach to the qualitative data analysis, as this bottom-up approach will allow for additional knowledge of the subject area to be learned, thus gaining valuable insight in order to draw conclusions.

4.3 Method

For the purpose of this study, it seems fitting that qualitative research is adopted as semi-structured focus groups would be an appropriative setting to collect participants' opinions and experiences of visual branding in events. The researcher constructs an interview schedule of topics that follows a logical order but also allows for related topics and discussion that may not occur to the

Table 9.1   Typology of planned events

Cultural celebrations	Business and trade	Arts and entertainment	Sports competitions
Festivals	Meetings and conventions	Concerts	Amateur/professional
Carnivals	Consumer and trade shows	Award ceremonies	Spectator/participant
Commemorations			
Religious events	Fairs and markets		
Political and state	Private events	Recreational	Education and scientific
Summits	Weddings	Sport or games for fun	Conferences
Royal occasions	Parties		Seminars
Political events	Socials		Clinics
VIP visits			

Source: Getz (2007)

researcher (Ivey, 2011). In order to follow this logical format, the research will follow the typology of events as set out by Getz (2005). Table 9.1 gives an overview of this framework.

For the purpose of this study and in order to keep the focus groups short, the author will only focus on Cultural Celebrations, Business and Trade, Arts and Entertainment and Sport Competitions. Focus groups are one of many qualitative research tools for social and market research (Masadeh, 2012). Their primary aim is to describe and understand the meanings and interpretations of a select group of people, to gain an understanding of specific issues from the perspective of the participants of the group (Liamputtong, 2009). Krueger and Casey (2000: 5) add that the defined area of interest must be discussed in a permissive, non-threatening environment. Furthermore, Barrows (2000) explains that a focus group enables the researcher to 'drill' more deeply to attain in-depth insights from a small number of people in a short period of time. In light of this, the average number of people in each group will vary between four and eight participants who will allow for rich discussion (Ziebland et al., 2013). Smaller groups of four/five participants afford more opportunity to share ideas but the restricted size also results in a smaller pool of total ideas (Krueger and Casey, 2015). The researcher will conduct 4–6 groups, and researchers recommend aiming for homogeneity within each group in order to capitalise on people's shared experiences (Kitzinger, 1995). This will allow multiple lines of communication which can be analysed and investigated appropriately.

(Continued)

(Continued)

Each group interview will last up to an hour or be subject to the contribution of the participants. A pilot study will be taken before commencing in order to investigate how respondents will react to the focus group. This will allow the researcher to highlight areas that will need subtle changes before the focus groups commence (see Appendix 1 for focus group layout). The questions that will be asked are seen in Appendix 2 and show how the questions link to the literature, as well as to the expected themes.

4.4 Sample

In order to gain rich data, a sample of willing individuals was required to complete the study. The sample will be chosen to reflect those segments of the populations who will provide the most meaningful information in relation to the project objectives (Millward, 2012). The study requires no specific gender as it is focused on consumers who attend events, thus the study will require all participants to have attended an event at any time. Due to time constraints and access to an ample sample, the sample will be conducted using University of Plymouth students. The probability of being chosen was unknown and relies on the researcher's discretion (Zikmund et al., 2013). Due to the nature of events, using a sample of Generation Y would allow the researcher to understand how consumers of this generation see branding. Unlike previous peer groups, they have grown up alongside smartphones and tablets and are the most eager adopters as new technologies are released (Eventbrite, 2015). With this in mind, this sample of the population (Generation Y) will be shaping the events market in the coming years, thus understanding what influences them to purchase events is key to selling events in the future. It is clear that some participants have specific expertise or experiences within the events sector that can help the researcher. Creswell (2014) notes that it is up to the researcher to decide on whether or not the participants need to be knowledgeable in the subject area. However, in order to make sure that everyone is aware of the research, questions will be emailed to each participant prior to the focus group. This will allow the participants to have some responses ready in order to provoke more wholesome answers (see Appendix 3).

4.5 Data analysis

Previous to the commencement of the dissertation, the researcher attended an NVivo software workshop in order to receive the necessary training for use of the software.

Due to the size of the sample, the researcher will conduct personal analysis on transcripts 1–4 (see Appendix 4 for transcript 2) and run an NVivo analysis on one focus group transcript (see Appendix 5 for transcript 5) in order to prove competency on the software. Once the primary data are collected, each focus group will be transcribed and read repeatedly in order for the researcher to fully comprehend the data collected and gain a sense of what the participants feel about branding. The researcher will follow the format as justified by Braun and Clarke (2013) in order to effectively analyse the data. Table 9.2 shows the breakdown of this process.

Table 9.2   Six phases of thematic analysis

1. Familiarisation with the data: the researcher must immerse themselves in, and become intimately familiar with, their data; reading and re-reading the data (and listening to audio-recorded data at least once, if relevant) and noting any initial analytic observations.

2. Coding: this involves generating concise labels for important features of the data of relevance to the research question guiding the analysis. The researcher codes every data item and ends this phase by collating all their codes and relevant data extracts.

3. Searching for themes: a theme is a coherent and meaningful pattern in the data relevant to the research question. Searching for themes allows the researcher to identify similarity in the data. The researcher ends this phase by collating all the coded data relevant to each theme.

4. Reviewing themes: involves checking that the themes work in relation to both the coded extracts and the full data set. The researcher should reflect on whether the themes tell a substantial and convincing story in relation to the data. It may be necessary to collapse two themes together or to split a theme into two or more themes, or to discard the candidate themes altogether and begin again the process of theme development.

5. Defining and naming themes: requires the researcher to conduct and write a detailed analysis of each theme, identifying the core of each theme and constructing a concise, effective name for each theme.

6. Writing up: writing is an integral element of the analytic process. Writing up involves joining of the analytic narrative and data extracts to tell the reader a coherent and persuasive story about the data, and contextualising it in relation to existing literature.

Source: Braun and Clarke (2013)

The data will then be applied to a coding scheme (see Appendix 5) in order to isolate themes from the data, which will allow the leader to conduct a thematic analysis of the data in relation to the literature and the framework by Crowther (2011). A theme captures something important about the data in relation to the research question and represents some level of patterned response or meaning within the data set (Braun and Clarke, 2013). It goes beyond word or phrase counting to analyses involving 'identifying and describing both implicit and explicit ideas' (Guest et al., 2012; Fugard and

(Continued)

(Continued)

Potts, 2015). The data will then be analysed with the aims and objectives in mind as well as including relevant literature (see Appendix 6). Analysis of focus group data must be driven and consistent with the study's overall research aims for optimal discovery and exploration (Duggleby, 2005; Morgan, 2010). As a basic method of analysis, it works with people's experiences and understandings about a particular subject area within the confines of a focus group or interview. Recent guidelines for thematic analysis (Braun and Clarke, 2013) detail that the size of the project is completely versatile; it can be small, medium or large in nature and still produce sufficient results.

4.6 Ethical considerations

According to Plymouth University, it is committed to maintaining and promoting the highest standards of integrity and probity in scientific research. Ethical values are central to its structures and practices of research governance (Plymouth University, 2015). Attention to the ethical consideration and approval of participants is crucial. These considerations are detailed below.

4.6.1 Consent for recording

All participants in the focus groups were asked for consent to use their information afterwards and the right for the researcher to record them both by audio and visual devices (see Appendix 7).

4.6.2 Right to withdraw

Participants were informed from the outset that their involvement was voluntary and they had the right to withdraw from the focus groups at any time without penalty.

4.6.3 Confidentiality

Except for the consent of the participant in the study, all information collected will be kept confidential. All transcripts and audio recordings will be deleted once the dissertation has been completed. Names of participants will be changed to a pseudonym in order to keep participants' identities confidential.

Source: 'The significance of brand design and colour on event purchase and participation amongst Generation Y' by Emma Macphie, undergraduate dissertation, supervised by Susan Horner, Plymouth University, 2016.
Note that references are for illustration purposes only.

Illustration 9.5   Example of a methodology from a student conference paper

Methodology

Workplace bullying is a complex multi-discipline topic involving human resource management, education and psychology. Hence, the interpretivism philosophy, with an inductive approach of reasoning, is suitably employed to guide the collection and interpretation of qualitative data (Saunders, Lewis & Thornhill, 2012). Due to the sensitive nature of WB, this study engages in-depth telephone interviews to gather qualitative data (Keats, 2000) and adhering to ethical practices (Saunders et al., 2012). Five unbiased interview questions were first developed through thorough literature review, then, pre-tested and pilot tested to strengthen reliability and validity (McBurney & White, 2007). These questions aim to provide interviewees a platform to share their perceptions of WB, and to voice out bullying incidents they have encountered/seen/heard in their workplaces and those associated causes and consequences. The interview conversation will be analysed using interpretative phenomenological analysis (IPA) (Smith & Osborn, 2003). This method is frequently adopted by psychological studies as it can flexibly and non-prescriptively use to identify, analyse, collate and summarise key themes and subthemes, collectively, that capture interviewees' perceptions, accounts, experiences, emotions, responses and phenomenon of hotel WB (Millward, 2006; Smith, Flowers & Larkin, 2009).

Due to the qualitative nature of this study, statistical significance was not the purpose. Hence, purposive sampling technique was employed to select 10 suitable interviewees from front of the house and back of the house departments of 10 different five stars hotels to participate in this research. Managers from ten different five stars hotels were preferred due to the high possibility of them able to comprehend and converse in English. These participants must i) include both genders; ii) hold Taiwan nationality; iii) have at least six months of work experience in their hotels; iv) be able to converse in English. These criteria are important to support a thorough investigation of hotel WB issues from the perspectives of female and male Taiwanese managers working in different departments. The background of the interviewees is summarised in Table 9.3.

(Continued)

(Continued)

Table 9.3   A summary of the hotel managers' background (n = 10)

Fictional name	Gender	Age	Position	Education	Work experience in current hotel
Thi-Ben	Female	27	Reception Manager	Postgraduate	2 years
Lu-Pei	Female	27	Front Office Manager	Postgraduate	1 year
Bau-Ya	Female	33	Duty Manager	Vocational	3 years
Yee-Fang	Female	25	Front Office Manager	Postgraduate	6 months
Wei-Lun	Female	45	Human Resource Manager	Vocational	18 years
Yea-Hui	Female	27	Sales Manager	Postgraduate	3 years
Lin-Yu	Female	32	Rooms Division Manager	Bachelor	2 years
Lee-Wei	Male	29	Front Office Manager	Postgraduate	2 years
Mai-Bou	Male	26	Food and Beverage Manager	Bachelor	1 year
Mo-Yu	Male	27	Recreation Manager	Postgraduate	1 year

Source: Hotel Workplace Bullying in Taiwan EuroCHRIE, Dubai 7–9th October, 2015 p 3. Matthew H. T. Yap, Susan Horner, Monica T. Y. Hsu, and Candy, M. F. Tang (2015). Note that references are for illustration purposes only.

Results

The results sections are at the centre of a report and will vary in length and format in relation to the scope and aims of the project. In the case of a market research report where a survey was involved, there needs to be a distinction between a statement or description of the results and any statistical (or other) analysis.

When describing results, care should be given to do just this and not to overlap with the later sections of analysis and interpretation. For example, where a structured questionnaire was used the description of results relates to a statement of the frequencies for each question. Here, consideration should be made to how best to illustrate the data. Tables, charts and graphs are often used to guide the reader through the results. It is unnecessary to repeat verbatim all that is shown in a table or chart in any accompanying text. However, salient points should be described additionally in the text. Rather than treat each answer to a question on the questionnaire consecutively, grouping results around a theme within a sub-section is generally worthwhile. The theme of a sub-section could relate back to a specific project objective (or part of one). This way the reader can follow your logic in how you are beginning to satisfy the aims and objectives stated in the earlier section of the report.

When this moves to the analysis of the results, where statistical tests are applied, relation to the project aims and objectives is again advisable as a structure. Reiterating objectives, or in this case hypotheses, can provide a structure to the section and the reader can follow the purpose of the analysis.

You can see an example of the results section from a paper based on an undergraduate dissertation research that was carried out in India in Illustration 9.6.

Illustration 9.6   Example of a results section from a student paper

Results

Key findings from the questionnaires

The first question was designed to get a clear picture of the preferences of an agritourist's activities. When data collected from the questionnaires was analysed, it was clear that a majority of the participants wanted a fair mix of all the activities. One participant said that he felt as though the development of agritourism in India was a splendid idea and that he would come back to India to be a part of the agritour as he felt that he would learn a lot from that type of tour. Others gave valuable suggestions like going into intricate details about the kind of activities they would like to take part in. One of the respondents, an Indian, had been on an agritour to Baramati and commented that it was one of the most splendid trips he had been on with his family and also said that the trip was enjoyable because the hosts provided them with a fair blend of activities.

The second question was designed to address the type of agritourist spaces that would be preferred by a prospective tourist. Sznajder, Przezborska and Scrimgeour (2009) stated that, according to a survey in the USA, people there preferred natural wilderness followed by beautiful landscapes. Our study revealed, however, that prospective tourists preferred to take part in activities that are held on the farm. There was also a participant who said that – apart from the spaces mentioned above – it would be great if agricultural universities, museums and research areas could be included.

The next question focused on potential top attractions to prospective tourists. From the questionnaires it became clear that the participants in this study wanted to take part in activities that are a perfect blend of all possible activities. There were also comments saying that agritourism is like an educational programme on the farm where the tourists learn about farming and livestock and it would be right

(Continued)

(Continued)

only if the package comprised of a blend of all that happens on the farm. Another respondent said that he would be very upset if he chose something and missed out on another and thus he felt that a perfect agritourism package is one where the tourists live like a farmer and learn about the activities that go on in that farm. There was another respondent who replied saying that not all tourists would be interested in all the activities, so it is correct that the host offers a choice of activities to the tourists and they could choose what they want to do.

Understanding that customer segmentation plays a very big role in the success of an agritourism unit, the last question hence explored the ideal duration of a stay. The results of our investigation in India show that there was almost a unanimous choice in so far as tourists would prefer to stay on the farm over the weekend. It was also surprising that some of the prospective tourists did not mind being part of an agritour for more than a week. The interesting part of this result is that the majority of the people who wanted to stay longer on the farms were corporate workers from Europe, including British nationals who particularly favoured a longer stay. Some tourists also felt that staying on a farm for just a few hours is enough.

Key findings from the interviews

Summary of the interview with respondent A1

The reason why respondent A1 was chosen is because he is the founder and managing director of the Agritourism Development Corporation of India. In addition, he is the National Tourism Award Winner for 2008–09, for the development of the unique technique of combining agriculture and tourism in the Baramati district (Taware, 2010). He mentioned during the interview that agriculture is the backbone of the Indian economy and also that tourism is one such sector that brings in a lot of income, especially in the form of foreign exchange. He also mentioned that only if villages are self-sufficient will the nation develop, because more than 50% of the population of India live in villages. On asking him to share his feelings on the development of rural tourism, he remembered his childhood memories in a small village, Sanghavi in Baramati taluka:

> I was lucky to be brought up as a part of the joint family in the agri and rural setup in the small village. Unless the villages are self-sufficient, nation cannot progress. We must go to villages in order to achieve development of villages, the mantra given by Mahatma Gandhi still holds true. ATDC's mission is to promote agriculture tourism to achieve self-reliant,

employment and economic stability in rural communities and to attract urban people to get back to the roots, he said. ATDC has been celebrating May 16 as World Agritourism Day since 2008 and the United Nations World Tourism Organization (UNWTO) has now acknowledged these efforts by ATDC and declared May 16 as World Agritourism Day.

He even mentioned that it is apt and possible to start an agritourism project in any part of India as it has a high scope and also requires little investment. He also noted that anyone with the interest can start a project because the three major factors that contribute to the success of agritourism are: (i) the farmer, (ii) the village and (iii) agriculture – all present in India in abundance. He also said that it is important for the organiser to be sure that the tourists have something to see, do and buy. The respondent also gave information about the initial investment required and the return on investment, saying that an individual farrner could obtain a loan from the bank, invest a small amount of money himself, and as a result could make a steady income from agritourism.

Summary of interview with respondent B1

Mr Sekar is the Managing Partner of GRT Nature Trails, Sky Rocca, Yercaud. This hotel focuses on nature trails combined with luxury.

In the interview, Mr Sekar mentioned that 'Agritourism is a kind of tourism where the farmer gets the opportunity to entertain and educate those interested in what is his primary source of income'. He also said that in the present-day scenario, agritourism will help the farmers as it will give the tourists new options. Mr Sekar said that he had read in the in-flight magazine on his way back from New Zealand that today's tourists are more health-conscious and they want to learn about how the food that they consume is produced. They even want to know about how the cows are fed because that affects the quality of dairy products. He also said that as people want to go back to their roots and learn about the process of food grain production, milk production, meat and poultry, etc., it is a wise choice to start an agritourism unit within an existing hotel. When asked about his experience during his recent agritour, the respondent said:

I think this is the best holiday I have been to. The reason I am saying this is that it is very peaceful and I learnt many things during the entire trip. Not many people know about why the milk of the cow is thick and why it loses

(Continued)

(Continued)

its thickness. I love cheese but to date I have never gone into the details of cheese making and this trip has actually got me thinking. In India, in spite of all the resources available, people of our age group think it is 'uncool' to be an agriculturist but they do not realise that it is that agriculture that gives them food. I have been pondering so much to the extent that I feel that every child should be sent on an agritour from time to time; it is only then that they learn about the trouble the farmer takes to provide us with food. I feel agri-tourism is a splendid thing, as it opens one's eyes not only towards agriculture-based education but it also instils important values.

When asked who the target market would be, if he were to start agritourism in his hotel, he said that it would be anyone who would like to have a different kind of holiday. He also said that he would start by marketing it to areas around and then he would like to go on a broader scale. Mr Sekar was confident that agritourism would be successful in India because India is an agriculture-based country and, due to the recent problems of water scarcity, farmers are taking drastic steps like commit-ting suicide and, hence, agritourism would be a great economic idea for them. He also mentioned that according to some recent tourism surveys, Indian tourists are no longer prejudiced towards new kinds of tourism and are ready to visit new places. He also mentioned that agritourism would have some teething problems but should be ready to face this because every business has problems till it is well established.

Summary of interview with respondent B2

Respondent B2 is one of the managing partners of Casino Group of Hotels (CGH), Cochin. Though its pilot hotel is located in Cochin, this group has ten other proper-ties around Kerala. The hotel in Cochin has a different theme, and, most of all, CGH focuses on eco-friendly techniques of hotel management. The respondent said that he had not really thought about introducing agritourism into any of the hotels but also mentioned that it would be a great idea. He shared his views about how peo-ple are losing their family values in India and how they are now busy and hence they do not have time for each other. He also mentioned that he had heard about Baramati and from his point of view it was a beautiful concept, as it was located in a place where people get good food, knowledge, clean air to breath and also that it is a place where people are reminded about their family values.

When asked if he had been on an agritour, the respondent mentioned that he had always tried to go on one but his busy schedule had not permitted him to do so. He also said that he would grab any opportunity available to be a part of an agritour. He said that if it is impossible to introduce agritourism as a part of any of the existing hotels because they all have a different theme, then he would introduce a new property. He said that *Kalari Kovilakam*, which is located in a rural area of Kolangadu, could be a good choice as well. He also mentioned that the present *Kalari Kovilakam* was the palace of the Vengunad rulers. The company is using this at the moment as a place for Ayurveda, Yoga and *Kalaripayattu* (an Indian form of martial arts originating from Kerala and also known as the Dance of Steel). The respondent also shared his views that he would like to implement agritourism but not immediately; he said that it would be a good idea to start an agritourism project and he would try to blend it with heritage and culinary tourism, so that tourists could learn a lot from one trip to India.

Summary of interview with respondent B3

The final interviewee was Mr Virender Yadav, the managing director of CozyDeepika Group, since 1987 in New Delhi. Mr Yadav first started a travel agency in the name of Cozy Travels Private Limited which now has branches in New York, Moscow, Frankfurt, Hamburg, London, Birmingham, and the latest addition to the list being Bergamo, Italy. Mr Yadav actually has an agricultural background and he is a native of a small agricultural village, Sikanderpur Ghosi, Haryana. The most recent projects of the CozyDeepika Group are two hotels – Umrao Resorts, New Delhi and Umrao Hotel, Amritsar.

Mr Yadav said that, 'Agritourism is the process of providing guests with non-expensive accommodation and food, providing maximum exposure to the traditional farmers' way of life to the tourists'. Mr Yadav then recalled the days when his children were little. He said that he did not want them to grow up without knowing the worth and value of rural life, so he used to take them to the 400-acre farm in Shona, Haryana, every Sunday so that they would spend time on the farm and learn various things from the farms, the farmers and the animal units. He said that this practice made his children more humanitarian; they knew the worth and value of agriculture and also valued the food that they consumed every day.

When MrYadav was asked if he would consider developing agritourism in one of his hotels, he said that both the present hotels are located in a very commercial area and it would not be right if he had to start developing agritourism in these hotels. At the same time, he said that he would like to develop agritourism on his lands in Shona. These were his exact words:

(Continued)

(Continued)

Developing agritourism has always been on my mind but I am not able to do it right now due to other commitments, which is I want to develop Umrao Resorts, New Delhi before the Commonwealth Games start in October. At the same time I would like to develop agritourism in Shona, because it is one of the most fertile lands in India. There is a saying that if you just drop a seed, it will grow on its own. I want to have an agri-resort that caters to different segments of people. I would like to focus on accommodation on the agricultural land, combined with off-the-farm education and on-the-farm practical experience. During the tour, the guests would live in simple style, yet they would have spent a great time on the farm. Just as my children have learnt many lessons from their weekly trip to the farm, I want other adults and children to learn a lot as well.

Mr Yadav also said that developing agritourism in India is a great idea as India has a lot of natural and agricultural resources. He also said that as India is a very big country with great geographic variations and in each area different crops are cultivated. This would help all the tourists learn about the different geographical areas and different crop varieties.

Summary of interview with respondent C1

Mr Vijayann P. Rajes is a leading agriculturist in Yercaud, India. He owns an estate where he cultivates coffee, pepper and other spices and fruits. Together with his wife, Mr Rajes also has a dairy farm, a vermicompost bed and a horticulture section where they grow flowers that are supplied to florists in Bangalore, Karnataka. Apart from this, they also have an artificially created lake, wherein there are different varieties of fish. Mr Rajes was the vice-chairman of the United Planters Association of Southern India in 1998 and was the chairman of the organisation in 2006. He is still one of the people at the helm of affairs of the organisation.

Mr Rajes had a lot of information regarding agritourism and he defined it as follows: 'Agritourism is the introduction of non agricultural semi-urban and urban people to the day to day life on a farm producing some agri or farm-based product.' Mr Rajes also mentioned that developing agritourism would create new employment opportunities in the rural areas that would add to the income of the farmers, and he also mentioned that agritourism prevails amongst coffee growers. When questioned on whether the development of agritourism would reduce the production of food grains, Mr Rajes responded by saying:

I do not believe that agritourism will reduce the availability of food products, because the public and policy makers are not aware of the hardships faced by farmers in rural areas, who without basic infrastructure and comforts under extreme sacrifice work to make food available. Agritourism will bring awareness to the public at large who will realise the contribution of agriculturists and the importance of food security to a nation. Policies of government usually follow public opinion, and therefore agriculture will eventually benefit.

Mr Rajes also felt that the development of agritourism in India would be absolutely feasible and his reasons were that many children in cities are not aware of the basic information of how or where their food comes from or how much effort goes into the production of the food they eat each day. They also have to be sensitised to how human beings depend on nature for their survival. Climate change, global warming and eco-sensitivity will have more relevance when seen from an agro perspective. Mr Rajes also mentioned that agritourism offers an opportunity to have a meaningful holiday combined with a learning experience. Apart from recreational activities, he said that on his estate he would give information to the tourists on farm management and also sensitise them to the dignity of labour. He also felt that there is a uniqueness offered by agritourism: 'One gets the unique experience of watching the day to day functioning of an operational farm by living with those who run it probably for the fourth or fifth generation and the passion with which they do things.'

Summary of interview with respondent C2

Mr R.K. Raghunandan is an agriculturalist and has turned into an exporter of agro-based products. He is the managing partner of M/s. Green India Exports, Pollachi, India and M/s Saffron and Green, UK. Green India Exports produces and exports many eco-friendly products such as coconut shell ice-cream cups, natural wild bird feeders, coir peat products (soil substitute) and natural vanilla beans.

When asked what, from his point of view, is agritourism, Mr Raghunandan replied, 'Agritourism is tourism at the agricultural farm level. The tourists will be a paying guest of the farmer, who will in turn charge a fee for food and accommodation and all the amenities provided by him to the tourist.'

He felt that agritourism would increase employment opportunities on a small scale because most of the farm work would be done by the host and the guest.

(Continued)

(Continued)

He also stated that the young professionals who no longer want to stay in India due to job scarcity would have a new choice. He felt that by implementing agritourism, the income of the farmer would increase as he would produce food and agro-based products, and in addition to that he would also host agritourists and this would be an additional source of income. The author wanted to know his point of view on the quantity of food products if the agricultural land is used for tourism purposes, to which Mr Raghunandan responded by saying that tourism will be a part of the farm but it will not take away all the farm lands. He also said that it would not reduce the amount of food grains produced because the farms where the tourists will be staying will produce up to 60% of their food requirements. Such farms will sell their surplus produce in the market, and hence will increase the food products' availability.

Mr Raghunandan also said that he would think about an agritourism unit in his farm which would offer a range of recreational attractions. Apart from the recreational activities, he also said that he would provide information to the tourists regarding successful management of farms, the process of food production and the importance of being eco-friendly. From his point of view, agritourism would be very successful in India because India is an agriculture-based country, where agriculture is more of a culture than a profession, but Mr Raghunandan also believed that immense efforts are required. His exact words were:

> Agritourism could be a success in the long run only if there is enough publicity, sincere efforts and meticulous planning by the agritourist promoters and managers, and most importantly agritourism should be advertised, promoted and encouraged by the Indian government. It would be successful because it is so different from the various types of tourism that exist at the moment. Agritourism gives to the tourists a first-hand feel of the cultural practices of each region, social customs, local lifestyle, and also helps the tourists to know about the agricultural methods and practices of regional farmers. Another important fact is that my friends, from the metropolitan cities, often comment that they want their children to know the value of nature, agriculture and the environment. They also say that they are envious about the fact that my children have knowledge about farm and agro activities and can also know how to handle issues on the farm. I would say that providing this knowledge to all the children and adults would be a great idea.

Mr Raghunandan also said that, 'Agritourism is personal, simple and ethnic. It is completely different from any other form of tourism, which makes the whole concept unique in its own special way'.

Source: 'Agritourism in India: the potential for sustainable development and economic growth' by Susan Horner, Eva Schuepbach and Avantikka Raghunandan. Paper presented at EuroCHRIE, Amsterdam, October 2010, pp. 5–9. Please note that the names of the respondents were included in the paper after written agreement was obtained.

Discussion

Following the description and analysis of the results, the findings can now be placed in a context and the implications evaluated and discussed. It is worth beginning the discussion section with a restatement of the aims and objectives and then going on to discuss how well the findings from the previous sections answer these research questions. It is important in student research projects that the discussion refers to past research identified within the literature review. Where any of the objectives have not been fully answered, this should be fully acknowledged.

It is also interesting for you to consider a summary of the research at this stage. Illustration 9.7 shows you how a student summarised their research in an abstract to their study, and the key findings within the conclusion. The study provided the student with a platform to publish his work at an academic conference in 2014.

Illustration 9.7   Example of an abstract, conclusions and recommendations from a student academic paper

Emotional intelligence (EI) has gained significance in hotel businesses as a predictor of improved organisational performance and individual career success. As such, this study aims to determine and analyse Bulgarian hotel managers' (BHM) understanding of EI and its influence on their careers and organisational success. Qualitative data was collected from the in-depth interviewing of 12 purposively selected BHM from four- and five-star hotels, and then analysed using interpretative

(Continued)

(Continued)

phenomenological analysis. In conclusion, BHM knowledge of EI was imperfect, although they could give practical examples of the implications of EI on organisational and personal success. They also provided new perspectives on ways to successfully implement EI in their hotels. The study recommends BHM enhance their knowledge on EI before employing EI initiatives in their workplaces.

Conclusions

In conclusion, BHMs' understanding of EI was not well developed as they could not provide an in-depth explanation of the term; their definitions were only limited to the physical manifestations of emotions, what can influence them and how managers can balance or control those emotions. The participants were able to explain ways to detect emotions by observing body language; they also understood the basic factors that can influence EI such as gender, age, culture and experience. The main issue was that they were unable to identify the specific processes that connect emotions and intelligence. Furthermore, the four skills of perceiving, using, understanding and managing emotions were not individually identified and explained; the participants were mostly discussing them altogether as EI and only sporadically mentioned them separately, focusing only on the most visible ones, namely using and managing emotions (Brackett et al., 2011).

Despite these limitations, it can be concluded that BHMs have quite accurate and very detailed perceptions on the connection between EI and organisational and career success (Groves et al., 2008). They were able to understand and identify specific customer service issues that can be resolved through EI and also propose specific ways to increase sales by using EI (Prentice and King, 2011). It was established that employees and managers who possess EI can resolve guest issues by understanding the clients' emotions, thus improving customer service. Participants were also able to pinpoint the connection between EI and sales – the ability to understand guest emotions can help find the best time to offer specifically designed sales propositions that are adapted to the mood of the guests, thus increasing hotel sales (Cherniss, 2001).

Interviewees also commented on the connection between EI and career success. They suggested that managers who are skilled in EI are in general more capable of doing the job, able to communicate the company's vision and more prominent for career advancement (Groves et al., 2008).

The respondents suggested that EI should be first defined, then the need for it should be identified through reflection and analysis, and only then could the managers proceed with integrating it into the hotel (Brackett et al., 2011). The training sessions should be based on interaction with the participants and should cover topics such as the connection between EI and desired behaviour and manners; coaching and team building were also proposed as alternatives.

Recommendations

There are several recommendations that can be suggested based on the research. First, BHMs should seek to better understand EI and should reflect on each level and understand the specific skills associated with it. This would help them understand the concept better and would assist them in further explorations of the phenomenon. According to the literature, there are many implications for EI in the hotel business and it is hotel managers who should be responsible for integrating the concept and learning how to benefit from it (Tsai, 2009). It is therefore recommended that BHMs should take the initiative and propose the concept to hotel owners; they should be able to assess the needs of their hotels and find the areas where EI can help solve some of the existing problems (Cherniss, 2001; Groves et al., 2008).

BHMs should first turn to specialists in the area in order to develop more detailed and scientific understanding of EI. Some ideas include formal educational institutions such as colleges and universities; also guest speakers, trainings offered on-site or in specialised training centres; last but not least there are many EI associations whose function it is to assist industry professionals (Brackett et al., 2011; Prentice and King, 2011).

This could be followed by careful reflection on the meanings of EI and the factors that can influence EI. In the light of the local culture and other demographic factors such as age, experience, upbringing and education (Chopra and Kanji, 2010), BHMs should also carefully examine EI implications for organisational and personal success. Kusluvan et al. (2010) recommended that managers in the hotel industry increase their EI, as it can help them perform better at their job and improve the overall performance of their departments and hotels. The respondents connected EI with several positive outcomes such as improved customer service, increased sales, increased staff motivation and retention, fewer conflicts and less stress (Cherniss, 2001; Groves et al., 2008). Comprehending these connections and implications will enable BHMs to use and develop EI in the most optimal ways (Kilduff et al., 2010).

Source: 'Emotional intelligence of hotel managers in Bulgaria' by Susan Horner, Matthew Yap and Goran Yordanov, pp. 1, 5–6. Paper presented at EuroCHRIE, Freiberg, 16–18 October 2013.
Note that references are for illustration purposes only.

Recommendations

In some student research reports, it is necessary to make recommendations. In the case of a consultancy project, this is most applicable because of its applied nature. In consultancy projects, the research will most likely have practical implications, however in academic research recommendations will also refer to future research that could come from the study. Recommendations should be brief and precise and must relate to what has been found from the research. Where the research was limited, recommendations for future developments or other projects can be expressed.

Conclusion

The final section is a brief and straightforward summary of the methods, results and their implications. It should also be stated how well the research satisfied the aims and objectives set. In short, it is what you can justifiably conclude from what you have done and what you have found out. Remember that it is a summary and so you should not introduce new ideas.

References or Bibliography

A list of references is all the books, journals and other sources you have 'referred' to in the text. A bibliography includes these and other sources you consulted but did not actually refer to in the report. Which you select is perhaps a matter of choice or may be specifically dictated (as in the case of reports supporting qualifications or journal articles). Two methods of referencing work in the text and the organisation of a bibliography or reference list are explained in a following section.

Appendices

Additional information which is relevant to the research but not included in the report (to keep it uncluttered) can be appended to (put at the end of) the report. This may include a copy of the questionnaire, interview transcripts, coding scheme, interview schedule and any other relevant material. Somewhere in the text each numbered appendix should be referred to so that the reader is aware of its presence and can make a judgement as to whether they need to refer to the additional information provided.

9.2.2 Organising sections of a research report

Numbering

In most reports, there is a numbering system applied to each major section, and sometimes also to sub-sections, such as:

Section 3   Methodology

    3.1   Sampling

        3.1.1   Introduction

        3.1.2   Sampling method

        3.1.3   Sample selection

        3.1.4   Sample size

    3.2   Data collection etc.

It is recommended that no further sub-divisions are used as the numbering system can become too cluttered and may distract the reader. In the example given, the major section or chapter is divided first into the main topic areas (sampling, data collection, etc.) and then each of these are sub-divided into the discussion of more specific aspects. In some reports where particular references are required, such as government reports, an alternative is to number each paragraph. Unless instructed to do so, it is normally unnecessary to go this far.

The pages of a report should be numbered (as shown on the contents page). It is convention in books for the introduction to begin as page 1, in Arabic numbers (1, 2, 3, etc.) and for sections prior to this (acknowledgements, summary, foreword, etc.) to have roman numbers (i, ii, iii, iv, etc.). This is reasonably straightforward if a word-processing package is being used. In some reports and with some educational institutions, it is a requirement that all pages are numbered consecutively beginning with 1.

With appendices, it may be more difficult to page number because some of the material may not be available electronically. Whilst it is essential to number each appendix, the use of page numbers varies. It is important, especially where readers are likely to need to refer to the appendices, that page numbers extend to this section.

Referencing in a research report

When compiling the list of references at the end of the report and formatting in-text citations throughout, it is important that style guides are adhered to. In the case of student research projects, it is necessary that you follow the referencing style specified by your institution. Two common referencing styles are detailed below for in-text citation and the reference list.

In-text citation using the Harvard System

At every point in the text of a book, essay or report at which a citation (a reference to a particular document) is made, it is essential that the source can be identified. One method, called the Harvard System, requires the author's name and the year of publication to be inserted after each reference in the text. If the author's surname occurs naturally in the sentence, then only the year is given in brackets:

Mansfield (2015) describes…

If not, then both author and date are included in parentheses:

In an earlier study (Agarwal, 2002) it is described as…

If the author has more than one document published in the same year cited in your work, it is identified by adding lower-case letters after the year and within the parentheses. For example:

Huang (2008a) discussed the subject … In a further article (Huang, 2008b), it was suggested…

If there are two authors, the surnames of both should be given before the date:

Semley and Busby (2014) identify…

If there are more than two authors, after the first reference, where all authors are named, the surname of the first should be given followed by 'et al.' (this is an abbreviation of 'et alia' which means 'and others'). First appearance:

…as acknowledged in existing studies (Brunt, Mawby and Hambly, 2000).

All references thereafter:

…as noted by Brunt et al. (2000).

When citing references in the text, you should not include the authors' initials, unless to distinguish between more than one author with the same surname and date. If no person is named who can be treated as the author, and the title or title page implies that an organisation is mainly responsible for the publication, this body may be treated as the author. This may include certain publications by Visit Britain or the Office for National Statistics, for instance. On *very* rare occasions, there may be neither an author nor an organisation – this may be shown by 'Anon.' in place of the author's name, meaning anonymous.

To further complicate matters, if different parts of a document are cited in different parts of the text, the appropriate page or section number(s) may be given in the text, following the date and within the parentheses:

Semley and Busby (2014: 27) describe…

In-text citation using the numeric system

With this system, instead of the name and date, a number in the text refers to the origins of any sources used. Numbers are either placed in parentheses or in superscript. If the same source is used more than once in the text, then the same number first cited is used in each subsequent citation. A list of references showing the full details is provided at the end of the report. For example:

> Science and technology are continually providing new means of stretching the limits of the ecosystem (1). This created the illusion that the negative side-effects of economic growth can always be eliminated by modern technology (2).

Alternatively, this format can be used:

> Science and technology are continually providing new means of stretching the limits of the ecosystem.[1] This created the illusion that the negative side-effects of economic growth can always be eliminated by modern technology.[2]

Reference lists using the Harvard System

Books and reports always give a list of references for the information used by the author in preparing the paper. This allows those reading the work to check the sources and decide for themselves whether the conclusions drawn are valid, as well as to find more information on a subject.

The reference list should be presented at the end of the text, the list to be arranged in alphabetical order of authors' surnames, and then by year and letter, if applicable. References should be produced following the layout given below. The way in which a reference is given depends on the nature of the source:

Reference to a book:

> Author(s). (Year of publication). *Title*, edition number (if relevant). Page or chapter number(s) (if relevant). Place where published: Publisher.

For example:

> Horner, S. and Swarbrooke, J. (2016). *Consumer Behaviour in Tourism*, 3rd edition. Oxon: Routledge.

Reference to a report:
Similarly, a reference to a report should be shown thus:

> Visit Britain (2015). Foresight – Issue 141: Football tourism in Britain. Foresight.

Reference to a contribution in a book:

> Author(s) of contribution. (Year of publication). Title of contribution followed by 'In' Author(s) of book. *Title of book*, edition number (if relevant). Place where published: Publisher, Page number(s) of contribution.

For example:

> Busby, G. (2005). Work Experience and Industrial Links. In D. Airey and J. Tribe (eds). *An International Handbook of Tourism Education.* London: Elsevier, pp. 93–107.

Reference to a contribution in a journal:

When referencing from a journal, follow the same guidelines but remember to include the volume and issue numbers. This time, just to complicate matters, instead of writing the title in *italics* the title of the periodical is written in *italics*. So the order for a journal is:

> Author(s) of the contribution. (Year of publication). Title of the contribution. *Title of the Journal*, Volume number (Issue number): Page number(s).

For example:

> Agarwal, S. (2002). Restructuring seaside tourism: The resort lifecycle. *Annals of Tourism Research*, 29 (1): 25–55.

Reference to a contribution in the popular press:

This is similar to the way a periodical is referenced with the exception that because publications in the popular press rarely have volume numbers, the date of the publication is inserted in its place. For example:

> Smith, H. (2016). Miracle in Athens as Greek tourism numbers keep growing. *The Guardian*, 28 May.

The use of personal communications:

Sometimes your source will be a conversation, lecture notes or other unpublished information. In this case you write:

> Bell, M. (2016). Personal communication, 3 July.

Reference lists using the numeric system

All sources referred to in the numeric system are similarly listed at the end of the main text of a report. Here, however, entries are arranged in numerical order as opposed to alphabetical order as with the previous system. Following the number, the organisation of the reference is as for the Harvard System. For example:

1. Wight, A.C. (2006). Philosophical and methodological praxes in dark tourism: Controversy, contention and the evolving paradigm. *Journal of Vacation Marketing*, 12 (2): 119–29.
2. Agarwal, S. (2002). Restructuring seaside tourism: The resort lifecycle. *Annals of Tourism Research*, 29 (1): 25–55.

Use of referencing software

Referencing software is now widely available and can be very useful when compiling a reference list for student research projects. Examples of commonly used referencing software include Endnote, Mendeley and Refworks. Use of such software enables the user to create a database of references. These references can then be inserted into any document as an in-text citation and will automatically provide the full reference in the format specified.

9.2.3 Other aspects of report writing

Getting in the mood for writing

Writing reports is not particularly easy and every writer has moments when things seem to fall into place and other times when nothing seems to go well and writing anything is an uphill struggle. For some, the approaching deadline helps and they can 'burn the midnight oil' but this is a risky strategy, especially if you are likely to fall asleep. You must work out what strategy works best for you and plan around this. It can be particularly difficult if many other work commitments occur at the same time as you are trying to write your report. This is because it is easy to deal with minor things and leave writing (which is more difficult) aside. Ideally, you should plan ahead and make some space where you can concentrate on the writing. This is because you need time to think as well as write, so allowing yourself the odd hour before lunch (or before going out) is unlikely to be very successful. Other aspects which you may find useful are listed below:

1. Planning – plan a whole section in advance and think about how the sub-sections fit into it. Then give yourself deadlines for completing each part. This way you can monitor your own progress.
2. Routine – try and get into a routine of writing something each day, so you feel as if you are progressing and getting nearer the end. Once a section is planned, write it up as soon as possible so that you remember what you intended.
3. The flow – when things are going well and your ideas are flowing onto the page, capitalise on it. Do not stop to check a reference or design a table, keep

going. Checking and minor jobs can be done later. Remember, some sections (results and discussion) are better written in one go rather than broken down over a longer time period, so plan for this if you can.

4. Stopping for a break – when you stop writing, think about where you are going to start the next time. If you have come to an abrupt halt because of a difficult section, try and make a few inroads into it before you stop. Otherwise, the thought of starting again may be much harder.

5. Workplace – find a place to work where there are few distractions and where it is quiet. You may need to tell others what you are doing and ask not to be disturbed. If there are lots of things going on around you, it may be more difficult to get into a rhythm of writing.

6. Drafting – you are highly unlikely to have everything perfect in a first draft. Several drafts may be needed, so you should allow time for this in your plans. Once a section has been written as a first draft, some writers find it worthwhile to put it to one side and do other jobs, returning to it later with a fresh mind to check to see if it makes sense and then make amendments.

7. Get help – ask a colleague to look over your work to see if what you have written is easily understood. If possible, ask someone who has not been closely associated with your research. This way they can better comment on whether your explanations can be followed than somebody who already has a fair idea of what you are trying to say.

8. Reward – reward yourself for a job well done. Whether this is a celebratory drink at the end of a busy afternoon or socialising with friends, take time out and treat yourself. Giving yourself treats when you have achieved your own deadlines or targets can help with your own motivation – you deserve it after all.

Is it any good?

Before beginning the final draft, you should look back over the whole report with a critical eye. The following questions may help you as a guide, but others, specific to your project, will need to be added:

1. Title and introductory sections

    - Is the title relevant?
    - Does the introduction set the scene?
    - Are the aims and objectives clearly stated?
    - Is the summary fair and concise?
    - Have all the sources in the literature review been properly recorded?
    - Are the reasons for the project clear?

2. Main sections

    - Are the sections clearly presented?
    - Are the sections in a logical sequence?
    - Is your report easy to follow (e.g. are the aims and objectives developed as consistent themes)?
    - Are all tables, figures, appendices and references labelled and referred to properly?
    - Is your conclusion brief, related to the main findings and to the purpose of the research?

3. Paragraphs

    - Are paragraphs complete mini topics in themselves?
    - Do they start with an appropriate topic sentence?
    - Do they contain information relating only to the paragraph topic?
    - Do the paragraphs link the section together?

4. Writing clearly

    - Do your ideas emerge clearly?
    - Will your language be understood by the readership?
    - Are sentences too long?
    - Have the spelling and punctuation been checked (do this after the final draft too)?
    - Are certain words repeated too often?
    - Have you been consistent in the tense you have used?

5. Layout

    - Is the layout appropriate for the readership/instructions given?
    - Has a consistent system been used for headings and section numbering?
    - Is the contents page still accurate?
    - Is the style of font, size and printing finish clear and easy to read?

9.3 Giving presentations

9.3.1 Introduction

A presentation is a form of communication where a speaker talks on a given subject to an audience. There are numerous types of presentations within this definition, from a student presenting their research, through an employee reporting back the interim findings of a project at a meeting, to the after-dinner speech or conference presentation. The size and nature of the audience listening to the presentation are dependent on the context of the presentation. This context will ultimately determine how the presentation should be pitched. There are, however, some basic guidelines which are important to recognise when speaking to an audience. This section provides key pointers for giving a good presentation and investigates some of the main issues that can be encountered.

9.3.2 Planning: first thoughts

1.   The purpose

Throughout this text, the theme of returning to your aims and objectives has been a constantly recurring one. Giving a presentation is no exception. The first question should be to determine the purpose of the presentation and to develop a specific aim and objectives for it. This could be in the form of a particular title, question or recommendation such as 'to explain how research findings can inform tourism strategy'. Even this may be too general, but whatever the aim of the presentation it should remain as a focus for the whole planning procedure.

2.   Who is the audience?

Closely bound with the first point, what you aim to talk about, is considering who is going to be listening. This will influence the later stages of the planning process in terms of the content of the presentation, its length, and the use of visual aids. To a small technical audience of fellow researchers, their knowledge of your research and its methods may be high compared to a large general audience or one which is mixed. Whatever your circumstances, you should ask the following questions:

- What does the audience already know about my subject?
- What are they coming to learn, or what interests them?
- What are their feelings (or prejudices) likely to be about my subject?
- Do they all feel/think/know the same?
- What resistance are they likely to have towards me or my subject?
- What is the likely size of the audience?

Keeping in mind what you aim to present whilst being sensitive to the type of audience will help establish the emphasis of the remaining preparatory stages.

3.   Major topics and the structure

This stage involves identifying the major topics which will form the principal content of the presentation. Obviously, this is determined by the subject of the presentation, however there are three aspects you should be mindful of. First, how can each major topic be divided into more manageable sections? Second, how large are these sections? If possible, each major topic and the sections within it should be of equal length. For example, if there are two major topics and each is divided into three sections, making six in total, all six should be roughly similar in duration. Third, consider a logical sequence for the sections. In doing this, you should always be aware of how you will be able to relate each section back to the major topic and of course back to the aim of the presentation.

4.   Content and length

The amount of time given to you for the presentation may well have been decided in advance and, once known, it is necessary to think carefully about how much you have to say. You will have already identified the sections and put them in a sequence; now you can actually write down the contents of each section whilst being mindful of how long you will have to speak. It is worthwhile at this point attaching a ranking system of priority to each section. This will help if later it becomes clear that the presentation will be over-length and you must make some cuts. Do not worry too much about writing the finished version (see later with scripting) but aim to be short. This will allow you time to speak of 'signposts' – reminders of where you are in the structure of the presentation. Remember that an audience is quickly irritated by a presentation which overruns into the coffee or lunch break, but few are similarly irritated by a good presentation which is a little short.

5.   How to start

When beginning a presentation, the initial moments are quite crucial. The audience must accept you as the speaker and feel comfortable with you. Some people are naturally humorous and confident enough to begin with a joke. This can work well, but if the joke is unrelated, not funny or in some way inappropriate, it can ruin the whole presentation. With large, unfamiliar audiences, this strategy is particularly treacherous. A safer alternative is to express how pleased you are to be there and to have the opportunity to speak. In other words, you are not presenting yourself as the best orator the audience will ever come across; rather you are an interesting, hard-working person, like themselves, who is worthwhile listening to.

   Explaining the layout/structure of your talk is also crucial. You should start with what you are going to talk about in general terms and how you are going to divide the subject into sections. Essentially, you are establishing the signposts, previously referred to, so the audience will know where they are at any time during the presentation. For instance, if they know that you are talking on the fifth of six sections (which have each lasted about five minutes) and their empty stomach starts to rumble, they have an idea about how long they have to wait before lunch.

6.   Relating to the audience

Every so often, it will be necessary to reflect on how the audience is coping with the subject of your talk. You should have frequent summaries where you clarify where you have come from and what must still be done to satisfy the aim of the presentation. This helps the audience to follow your logic or line of argument. Presentations which are a string of facts or technical terms become progressively more difficult to follow, unless the audience is repeatedly reminded of the structure and purpose.

7.   Telling them a story

When writing a presentation, if you believe that it will be difficult to develop a logical sequence, consider telling a story. Very factual information can be made more interesting if you explain how you went about doing the investigation. For example, 'the data collection method, focus groups, gave us problems selecting the right people to take part … first we tried …. then when this didn't work in the pilot we … found we couldn't … so finally we managed to…'.

   When making a presentation, you should be talking to an audience and not reading to them. If a written report accompanies your presentation, the interested in the audience can read this on their own. A presentation and a written report are different tools of communication; the former could motivate an individual to read the latter. However, a presentation quickly becomes boring if basically all you are doing is reading out your report. Hence, developing a storyline can go a long way in making rather plain research findings into something which is pleasant to listen to and easy to follow.

9.3.3 Planning: second thoughts

Having decided what to include in a presentation, reflected on the type of audience, decided what the main topics and sections are, given them an order, written down what is involved whilst being mindful of how long you will have to speak, signposted where necessary and decided on a narrative style, are you ready to go? Possibly, but there are some other aspects worth contemplating:

1.   The attention span of the audience

It is well known that for a presentation of, say, 45 minutes, the attention span of the audience drops sharply after 10 minutes, continues to fall and rises for the last 5 minutes or so. To overcome this, to a certain extent dividing the presentation into smaller manageable parts helps. However, even the best speaker realises how an audience loses concentration and makes their important points at the beginning and end of a presentation. Moreover, knowing this can help to inform you of when to show slides or use other visual aids. Changes in the style of delivery can also assist in the revival of sagging attention.

2. Taking a break

Having a break rarely annoys anybody. If you have structured your presentation as outlined here, then there should be natural points where a break can occur. It is probably better to have several shorter breaks than a single long one. If, however, you are committed to having a single break part way through your presentation, it may be better to have it a little way past the half-way point. That way the audience knows that they have less to come back to than before the break (assuming you keep to time). You should clearly signpost where breaks are to occur and remind the audience of what is to be done after the break. Remember that a break means getting up, moving around or having a coffee, and does not mean pausing in your talk to ask if there are any questions.

3. Audience participation

The type of presentation which is envisaged here is unlikely to involve splitting the audience into smaller groups and sending them away to complete a particular task. With very large audiences, participation is difficult, however with smaller ones the passing round of brochures or other physical objects may be worthwhile. The main form of participation comes in the form of questions. As the presenter, you should take the lead in inviting questions at suitable points in the presentation. Assuming you have used up all your allotted time, it is unlikely that asking questions at the end, as an afterthought, will result in anything fruitful being asked. It is better to be specific and ask for questions at the end of a particular topic to see if further clarification is necessary. With this in mind, there may be certain scenarios which arise when you ask, 'are there any questions concerning…?':

a. Silence – this can feel quite awkward but you should allow a sufficient pause, which may feel like an eternity, before proceeding.
b. The question which helps – this is a question from the audience which seeks relevant clarification. This type should be welcomed and answered immediately.
c. The irrelevant question – this type of question is so specific or technical that you sense that the majority of the audience is uninterested or that to answer it would take too long. In this case, indicate that to properly answer the question would take too long but that you would be happy to discuss the matter with the questioner and anyone else interested at the next break.
d. The awkward questioner – occasionally, questions are asked which are deliberately off-putting. It is not recommended that you enter into an exchange with somebody out to damage you. In a similar way to type (c), offer to answer the question individually and informally following the presentation.

It may be every presenter's nightmare to have somebody in the audience out to make you appear stupid. It is also very annoying to you, however you must appear absolutely reasonable and unruffled. If you anticipate that this type of questioner may be in your audience, prepare an answer in advance. You could say, 'I will need more time to properly consider such an interesting question; perhaps we could meet informally before lunch and discuss things fully. Now returning to the next section...'. In short, you have put the questioner down politely, but have not entered into an exchange (in not seeking a response to your invitation of a discussion before lunch). In this prepared answer, you have taken the lead, indicated how and when you will answer and then immediately got on with the presentation.

4. Using a script

It is difficult to know how much of the content of a presentation needs to be written down in advance and used in the presentation. There are two extremes – giving a spontaneous presentation without notes or visual aids and reading out loud a written paper. The former is extremely dangerous and risks going either over length, quickly running out of things to say or forgetting a memorised speech. The latter can be very tedious, and some would say insulting, to listen to. The most interesting style of delivery is where somebody appears to be talking to you, but mimicking this is not easy. When writing your presentation, you should write it as you would speak, not as you would write a research paper. Probably the best way to do this is to think, when writing, how you would say something if explaining it to another person and transcribing this. It is also a good idea to continually practise reading out loud what you have just written.

As you head towards a final version, you may find that you have almost memorised what you have written. The question then is to decide how much written material you will need with you when giving the presentation. Having a whole script enhances the likelihood that you will end up reading it, which is what you are trying to avoid. You should be able to condense a script down into sections with key words and phrases to prompt you. Placing these onto cards is a good idea.

In short, the process of developing the actual script involves, first, writing it out in full using spoken rather than written English; second, reciting this and refining as necessary; and finally, placing what you need onto cards to guide you during the delivery.

5. Your mannerisms

Nobody likes their particular mannerisms pointed out to them, but occasionally nerves make us do things which would be distracting when giving a presentation. It is worthwhile, particularly for the beginner, to have oneself videotaped or watched by others who are looking for just such distractions. The most common of these include:

a. Physical distractions – repeatedly moving around, scratching your nose, con-stantly adjusting a transparency, etc.
b. Verbal distractions – repeatedly using the same word or phrase, such as 'basi-cally', 'actually', 'the thing is', 'you know'.
c. Eye contact – maintaining eye contact with the audience is important. Head down reading notes is distracting, but a fixed gaze on the back of the room can be equally so.
d. Speed – often, presenters speak far too quickly. Remember that the content is very familiar to you but will not be to the audience. They will need time to understand it.
e. Pitch – some speak too loud and others too quietly. Others have the correct pitch most of the time but drop it towards the end of a sentence. Practice and being aware of this aspect help.

9.3.4 Visual aids

Using some sort of visual aid to support a presentation is common practice but, as with other areas of presentation, there are also some pitfalls. At a general level, you should be aware of the following guidelines:

Relevance: the visual aids used should be clearly linked to the purpose of the presentation or the point you are trying to make, and should be appropriate in terms of the level of understanding of your audience.

Simplicity: visual aids must get straight to the point. If you have to spend too much time explaining what is shown, the purpose and value of them can be quickly lost.

Emphasis: you must use your visual aids to emphasise a particular point, stress an important idea, indicate a change in the structure or identify a new concept. They are there to ease understanding.

Consistency: it is best to develop a consistent style in your use of visual aids. Constant changing from one type to another can be confusing.

Some of the main types of visual aids include:

1. PowerPoint – presentation software such as PowerPoint is very useful in provid-ing the audience with written and visual information. When using presentation software, there are a number of considerations which need to be made regard-ing technology, formatting and content, and the presentation space:

    • Technological considerations: if using presentation software, it is impor-tant that you have access to the correct audio and visual equipment including a projector, screen and sound if required. It is also important to ensure that you have access to the software in the location you are giving the presentation. To avoid any technological problems, it is worthwhile having a laptop with you, which you can run the software from, as a back-up. It is also important that you have the presentation saved in a number of places: online, on email, on a memory stick.

- Formatting and content: it is essential that attention is paid to the formatting of presentation content. Ensure that any text or images are a suitable size for the audience to read easily. Use a sans serif font in a bold colour that stands out from the background. Opt for either dark text on a light background or light text on a dark background and avoid clashing colours as these can be difficult to read. A common mistake in presentations using presentation software is the provision of too much information. Avoid putting too much information on a slide; instead, provide a few key points or a diagram for the audience to digest. Furthermore, give the audience time to read the information you provide them with. Any images that are used should add to the audience's understanding, rather than detract from the presentation content.

- The presentation space: if you have the opportunity, familiarise yourself with the room or space in which you will be giving your presentation. Identify where you will stand so that you can address the audience without getting between the projector and the screen. If you need to move around the room during your presentation, use of a wireless presentation remote is recommended as this allows the presenter to change between slides without being in a static location.

2. Whiteboards and flipcharts: these can be used to highlight particular points as the presentation progresses; it is less common that they are prepared in advance. When using whiteboards and flipcharts as a visual aid, consideration needs to be given to their presentation:

    - Materials: if you are planning to make use of these visual aids, ensure you have access to the right materials including pens, flipchart paper and, if using the whiteboard, a board rubber. It is important to remember that felt pens used on whiteboards can also be used on flipcharts but the same is not true in reverse. Whiteboard markers which can be removed must be used if you wish to use the board more than once in a presentation. If you are using a flipchart, make sure there is additional paper to allow for errors.

    - Clarity of the information: when using these visual aids, it is important that you present the information clearly so that it is visible to every member of the audience. To improve the clarity of the information presented, always start with a clean board or page, take your time and write clearly in large letters. Ensure that you use a bold-coloured pen – black or blue will stand out against the white background whereas green, red, yellow or orange can be more difficult to see. If possible, practise using these visual aids beforehand to see if what you write can be read from the back of the room.

- Presenting to the audience: using a whiteboard or flipchart will require you to turn your back on the audience. If the information can be prepared in advance, you may wish to do so. Avoid talking to the board when you are writing; wait to explain the information once you have finished. Pausing briefly whilst you write will not lose the attention of the audience. Remember to pause and stand clear of the board once you have finished so that your audience can see what you have written and take it in.

3. Film – a good film as part of a presentation can be a great success but the more complicated your visual aids become, the more room there is for error. Before using film in a presentation, consider both the suitability of this medium to illustrate your point and the content and presentation of the film:

- Suitability: only use film if it is relevant, simple and helps to emphasise an appropriate point. Pay attention to timing and do not make the film too long, otherwise it may take over the presentation. Consider carefully when, during the presentation, it is best to show the film as its message can be lost if it is shown at an inappropriate point. When determining the suitability of this medium as a visual aid, ask yourself:

  o   Why is this video being substituted for me in the presentation?
  o   Is a video or film an appropriate technique to achieve my aims?

- Content and presentation: if creating the film yourself, be aware that this requires training. It can easily look like a home movie and the audience can quickly become more aware of its shortcomings than of the message you are trying to give. If you are unable to create a film that looks professional, it may be better to omit this element of your presentation. If you are using film to supplement your presentation, it is important that you do not perform in it. However much you may have liked to have been a television presenter, doing so well requires skill and training. Most film commentaries performed by untrained presenters have a habit of appearing like something from a Monty Python sketch. If you do appear in a film, get an honest opinion from a trusted colleague before you decide to use it. When showing the film, take care in making additional comments. With any type of sound film, you probably will not be heard by everybody. With a silent film, rehearsal is vital, so that your comments match the appropriate point in the film and also finish in the right place.

9.3.5 Poster presentations

Another form of presentation is the poster presentation which is often used in an academic context. In this instance, a poster will provide an overview of research that has been conducted. In most cases, the audience will read the poster and the researcher will be on hand to talk them through the work. In other instances, the poster will be presented by the researcher. When creating a poster, it is important to provide only the key points to keep the readers' attention. Small blocks of text, clear diagrams and images should be used to convey the information. Careful attention needs to be paid to formatting, particularly in relation to font size, style and colour to ensure readability.

An example of a poster which was presented at an academic conference is shown in Illustration 9.8.

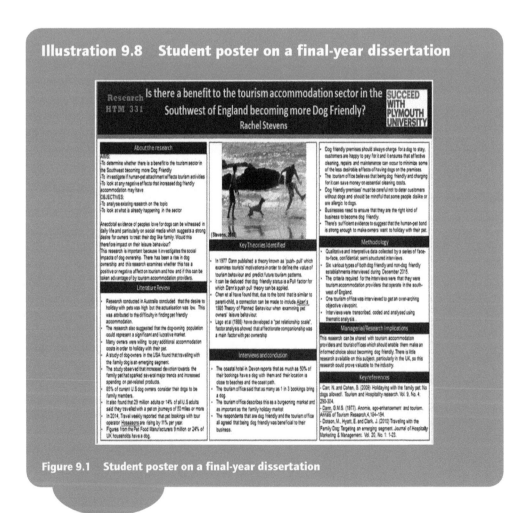

Illustration 9.8   Student poster on a final-year dissertation

Figure 9.1   Student poster on a final-year dissertation

9.4 Publishing your research

As an undergraduate or postgraduate student, you may wish to publish some of the research you have conducted. There are a number of options for publication so you will need to determine the most suitable format for your work. Popular publication channels include conference papers, book chapters and peer-reviewed journal articles. Each of these publication types will be discussed in this section using examples from undergraduate students.

9.4.1 Conference papers

Conference papers are perhaps the most accessible form of publication for under-graduate and postgraduate students as there are a large number of academic conferences each year which address a wide range of research topics. Although aca-demic conferences tend to be multidisciplinary, the papers, delivered by researchers from different disciplines or research areas, will share a common theme. Attendance at academic conferences permits exposure to the most cutting-edge research in a par-ticular field. Furthermore, as an undergraduate or postgraduate, academic conferences provide the opportunity to present your research and to network with those who possess similar research interests to you.

As a researcher, the first stage is to decide on a suitable conference for your research. It is important that your research fits with the theme of the conference, but considerations may also be made based on location and the extent to which the conference welcomes student research. Once a conference has been selected, you will need to prepare an abstract for the research you wish to present. An abstract is a short document, usually ranging from 200 to 500 words, which pro-vides a clear outline of the topic, identifies the methods used and highlights key findings from the research. The abstract will be reviewed by the conference com-mittee and either accepted or rejected so it is important that this document engages the reader. Depending on the conference, an extended abstract or the full paper may be requested; if this is the case, a style guide will be provided and must be adhered to. Conference papers are typically published as a collection of conference proceedings; for those conferences that do not request the full paper, the abstract is published. At the conference, the researcher will be allocated a time slot, usually allowing 15–20 minutes to present their research. We have already considered examples of these earlier in the chapter. The publication of a conference paper can provide you with an introduction to the academic world if you want to continue to postgraduate level, but it can also bring you and your university or college the opportunity for publicity that can be useful to you in finding a job since it adds value to your curriculum vitae. See Illustration 9.9 which shows an example of publicity that resulted from this type of activity.

Illustration 9.9   Example of publicity from student presentation

Image 9.1   Hospitality team: Rebecca Makepeace, Craig Wight and Susan Horner (from left to right)

Susan Horner delivered an academic paper at the Council for Hospitality Management Education (CHME) conference in Manchester on 21 May that was written on the basis of the undergraduate dissertation researched by Rebecca Makepeace in 2014. The details of the paper are: 'Culinary tourism in Devon and Cornwall: a supply-side perspective' by Rebecca Makepeace, Craig Wight and Susan Horner. The paper explores the research that was carried out with hospitality producers across the two counties and suggests a theoretical model that can be used for future research on the topic.

The subject was well received by the international audience and many commented that it was excellent to publish student research at all levels of study. This is something we are making ourselves a name for and will continue to do at the School in the future.

Rebecca (Becky) is now an alumni of the School and is busy working in her family hotel business in the same region.

9.4.2 Book chapters and case studies

There is also an opportunity for you to write a short chapter or case study for a book. This can happen when your lecturer publishes regularly in books and suggests that you might like to contribute. The style of writing and the content will depend very much on the type of book.

9.4.3 Peer-reviewed journal articles

Publishing your work in a peer-reviewed journal is important if you want to pursue a career in academia but can also be a very rewarding experience for undergraduate and postgraduate researchers, highlighting the quality of the work they have produced during their time at university. In the case of student research, it is likely that the project will not have originally been intended for publication so the original research will need reworking according to the journal's style guide.

As with academic conferences, journal titles publish on different themes so the first step when seeking to publish a journal article is to identify which journal is most suitable for your research. The nature of the topic, the methodology and findings of the research will determine the suitability of different journals. It is important that the theme of the paper is one of those published by the journal. To determine whether or not your topic is suitable for a particular journal, familiarise yourself with some of the articles that have been published in it in the past. Once you have selected the journal, you will need to write the paper in accordance with the journal's style guide, including formatting and word count. After the paper has been submitted, it will be peer reviewed and either accepted, accepted pending revisions or rejected. Should the paper be rejected, make use of any comments or feedback that are provided and rework the paper for another journal. An example of an abstract from a paper that was published in an academic journal following the completion of an undergraduate dissertation is shown in Illustration 9.10.

Illustration 9.10   Example of an abstract from an academic paper based on an undergraduate dissertation

This study investigates the relationship between film-induced tourism and the concept of destination image via a substantial primary data collection exercise, followed by content analysis of television episodes. Port Isaac, on the north coast of Cornwall, in the west of England, is the setting for the popular ITV television series *Doc Martin*, starring Martin Clunes and Caroline Catz. Television can enhance the attractiveness of an area, especially when building on images of small-scale fishing and quaint customs. Findings showed a visitor profile fairly consistent with those of previous academic studies whilst frequency tests indicated that many respondents had clear destination images of Port Isaac prior to their visit. Consequently, content analysis of *Doc Martin* episodes was further undertaken; the results of which confirm there are links between images depicted in the television series and those pertaining to Port Isaac. Key features of the village are

(Continued)

(Continued)

apparent in both forms of research undertaken. With primetime screening on national television, the series acts as a display window for the village and surrounding area. The research indicates the series acted as a key influence on intention to visit, not surprisingly, for British tourists. Almost 76% of respondents associate Port Isaac with a specific image. The study is unusual, in film tourism research, in using two distinct forms of data to contrast the situation.

Key words: film tourism, destination image, Great Britain

Source: '*Doc Martin* and film tourism: The creation of destination image' by Graham Busby and Callum Haines, 2013, in *Tourism*, 61 (2): 105–20.

To finish this chapter, it is good for us to consider an extract from an academic paper published by one of the authors and his student. We can see in Illustration 9.11 the type of writing style and approach which lead to journal articles being accepted. Jennifer has just submitted her PhD as we write this, which shows the type of outcomes that can be achieved if you pursue the publication route.

Illustration 9.11   Analysis from a student academic paper based on an undergraduate dissertation

Cluster analysis

To detect respondents with similar characteristics a K-means cluster analysis was conducted using the 9 factors as composite variables. K-means cluster analysis was chosen over hierarchal clustering due to its usefulness in grouping large sample sizes and cases with similar characteristics (Hair et al., 1998). K-means clustering divides data into the number of clusters specified, therefore the most meaningful solution needed to be found. Cluster solutions varying from 2 to 8 were tested, however a 6 cluster solution was deemed the most appropriate in terms of significance.

Table 9.4 displays the 6 cluster solutions and the results of ANOVA tests. ANOVA results show that 8 of the 9 factors make a significant contribution to the cluster process at $p<0.001$, with one factor significant at $p<0.05$. F-statistics show the factors/variables which differentiate the groups most significantly. European resort variables are deemed most important in differentiating respondents where $F = 218.857$, followed by social variables, where $F = 138.623$. Snow variables were also significant at $F = 87.284$. Destination ($F = 8.656$), Motivation ($F = 6.801$), Cultural ($F = 6.156$), Activity ($F = 4.590$) and Sports variables ($F = 2.431$) have less effect. This identifies that European, social and snow variables can be used to differentiate between the behavioural characteristics of British winter sports tourists.

Cluster 1 accounts for 14.6% of sample respondents, to whom social aspects of winter sports holidays are of highest value; tending to travel in larger groups and participating in non-ski activities, snow variables are less important to these respondents. With social variables the most differentiating factor amongst this cluster, it was named 'Après Scene'.

Cluster 2 represents the smallest number of respondents (1.7%) where relaxation is important in their motivation to travel; this group are frequent winter sports tourists with high quality equipment, social aspects are unimportant and respondents travel in smaller groups. The importance of cultural activities and sightseeing is also evident, suggesting the importance of the vacation aspect of the trip. This group does not travel to European resorts, however the low importance of other destination variables identifies the prominence of skiing in the UK amongst this market. With relaxation and vacation variables differentiating this cluster, it was labelled 'Relaxation Seekers'.

Cluster 3 represents 15.1% of respondents, where socialising, getting away, developing skills and exercise are central motivations. Although respondents travel in larger groups and social motivations are prominent, differentiation can be made between Cluster 1 and Cluster 3 where the latter are more likely to travel with children and non-ski activities are less important. Traveling far afield is not a defining characteristic of this group, however the use of off-piste and freestyle terrain is prominent, suggesting sport motivations are also central. Socialising is important, but the lack of interest in events and nightlife suggest socialising is engaged in on piste, resulting in the name 'Social Skiers'.

Cluster 4 represents the largest group of respondents at 25.6% who have been named the 'Anything Goes' group. These respondents tend to travel in smaller groups, to European resorts where non-ski activities and motivation variables are important and social and snow variables are less important.

Cluster 5 represents 21.9% of respondents, for whom snow variables are most important. This group has been appropriately named 'Enthusiasts', as this group is less concerned with social, cultural and non-ski activities. Groups tend to be smaller

(Continued)

(Continued)

and with far afield destinations unimportant, this group can be identified as part of the European market. Exercise is also important as a motivation in this cluster, supporting the notion that participation in the sport is the main focus for the trip.

The final cluster, also representing 21.9% of respondents, is the 'Jet Set Enthusiasts'. This group again is concerned with snow variables, however destination is of greater importance than in cluster 5. Furthermore, social aspects and dining out are important, giving evidence of the 'vacation' aspect of the trip. This is also reflected in their desire to travel whereby exercise and getting away are important motivations. Group size tends to be smaller and less likely to include children.

Table 9.4   Cluster analysis categories of British winter sports tourists

Variables	Après Scene N = 87, 14.6%	Relaxation Seekers N = 10, 1.7%	Social Skiers N = 90, 15.1%	Anything Goes N = 48, 25.6%	Enthusiasts N = 131, 21.9%	Jet Set Enthusiasts N = 131, 21.9%	F	Sig.
Snow variables	0.85	−0.26	−0.41	0.78	−0.59	−0.55	87.284	0.000
Equipment	2.99	3.80	3.59	2.89	3.97	4.18	39.513	0.000
Off-piste	1.46	1.40	1.21	1.57	1.14	1.14	23.428	0.000
Terrain	5.98	2.6	2.95	4.86	2.30	2.51	162.602	0.000
Frequency	2.41	3.00	2.77	2.27	2.83	2.88	19.305	0.000
Freestyle	1.70	1.90	1.68	1.90	1.75	1.63	6.534	0.000
Social variables	−1.34	0.14	−0.40	0.58	0.82	−0.31	138.623	0.000
Après	3.62	6.20	6.39	7.06	7.36	4.98	186.420	0.000
Nightlife	1.33	2.20	1.70	2.17	2.16	1.58	42.244	0.000
Socialising	1.34	1.70	1.31	1.72	1.92	1.52	20.155	0.000
Events	2.25	2.50	2.54	2.59	2.61	2.43	5.748	0.000
Activity variables	0.03	−0.15	0.25	−0.31	0.07	0.09	4.590	0.000
Ice skating	2.59	2.70	2.68	2.77	2.77	2.72	2.158	0.057
Tobogganing	2.54	2.80	2.56	2.42	2.62	2.56	2.545	0.027
Sightseeing	2.37	1.70	2.48	2.42	2.77	2.26	4.057	0.001
Non-ski	7.52	6.60	7.60	7.60	7.20	7.53	11.194	0.000
Motivation variables	0.22	0.34	−0.06	−0.33	0.27	−0.03	6.801	0.000

Variables	Après Scene N = 87, 14.6%	Relaxation Seekers N = 10, 1.7%	Social Skiers N = 90, 15.1%	Anything Goes N = 48, 25.6%	Enthusiasts N = 131, 21.9%	Jet Set Enthusiasts N = 131, 21.9%	F	Sig.
Get away	1.76	2.00	1.74	1.84	1.72	1.56	8.419	0.000
Relax	1.67	1.70	1.98	1.97	1.97	1.91	4.430	0.001
Exercise	2.08	1.90	1.71	1.78	1.60	1.53	1.643	0.147
Dest. variables	−0.04	0.43	0.34	0.08	0.11	−0.44	8.656	0.000
USA	1.84	1.90	1.74	1.84	1.72	1.56	7.461	0.000
Canada	1.78	1.60	1.71	1.78	1.60	1.52	6.127	0.000
Asia	1.98	2.00	1.99	1.97	1.97	1.91	2.737	0.019
Cultural variables	−0.01	−0.36	0.26	0.14	0.07	−0.37	6.156	0.000
Dining out	1.60	1.50	1.70	1.65	1.72	1.46	4.088	0.001
Shopping	2.01	1.60	2.27	2.15	2.33	2.12	6.153	0.000
Sports variables	−0.12	−0.03	−0.18	0.22	−0.01	−0.03	2.431	0.034
Develop skills	1.51	1.20	1.41	1.68	1.54	1.55	3.224	0.007
Group variables	−0.22	0.23	−1.05	0.17	0.15	0.49	37.784	0.000
Children	1.76	1.70	1.66	1.68	1.78	1.90	5.214	0.000
Group size	3.31	1.80	4.07	1.88	1.72	1.77	128.495	0.000
European resort variables	−0.04	6.16	−0.13	−0.14	−0.10	−0.09	218.857	0.000
Europe	1.00	2.00	1.00	1.00	1.00	1.00	–	–

Cluster characteristics by sport

Segmentation by snow sport has yet to be investigated, yet as identified in this study (Table 9.5) it is significant in determining and grouping skier characteristics (p<0.005). Skiers as a population are well represented in those clusters where social-ising is a key determinant (Après Scene and Social Skiers). It is also prominent in the Anything Goes group where vacation aspects are central in motivating trips. Comparatively, snowboarders are more evident in the Enthusiast market and are clas-sified into clusters where snow-related variables are key determinants (Enthusiast and

(Continued)

Table 9.5 Cluster analysis characteristics

(Continued)

Characteristics		Après Scene N = 87 14.6%		Relaxation Seekers N = 10 1.7%		Social Skiers N = 90 15.1%		Anything Goes N = 48 25.6%		Enthusiasts N = 131 21.9%		Jet Set Enthusiasts N = 131 21.9%		Chi-sq.	Sig.
		N	%	N	%	N	%	N	%	N	%	N	%		
Sport	Skier	60	15.3	6	1.5	62	15.9	115	29.4	76	19.4	72	18.4	25.511	0.004
	Snowboarder	17	11.8	4	2.8	17	11.8	25	17.4	38	26.4	43	29.9		
	Both	10	16.7	0	0.0	11	18.3	7	11.7	16	26.7	16	26.7		
Skill level	Beginner	7	46.7	1	6.7	0	0.0%	5	33.3	2	13.3	0	0.0	65.665	0.000
	Intermediate	48	16.6	3	1.0	40	13.9	98	34.1	58	20.2	40	13.9		
	Advanced	32	10.9	6	2.0	49	16.7	45	15.3	71	24.1	91	31.0		
Age	15–24	33	35.9	0	0.0	18	19.6	17	18.5	11	12.0	13	14.1	70.506	0.000
	25–44	36	10.9	8	2.4	41	12.4	84	25.4	72	21.8	90	27.2		
	45–64	15	9.4	2	1.3	25	15.7	46	28.9	44	27.7	27	17.0		
	65+	2	16.7	0	0.0	6	50.0	1	8.3	2	16.7	1	8.3		

Jet Set Enthusiast). The importance of destination to this group is also evident with a higher number of snowboarders being classified as Jet Set Enthusiasts, who travel further afield to participate. Respondents who participate in both sports show a cross-over, motivated by the social aspects of the trip, yet are still snow enthusiasts, belonging to the Social Skier, Enthusiast and Jet Set Enthusiast categories.

Source: 'Tourist differentiation: Developing a typology for the winter sports market' by Jennifer Phillips and Paul Brunt, 2013, in *Tourism International Interdisciplinary Journal*, 61 (3): 219–43.

9.5 Summary

This chapter has attempted to provide some useful guidelines when writing a report or giving a presentation and publishing research. To summarise, four key points should be remembered:

1. Have a purpose, so that you know exactly what you want to achieve and pass on to your reader or audience.
2. Realise that your reader or audience will not remember everything you have said or written. Identify three or four key ideas that must be remembered and that they can take away with them.
3. With presentations, speak with enthusiasm for your topic and consideration for your audience.
4. If you choose to publish your research, ensure that you choose the most appropriate format for your work.

The essence of an excellent student publication relies on an excellent abstract. We can consider a final one of these in the last illustration of the book (9.12).

Illustration 9.12   Final example of an abstract

This research project has taken a further step towards explaining what might inspire cruise passengers to tip whilst on a cruise. This research project provides a valuable

(Continued)

(Continued)

insight into the tipping motives of 232 cruise passengers. An online self-completion questionnaire was used to identify what motivates cruise passengers to tip. The results obtained in this study show that cruise passengers interpret tipping as a good way of showing gratitude to those providing the service, and furthermore they tip because the service they received whilst on a cruise ship was beyond extraordinary and it's their way of showing gratitude. Cruise passengers believe tipping on a cruise should be voluntary; they also prefer to leave a cash-based tip rather than conform to the automatic tipping policies.

Source: Malwina Osmelak, undergraduate dissertation, Plymouth University, 2016.

Exercises

1. Select journals from different disciplines and contrast the different approaches to the writing of articles.
2. Using reports produced by Visit Britain, where surveys have been used, identify how the authors have divided the information into major and minor sections. How are they numbered?
3. Prepare a short presentation (of 10 minutes duration) on how to correctly cite authors when writing reports and how to prepare a reference list. If possible, try out the presentation within a group. Other topics could include how to number sections in a report, writing the first draft, and the do's and don'ts of giving a presentation.
4. Choose two academic journals and identify their style guides. Compare the differences in requirements as if you were planning to submit a paper to either of these journals.

Further reading

Bell, J. (2014). *Doing Your Research Project: A guide for first-time researchers*. 6th edition. Maidenhead: McGraw-Hill Education.
This is a very useful reference book for the first-time student through to those undertaking a higher degree. There are valuable ideas from initial project preparation through data collection to writing a report.

Berry, R. (2004). *The Research Project: How to write it*. 5th edition. Oxon: Routledge.
This book was developed from an original work called 'How to write a research paper', written by the same author in 1966. Its emphasis is on research reports of a more academic rather than consultancy nature. The book is concisely written with sections on choosing a topic, using the library, making notes, comparing and developing the text and how to avoid some common errors.

Walters, L. (1993). *Secrets of Successful Speakers*. New York: McGraw-Hill.
This text covers 11 steps to giving successful speeches and presentations. These include setting objectives, considering the audience, conquering fear, being credible, developing a theme, organising material, motivating an audience and how to avoid some common pitfalls.

Reference

Clarke, V. and Braun, V. (2013). Teaching Thematic Analysis: Overcoming challenges and developing strategies for effective learning. *The Psychologist*. 26 (2): 120–3.

INDEX